D0929810

BEST FRIENDS AND
MARRIAGE

BEST FRIENDS AND MARRIAGE

Exchange Among Women

STACEY J. OLIKER

University of California Press
Berkeley   Los Angeles   London

University of California Press
Berkeley and Los Angeles, California

University of California Press, Ltd.
London, England

Library of Congress Cataloging-in-Publication Data

Oliker, Stacey J.
    Best friends and marriage: exchange among women / Stacey J.
Oliker.
        p.   cm.
    Contents: Bibliography: p.
    Includes index.
    ISBN 0-520-06392-9 (alk. paper)
    1. Women—California. 2. Friendship—California. 3. Marriage—
California. 4. Women—California—Family relationships.
I. Title.
HQ1438.C2055   1989
305.4'09794—dc19   89-4890
                                                                     CIP

Printed in the United States of America
1   2   3   4   5   6   7   8   9

To my parents,
Ruth Bahm Oliker and Albert E. Oliker

Contents

Acknowledgments

I thank the women and men who granted me interviews and who talked so thoughtfully and honestly about their friendships and families. I am extremely grateful to Claude Fischer for his close, critical readings of several drafts of the dissertation that became this book. His counsel was straightforward, incisive, and always helpful. Arlie Hochschild and Robert Blauner also braved rough drafts of dissertation and provided very helpful criticisms. Others who gave me invaluable comments include Ellen Reier, Lew Friedland, Peggy Pascoe, Ann VanDePol, Rivka Polatnick, Linda Collins, Carole Joffe, Laura Pinsky, Barbara Cushing, Elizabeth Colson, Susan Ervin-Tripp, Susan Phillips, and Ruth Milkman. U.C. Press editor Naomi Schneider offered steady encouragement and direction. At progressive stages of editing, Warren Reier, Betsey Scheiner, and Edith Gladstone were talented and generous teachers. Kathy Ringwood typed flawlessly. I thank all these people for their help, some of which I might have used better.

Among the friends who encouraged, supported, and distracted me during the years I worked on this project, I owe special thanks to these whom I have not yet named: Khamisah Aspar, Lynn Cooper, Aaron Cozen, Myrna Cozen, Caleb Cushing, Milton and Ruth Friedland, Linda Fuller, Carol Hatch, Su Mei Huang, Sandy Jacoby, Gail Kaufman, Greg McLauchlan, the Marino family, Bev Purrington, Erika Reier, Marcy Whitebook, Alice Wolfson, and sisters in the CDRR. Because I wrote this book far away from most of these people, I depended very much on Lew Friedland for the technical, intellectual, emotional, and practical help that allowed me to finish this work. To Lew; to my parents, Ruth and Al Oliker; to my sister, Nancy Oliker; and to my beloved friends—especially Ellen Reier, Laura Pinsky, and Linda Collins—thank you for everything that enabled and encouraged me to write this book.

I gratefully acknowledge the dissertation fellowship from the American Association of University Women that supported a year of my research.

Introduction

People are talking about friendship again. For the first time in this century it has kindled lively interest, although it engaged imaginations in past centuries, when the noteworthy friends were men. Women as friends were invisible, their friendships maligned. Women friends were heralded once, however, in the nineteenth-century sororal raptures of "romantic friendship." Today, scholars and journalists show women's friendships as positive once again and in many cases even contrast them to poorer relations among men. Canny advertisers now use friendship to pluck at heartstrings and pocketbooks. And filmmakers have seized upon friendship as a theme of regeneration.

This is a heady but confusing time to study women's friendships. As ideals about relationships form, they overshadow actualities and tempt us to treat friendship sentimentally, like other approved, private, and sentimental relationships—modern marriage in particular. And other issues cloud the field. Recent attention to friendship grows in part from a resurgent concern with "community." Nostalgia and yearning for community are widespread in politics, popular culture, and social theory. As in past revivals of concern about community, they follow a period of economic transition, ideological and political upheaval, and social experimentation.

The yearning for community as a source of stability, humanity, and unified and harmonious purpose has found expression along the entire political spectrum. On the left—where experiments in elective community once flowered—disillusioned writers now call for a return to older, traditional sites of community; the family appears to them most accessible for rebuilding. Progressive writers frequently echo those on the right, who focus their idealism about community on the family while disparaging the domain of elective community.

I arrived at my questions about friendship in the charged atmosphere of contemporary concerns about community. We know too little about personal life and community outside the nuclear family, and too little about the sources of persistence and change in family life. If we would revitalize traditional forms of community or build enduring new forms we need to study the wider realm of private life as well as the family. I selected an angle for studying women's friendships—as community and in relation to the family.

My study of contemporary women's friendships and marriages suggests that close friendships are vital and important relationships in women's lives and that they provide unique sources for intimacy, affection, identity, and community. Moreover, women's close friendships are abundant and appear to be even more widespread than marriages. Until very recently, certain that community had disappeared, sociologists have slighted friendship.[1] Their treatment of the communal realm fixes instead on the family as the crucible of personal integration and community. I bring women's friendships out of the shadow cast by the family, examine the culture of friendship and its internal dynamics, and link together women's friendships, families, and social change.

To learn about friendships among "ordinary" women, I selected predominantly working-class and middle-class women rather than members of an elite or representatives of a cultural avant-garde. I wanted to discover patterns that are widespread in contexts affecting most, rather than a few, contemporary women—at a moment when heightened ideals of friendship have not become prevalent. I interviewed twenty-one women; most are married and mothers. Although my sample does not statistically represent a population, it encompasses a variable range of contemporary women.

I asked my respondents plain questions about their friendships and marriages. Because friendship is still for most an unscrutinized institution, the women I interviewed had generally not considered these questions before. They spoke eloquently and with rich detail about the quality and meaning of their close friendships. The result was a fresh and energetic interchange.

My questions are about what characterizes women's close friendships and how they influence women's identities and commitments. I framed my questions as issues of gender stratification and private life. I sought to understand how women's beliefs, ideals, and actions are shaped in their public lives and in their families and close communities. Knowing that marriage and the family are important arenas of identity and motivation for most women, I explored wider personal realms that may condition experience in the family and constitute other sources of women's identity and action. Among these wider realms of private life—such as kinship, friendly sociability, neighboring, and voluntary organizations—close friendship has been least examined.

I analyze women's close friendships as an institution. Within relationships as personal and idiosyncratic as these, what patterns of value and practice justify the term institution? What beliefs, commitments, and positional constraints shape patterns of close friendship and connect close friendship and marriage? What is the correspondence between the ethos of friendship and larger cultural values and social authority? Do women's friendships involve personal and communal values that are believed to lie solely within the family? Do women friends compete with or undermine familial commitments? How does close friendship situate women in marital contests of power and privilege? How does women's place in public life influence their patterns of close friendship? These are the guiding questions of my research.

My study fits topically into the sociology of gender, of the family, and of community. As a sociology of gender, it aims to answer questions about the gender structure of private life, gender differences in modes of affiliation and individuation, and the dynamics of gender conflict in marriage. It views the family from one of its constituent viewpoints and explores "her marriage" and family (to use the phrase by which Jessie Bernard reminds us that marriage is different for men and women). It examines the structures of private life from which women draw resources for resisting gender subordination and forging change.

As a sociology of the family, this work fits into a tradition that examines the family in relation to community.[2] It challenges views of the family as a self-contained universe of private life—views that assume family life bounds the most significant emotional attachments of adult life and the most important relations of personal integration. It also challenges the belief that the modern family is bereft of communal ties of intimacy and moral authority, that the family and its members are pawns of distant social authority. In this way, the work enters the sociological debate on the meaning of modernity—to revise its underlying consensus on family and community change.

Finally, as a sociology of community, this study begins to reformulate the prevalent concept of community, which defines community by a set of historically specific social forms that are increasingly lost to modern society. In contrast, I identify elements of a more abstract conception of community that can be used to analyze modern social life. I aim to contribute to a sociology of community that encompasses the sites of modern private life that lie outside the family.

Two puzzling feminist issues influenced my approach to the topic. The first was a pattern I noticed in the early seventies among numerous women's "consciousness-raising" groups. In these grassroots groups in the second wave of feminism, women explored the politics of personal life, to develop a feminism that could transform both private and public life. Feminists have often been accused of intentionally undermining marriage and the family. But many consciousness-raising groups that I knew of—including the one I joined—spent the largest portion of their time helping members "work through" intimate heterosexual relationships.

Most of the men in these private relationships did not appreciate being discussed by an organized feminist group. And many relationships broke up in that period (like those of many other young educated women who deferred marriage until their late twenties and thirties). Looking back at these groups, however, I am struck by the strength of their implicit commitment to sustain male-female relationships. After all, our explicit concern was feminist struggle—often defined as uncompromising resistance to gender subordination and the irreducible conflict of interests between men and women. In fact, our explorations of how "the personal is political" were often also a collective effort to improve our individual relations with men we loved. Although we were helping each other to struggle against our men, we were also helping to sustain our commitments. Rarely did individual aspirations—like career ambitions—or public feminist politics receive the attention that our heterosexual relationships did.

The second puzzle involves the notion that women's networks are "cultures of resistance," a frequent theme in feminist political writing.[3] In one form or another, its central idea is that associations of women inherently generate resistance to male authority and domination. Yet in instances I knew of, female bonding seemed to generate cultures of accommodation or survival as often as cultures of resistance.

These puzzles directed me toward areas that interweave women's individualism, their commitments to other women, and their commitments to men. This mesh of interests, ideals, and desires seemed the significant place to look for nascent cultures of resistance and for enduring change. I sought to investigate how women's friendships form within the broader context of gender inequality and difference, and how these patterns of friendship articulate with women's other commitments.

I begin with a historical account of the development of companionate marriage and modern women's friendships. Chapter 1 thus provides a historical backdrop for the theoretical and empirical perspectives on contemporary marriage and friendship that I apply in this study. I argue that companionate marriage did not become a last repository of vanquished community but rather evolved intertwined with intimate friendship—twin and symbiotic cultures with a common ethos of "affective individualism." I discuss nineteenth-century romantic friendship as a unique culture of female friendships in this early era of companionate marriage. Romantic friendship provides a historical comparison for the contemporary relation between women's friendship and marriage and allows me to move from past to present, linking theory on the history of family and community with propositions about the contemporary situation.

Chapter 2 presents a broad introduction to my findings. I survey women's testimony on the unique and important aspects of close friendships. Here, women describe intimacy between close friends and how their friendly exchanges affect their marriages.

Chapters 3 and 4 analyze women's close friendships as an institution. Chapter 3 explores patterns of frequency, time, place, and permissible content in the friendships of the women I interviewed—how close friends establish commitment; the rules and expectations women apply to close friendship; and the wide realm of residual customs that gives friendship much of its recognizable form. These patterns reveal hierarchies of obligations and commitments that undergird both marriage and friendship.

Chapter 4 examines the classical link between friendship and individuation. I scrutinize my interviews for clues as to whether individuality and autonomy are engendered and reinforced in women's close friendships; I investigate how ideals of friendship and practices of individuality intersect with women's commitments to marriage and family.

Chapter 5 looks at the active involvement of close friends in each other's marriage. I consider how women friends talk about marriage, with what aims in mind, and to what effect on marriage and on their friendship. I consider the social context shaping women's "marriage work" and the implications of marriage work for power and authority in marriage.

Chapter 6 concludes by drawing together my historical analyses and my contemporary findings in a discussion of women's close friendships as community. Here, I attempt to disentangle a concept of community from classical assumptions that identify communal ties with premodern social forms. And I consider how the friendships I studied manifest elements of community.

Interviewing Women about Friendship

My exploratory aims and interest in friendship directed me to a method that would produce rich detail and adapt to evolving theoretical concerns: a focused interview, malleable enough to follow emergent leads and standardized enough to register strong patterns. Unobtrusive observation or participant observation in private friendships was, of course, impossible. Appendix A details this method of research and the associated problems of inquiry and inference. My interview elicited two kinds of information about friendship and marriage: women's self-descriptions of their friendships and their views on friendship and marriage; and more general information on the formal correspondence between friendship and marriage. To construct analyses of friendship independent of the women's own subjective understandings, I elicited considerable information about patterns and practices of friendship and prepared to interpret statements about reasons, needs, beliefs, and desires.

I directed most of my attention to middle- and working-class married, employed mothers, although I interviewed a wider variety of women. Because companionate marriage is a theoretical concern here, I might have focused on urban, educated professional women, the sector with which companionate marriage is most strongly identified in the literature. Yet the recent outpouring of writing on friendship—most of it about women in this stratum—suggests that under the influence of feminism, many of these women are reviving the ideology of romantic friendship; this posed a problem for me. As I explain in chapter 1, I believe that romantic friendship has always been more than just stylistic convention; it is rather a self-conscious culture of friendship. Still, like romantic marriage, romantic friendship is a realm where ideal and reality merge easily. I decided to learn about friendship from women who were less likely to idealize it.

Family scholarship since the sixties has amply documented the cross-class diffusion of the ideals of companionate marriage, at least among wives.[4] Given this evidence of widespread support for companionate ideals, I chose to focus on "average American" women and investigate friendships that should broadly represent contemporary women. (I did interview a few very low-income women. But in slighting their representation in my sample, I acknowledged the structural limitations of my propositions: under conditions of chronic unemployment and poverty and when a modicum of welfare benefits are available, poor single mothers may not find their long-term economic interests in marriage.)[5]

I focused on mothers for a few reasons. For one, a previous analysis of survey data on friendship suggested that motherhood constricts women's networks of friends considerably more than fatherhood does men's. Because mothers with small networks were unhappier than those with large ones, Claude Fischer and I took those contracted networks to reflect constraints on mothers' ability to conduct friendships rather than their preferences.[6] I wanted a closer look at that process. In recent decades, 90 percent of American women have married; 95 percent of all married women have expected to have children and, at least up to now, virtually all of these eventually have.[7] Thus, most women spend a fair portion of their adult life in that very involving role. I believed that examining women's friendships during a common period of constraint would uncover some of the stronger motives in friendship, and some of the persistent themes of community. In other words, a commonly experienced period of constraint might reveal—along with the particularities of friendship at that specific stage—the values and exchanges in their friendships that women would strive against odds to maintain.

I collected a varied sample of women to interview by contacting associates in various cities, towns, and suburbs in California (see appendix A for sampling details). All but a few of the women agreed to be interviewed. Although not statistically representative, the sample included women of various social classes, ages, races, and stages of life. Before describing this sample by categories, I offer sketches of a few of the women I interviewed. As I do throughout this book, I alter enough facts to preserve confidentiality.

Louise and her family live in a comfortable working-class neighborhood in a small city. She is in the first year of a very close friendship—her first since she and Gary married six years ago. Both Louise and her husband were born nearby, but her high school friendships faded—partly, she says, because her jealous husband discouraged them. Louise met Jan in a night class at the community college; their friendship seems to have added to Louise's growing sense of power in her marriage. School, work, and friendship have all added personal satisfaction as well as marital conflict to Louise's life. She feels that she and Gary are "working it out." He is now cooking meals for the children when Louise works, and he enjoys the company of Jan and her husband, the first couple Louise ever recruited into socializing as couples.

Cass had the help and encouragement of her large close-knit family in throwing out her husband, who beat her and tried to keep her away from her family. Lacking education, she works long hours, often at lonely, home piecework or household work, supporting her children on poverty-level wages. Her own family has provided friendship and support. One sister has always been her favorite confidante, and Cass has had few opportunities and little time to find friendships in other contexts. Cass and her children live in a very poor, ethnically diverse white neighborhood. Neighbors say hello; but only one has ever been invited into her tiny, impeccably tended home. Cass is reluctant to become friendlier with this one neighbor, who is also a single mother. Although Cass very much likes the woman, she is not eager to care for her children since Cass's own children are older and more independent.

Nancy lives in a comfortable suburban ranch home with her husband and teenage children. She is nearing forty and has worked part-time, off and on, at service jobs accessible to this articulate and personable woman with a high school education. She and her husband lead a very active social life with other couples, many of them friends she and her husband met in children's recreation. Nancy has two very close friends, including a longtime neighbor whom she calls her best friend. Nancy and her husband are also "best friends," and yet she keeps a very large sphere of interests and confidences for her close women friends alone.

Janine, her husband, and young children live in a basement flat in a deteriorating neighborhood of single-family homes in a small city. Like Janine, most of her neighbors are black. Many are formerly well paid industrial workers, now unemployed by industry shutdowns. Janine was recently laid off a kitchen job at a fast-food restaurant. Her husband is marginally employed; the job that brought them to this city ended when the company closed. Janine is still closest to one of her six sisters, and to the rest of her own family. "We're all friends. When we throw a party, we don't need to invite nobody, because everybody's already there." She also has a good friend in the neighborhood and spends a lot of time with her when their husbands are not at home.

Mary and Hal lead parallel lives. They have raised two children and have remained together through a thirty-year marriage, mostly by going their separate ways. Mary is bitter about her husband's lack of feeling for family, and his preference for his own friends. Hal does skilled industrial work, but Mary professes only the vaguest knowledge of his job of twenty years. For several years Mary has worked full-time at a large insurance company in an office with a stable staff of skilled clericals. She takes great pride and enjoyment in her work, and in sociable relations with her diverse office peers. Her best friend, Vera, is a divorced mother of grown children. The two friends socialize frequently during weekends and times that most of the other women regard as strictly "family time."

Thea is an urban mother of young teenagers. She is educated, very accomplished in and devoted to her full-time career. Work and family are her most important investments, although she and her husband lead an active upper-middle-class social life. Thea's marriage is the stereotypical companionate marriage; her "friendship" with her husband is still vital after many years of marriage. In recent years she has formed a very ardent friendship with another professional woman who also has strong family bonds. They consistently manage to find time together amid very busy lives.

The employed women in my sample worked in various parts of the "pink-collar ghetto." The household, clerical, service, and "women's professional" jobs (in fields where women dominate and educational requirements far outstrip salaries: teaching, nursing, librarianship, social work) were distributed among the women in a hierarchy of salary, working conditions, and prestige that roughly corresponded to the hierarchy of their husbands' jobs. The husbands' incomes and occupations varied much more than those of the women. Some husbands were low-paid unskilled service workers, others high double-digit professionals. Represented in between were blue-collar skilled workers, white-collar sales workers, small business owners, and corporate administrators. Mirroring patterns in society at large, these men were married to women whose salaries ranged by less than half the spread of their husbands'. The women's salaries constituted just over one-third of their family income, in the cases of the married women who worked full-time, and generally less than one-sixth of the household income, in the cases of those working part-time. Education among the women in my sample was more evenly distributed, because a majority had secured some community college education. Even the very low-income women had high school diplomas; Cass had just been awarded hers after several years of evening school.

Family cultural styles also only roughly corresponded to husbands' occupational status and income. Consumption patterns— evident in dress, household furnishings, organizational membership, and socializing and recreation patterns—were influenced also by wives' education and occupation and, it appeared, by their friendships as well. For example, Louise, a working-class woman by any standard, has upwardly mobile career aspirations; and her best friend is more prosperous and middle class. In her home, Louise has decorated one room—a living room—with the woodsy hues, nubby textures, and eclectic wall hangings that mark California's contemporary young middle class.

The bulk of my sample fell between stable working class and solid middle class. A few cases each were upper middle class and working and unemployed poor. Predictably, divorced women and black women were disproportionately represented in the latter categories. Since class categories for this sample were complex and particularly unpredictive for the relationships I studied, I use class designations loosely and attempt to specify which elements of stratification appeared to determine the behavior I am describing.

The women I interviewed range in age from early twenties to late fifties. Nearly half are in their thirties. All but two of the twenty-one women are mothers. Fourteen have children at home. Of these, nine have at least one child under six. Mirroring the national rate of employment, half the women with children under six currently do paid work: four work part-time, one full-time (and two others are on layoff or brief leave from full-time work). All six women whose children are older than six work, four women full-time.

Each interview took place in the woman's home and usually lasted two and a half hours. I kept the potentially long-ranging interview as compact as possible, because most women were carving out time for me amid a full day's responsibilities, and nearly half had young children at home with them. They were eager and willing to talk openly and at great length, with only one exception. Penny was a willing participant but said, "I'm the kind of person [who] can't explain myself." We both would have benefited from a longer and less structured exchange; in future exploratory work, I would probably include some multisession interviews.

The interview questions are reproduced in appendix B. Each interview entered a woman's close social world with introductory open-ended questions about self, family, and friends: Tell me a little about yourself. Then I asked for names and descriptions of those people with whom each woman felt most involved and closest. Eventually, I asked specific questions about the conduct and content of close friendships, probing for their cognitive, affective, and moral orientations. Most questions were open-ended, although often very narrowly focused; a good many invoked short or scaled forced-choice responses.

How should one read my conclusions? If I analyze individual conduct in terms of a group and report incidences of certain behavior among group members, I imply generalization. If a hypothesis generates rich detail, if the subject quickly strikes a resonant chord in a reader, if a theoretical argument is persuasive or uses the terms of a current discourse—then a reader may take an exploratory project as conclusive. I emphasize that I do not generalize the material I have gathered or confirm the propositions it generates or corroborates.

Perhaps the best way to remind a reader that I offer a hypothesis-generating exploratory study is to note its biases and limitations. I do so in appendix A. Assuming the reader is thus prepared, I curb my inclination to use very tentative language and frequent notes of caution. I can use bold interpretation to provoke theoretical refinement and confirmatory replication. As for the data this research method generated, I have presented a great deal—in the form of quotations and response counts—and I have discussed negative cases, so that the reader can judge the conclusions I have drawn. If I am successful, this book should stimulate new thinking and scholarship linking friendship to the social structures of gender.

Chapter One

The Modernization of
Friendship and Marriage

Like nearly everyone else, sociologists have paid little attention to friendship. They have tended to include it among the casualties of modernization, portraying modern friendship as a dessicated version of the richer intimacy of past times. Beyond sad comment on this "decline of community," they say little about friendship, except to note an occasional survival in street-corner society.

Marriage and the family, on the other hand, have received plenty of attention. The main task of twentieth-century sociologists of the family has been to chart the progress of companionate marriage, which is usually treated as fully evolved in whatever era the writer is situated. In these accounts, marriage now embodies the friendship and community that have been squeezed out of wider realms.

This chapter revises three accounts of changes in family and community that dominate sociological theory in these areas. As I create an alternate story of the modernization of friendship and marriage—one that fits better with recent social historical research—I can present my contemporary findings before a historical backdrop that may enrich and enliven their interpretation.

Two different sociological perspectives converge in the standard sociological accounts of community and family change.[1] The antimodernist perspective, generally conservative, echoes anti-Enlightenment alarm at the passing of the traditional family and the emergence of individualistic family norms. Writers like Carle

1

Zimmerman and Pitirim Sorokin, and later Robert Nisbet and Christopher Lasch, chart how individualism and the decline of community weaken the family. Emotionally and morally, the family collapses inward without the support of religious authority and intermediate communal institutions. Community is replaced by "pseudo-intimacy" and the "easy, nondemanding," and morally insignificant attachments of friendship.[2]

The modernist perspective—mostly liberal, and by far the predominant framework in American family sociology—generally embraces the transformation to modernity and views the family as resiliently adapting. Evolutionists, functionalists, interactionists have all contributed their particular versions of this change.[3] Sociologists in the modernist vein tend to agree with the antimodernists that the communal supports of the family have indeed eroded. But, although this shift has placed certain pressures on marriages, the family is able to adapt through internal changes and improve by functional specialization.

Although modernists and antimodernists draw different frameworks and conclusions for family and community change, they differ primarily in their attitude toward the change. Their accounts of the modernization of family and friendship converge remarkably. In the following portrait of this change, I incorporate a range of causal explanations, ignoring differences in framework among theorists, in order to depict this convergence.

Most explanations postulate a unidirectional flow of influence from larger institutions to the family (although important exceptions suggest a mutual interaction).[4] As industrialization and its attendant economic, political, demographic, and ideological changes—notably individualism—weaken traditional structures of kinship, a free market in marital selection emerges. Authority within the household democratizes. It becomes relatively greater than the authority of kin and community; yet it is simultaneously drained by an expanding state. In response to these changes, love, companionship, and the satisfaction of individual needs and desires become the standards for selecting and renewing commitments of marriage in an exchange between men and women as free agents.

As industrialism and urbanism infuse instrumentalism, impersonality, and transitoriness into social relations outside the family, the conjugal family becomes the last repository of emotionality, love, long-term commitment, altruism, and nurturance. Communal sentiment and responsibility contract from a wider circle of kin, neighbors, and friends to the realm of the household. Secondary institutions such as guild, church, and civic council lose their moral hold. The public sphere of sociality and community disappears; deep lasting friendship, communal exchange, and ritual are replaced by shallow instrumental sociability and neighborliness.

The sociological consensus on the modernization of family and friendship covers three favored stories. The first story recognizes the rise of individualism as a predominant modernizing ideology. It tells how a single powerful ideological current developed in politics and the marketplace and swept through private life, irrevocably transforming all relations there. Under the influence of individualism, modern couples marry and remain married for love; they look to marital intimacy for self-fulfillment and the satisfaction of their desires. Their friendships become casual, specialized, even calculated.[5] My research with women, however, contradicts what this story foretells about how marriage and friendship develop.

The second story concerns the rise of the privatized, sentimental conjugal family, built upon a romantic, companionate marriage. (A legal reformer, Judge Ben Lindsey, coined the term in the twenties for a proposed legal trial marriage; but it recently supplanted the awkward "companionship marriage.") In this story, a new marriage ideal arises and is realized through various social changes. In one version or another, this tale is the favorite of popular culture-makers as well as twentieth-century sociologists of the family. It asserts that free choice and romance make marriage passionate, sexy, fun, and equal—husband and wife are best friends and lovers.[6] My research, however, contradicts what this story foretells about texture and symmetry in contemporary marriage.

The third story is linked with the last one and in fact was taken up first by sociological theory. It describes moral-affectual changes in primary relationships outside the modernizing family. Here, the modern family partly responds to and partly abets the decline of intimate community. As community withers, relations with kin, neighbors, and friends become less intimate, warm, convivial, and committed until community no longer touches marriage and family life. Both husband and wife are pressured to meet all the other's needs. At least for women, my research contradicts what this story foretells about contemporary relations between family and friendship.[7]

In reviewing these stories in light of recent family and social historical research, I have assembled a speculative history of connections between women's friendships and family, to set the stage for my account of contemporary women's friendships. There are many patterns of family and gender behavior that structural and historical arguments explain well. Here and throughout, I emphasize these structural and historical explanations over psychodynamic ones. Much excellent work explains gender difference by socialization and internalization, and I shall turn to its theories as I progress. Certainly, I recognize that many aspects of friendships have psychological motives and roots in gender personality. Theorists who sensitively chart the psychodynamics of gender personality locate that process within the modern family.[8] The following discussion follows the social and family changes that consolidate gender differences.

Affective Individualism and the Family

Students of the rise of the companionate marriage hold that the spread of individualism and democratic values were and continue to be central forces of family change. Individualism, they maintain, decreases the authority of kin. Individual rights encourage individual choices and so marriages are contracted on the basis of affection rather than calculation. Family life becomes conjugally centered. Democracy in the family accompanies democracy in society. The equality of husband and wife promotes their empathy and friendship. Their conjugal isolation makes their communication and companionship unique and precious.[9]

William Goode and Gary Lee, among others, argue that exposure to individualistic ideas changes marital patterns; these ideas are so powerful that people who are exposed to them in education or travel incorporate them into family life even before they learn them in the marketplace or polity.[10] Edward Shorter writes, "Once the rules of marketplace individualism had been learned, they easily took control of the whole arena of conscious attitudes."[11] A clear account of how individualism "took control" of the family is hard to find, however. Sociological writers rarely tell the story. It appears rather as an assumption or as simple assertions of macrocauses and microeffects, as if some sociological classic had exhaustively explained how individualism altered family life and now only brief notes on that transformation were needed.

The emphasis on individualism in family sociology is not amiss. It is clear that over the past two or three centuries the family has been changing—leveling authority and favoring individual autonomy and other relational changes that are rooted in individualism. In our statements about individualism and the family, however, we must avoid a mechanistic view of ideological diffusion that obscures the ways that ideological changes in public life influence private life. Ideas that originate as market principles or civic ideals of political participation do not submerge old ideas and practices. Individualism and democracy did not simply or progressively replace communal and hierarchical traditions in family life. For the most part, they slowly, indirectly, and unevenly permeated family life and took diverse meanings there as they were mediated by religion, class, and gender. [12]

Writers who treat individualism in the family tend to focus on ways that individualism shaped the lives of men and women; but they pay little attention to the reverse process. By exploring how women and men have altered individualism as they adopted it, we can learn how communal and patriarchal ideologies found their last safe refuge in the modernizing family and how they bear today on companionship in marriage.

To revise the story of individualism and the family, I have adapted historian Lawrence Stone's concept of *affective individualism*. Stone holds that in sixteenth-century England, before the spread of individualism, "the family was an open-ended, low-keyed, unemotional, authoritarian institution," essentially an economic unit, short-lived because parents died early and children were fostered out in apprenticeship. Relations within all social strata were plagued with distrust, intolerance, habitual violence, and mutual litigation. [13] The affective chill of these times was a residue of harsh childrearing.

As the characteristic *mentalité* of modern culture, affective individualism changed relations of authority, thinking, and feeling among people. Awareness and expression of individuality, rights of autonomy, and emotional and personal intimacy replaced "distance, deference, and patriarchy" as the ethos of relations newly marked off as "personal life." The new, eighteenth-century family featured an "intensified affective bonding at the nuclear core," emphasized the pursuit of individual happiness, and valued sexual pleasure and privacy.[14] How affective individualism operated on wider social relations is less clear to Stone, but he finds evidence that people became more tolerant, sentimental, and distressed by cruelty and violence.

Economic, political, and psychodynamic influences combined to spread affective individualism among the eighteenth-century upper bourgeoisie and squirearchy.[15] Protestantism intensified the nascent individualism in Christian thought and undermined the patriarchal authority of husbands; the Renaissance and Calvinism diffused self-awareness. Capitalist markets and libertarianism augmented secularism, rationalism, and autonomy. The decline of patriarchy and repressive childrearing unleashed affection. A "complex of semi-independent developments, spread out over more than a century" initiated a "transformation of human consciousness" among the English elite, epitomized by these couplets from Pope's *Essay on Man* (1733):

> Thus God and Nature link'd the general frame
> And bade self-love and social be the same.
>
> . . . .
>
> That Reason, Passion answer one great aim
> That true self-love and Social are the same.[16]

Stone finds the central themes of individualism in these couplets: self-awareness and the autonomous pursuit of self-interest advance the social good; love and reason can reconcile (in marriage). He maintains that the social and familial changes that produced and responded to individualism evoked capacities for warm and intimate personal relations. People developed self-conscious, self-expressive forms of intimacy, and with introspection they found and expressed sentiment. Affective individualism thus appears as a coherent ethos.[17]

Like others who write about individualism in the family, Stone documents its appearance in the personal lives of men and women without noting how differently they adapted its ideas. Evidence from the past decade of social history suggests, however, that different patterns of affective individualism filtered through the differently cut prisms of gender. Self-consciousness and orientation toward self-interest advanced by political and economic individualism took different shape in the thought and relations of women, because women's identities formed within the small, separate world of the family. Much more so than men's, women's affective individualism developed within the communal constraints of family responsibility and collective gender identification. In formulating a gendered ideal-type, I refer to men and women of the middle classes (primarily in the nineteenth-century American Northeast), both because they are the subjects of most available data and because they were the avant-garde of individualism.

Colonial America, although never quite fitting the mold of traditional community, restrained the expression of individualism. In Puritan communities, for example, thorough authoritative regulation of family, work, and cultural life left little room for the elaboration of individual themes inherent in Puritan theology. Private life, as a realm distinguished from public life by uniquely personal and private relations, did not yet exist. Their boundaries vague, families were units of economic production—and thus work, play, childrearing, courtship, government, gossip, and mutual aid intermingled through time and space. In the course of these activities, people passed through one another's households—trading, visiting, boarding, apprenticing—and when residing there, they were considered family.[18]

Patriarchal authority, vested in the father, unified the government of family and society. Women and children contributed substantially to family and thus to social production; yet they had few individual rights and no formal political power. Centrality in production and social intercourse yielded a measure of respectful recognition and, very likely, informal sources of power as well. Nonetheless, colonial family and community allocated and enforced social roles that ceded little to individual rights and self-exploration.

In postrevolutionary America, waves of social change favored adaptations of affective individualism within an emerging realm of personal life. By the early nineteenth century, commercial capitalism and regional agricultural trade had vastly extended the reach of market relations. Many Americans, at least in the Northeast, had encountered the ideas of market individualism and the ideological currents of a centralizing national state. Although local communities continued to bound the moral space of social and communal ties, commerce and politics were conduits of Enlightenment and republican ideas of libertarian rights and the pursuit of happiness.[19]

Expanding commerce and factories fragmented the integrated world of family, work, and community. As men followed work out of the home, they entered the emergent public sphere of work and politics as access to wages became the measure of general value and status. Women continued their precapitalist domestic work, but now it became private, marginal to the dynamics of social reward in a cash economy.

While working-class and farm women continued to produce the goods and services of family subsistence, women of more prosperous classes were increasingly freed from activities of economic production. These middle-class women progressively enlarged their role in family nurturance and religious and moral tutelage. They did so with the blessing of religious authorities whose own public influence had been diminished by secular forces and who were glad to focus on regulating sexual and family relations. These newly allied middle-class women and ministers, joined by male veterans from the arduous public world of commerce, elaborated a new doctrine of separate spheres. They attributed a natural order and a moral equality to the responsibilities each gender would discharge in his or her own sphere. Men—tamers of nature, producers of value, warriors in the competition of each against all, providers of family material life, and citizens of public life—thereby rightfully governed families. Women—teachers of children, producers of domestic comfort, exemplars of purity and piety, providers of respite and consolation, and conservators of the values jostled out of public life—represented the heart of both society and family. In their separate spheres of endeavor, men and women adapted new relations of individualism.

Men of different classes were exposed and disposed to different degrees of configurations of individualism. By the eighteenth and nineteenth centuries, most men—merchants, laborers, farmers—found their work integrated into larger and larger markets that made the relation of self to work increasingly abstract and fragmented.[20] For men, *autonomy* became the salient aspect of affective individualism. Despite his brief cultural elevation in the eighteenth century, the "man of sentiment," whose moral self-awareness and humanist sensibilities imbued his participation in both private and civic life, had to step aside.[21] The eighteenth-century European bourgeois and, even more, the nineteenth-century American businessman were men of the market. Their self-interest, self-reliance, and competitiveness were core characteristics of the individualism formed in market relations. For husbands and fathers, their market self was reinforced in private life, as "provider" became men's central family role.

Good providers properly subordinated the affective self to the market self. Tocqueville, impressed with how the marketplace pervaded the thinking of nineteenth-century American men, pronounced, "Few of them are ever known to give way to those idle and solitary meditations which commonly precede and produce the great emotions of the heart."[22] For men, autonomy subsumed self-exploration and self-development. Men developed self-consciousness in terms of self-interest and expressed individuality primarily in autonomous achievement. They restrained emotional intimacy to give rein to independence. Thus, Georg Simmel characterized affective individualistic modern men as "differentiated" men of "secrets," who limited access to their whole selves even in the closest of friendships.[23]

For women, self-awareness and emotional intimacy became the salient aspects of affective individualism. Women's lives did not encourage independence and autonomy. Although liberty and equality were widespread themes of civic life in the eighteenth and nineteenth centuries, deference and the subordination of wives to husbands sustained less damage than other hierarchical social relations. Furthermore, the growing idealization of motherhood in these centuries and the barriers to participation in public life outside the newly separate "women's sphere" severely limited the possibilities of autonomy for women.

Individualism was a theme of the elevation of women's moral position in the family. Each woman was responsible for ensuring her family's piety and moral conduct; this calling encouraged her to claim she was the moral equal—at times the superior—of her husband. The moral equality attributed to women and men in the nineteenth-century gender ideal of separate spheres represented an increase in female stature over patriarchal ideals. Yet the new ideal by no means repudiated paternal authority. Barbara Welter, documenting the American cult of domestic "true womanhood," quotes a nineteenth-century women's magazine: "The man bears rule over his wife's person and conduct. She bears rule over his inclinations: he governs by law; she by persuasion."[24] In terms of individualism, this arrangement left women far more room for self-examination than it did for autonomy.

Similarly, the sentimental ideals of motherhood and childhood that diffused at this time promoted self-awareness and emotionality without increasing women's autonomy. As "angels of love and fidelity who first opened our senses to behold God in his works and word," mothers were increasingly viewed as forming their children's later character as well. And the most effective influence was now tender rather than repressive, as it had been in previous eras. In floods of diaries, magazines, and maternal associations, mothers examined their motivations and achievements. "It seems to me at times as if the weight of responsibility connected with these little immortal beings would prove too much for me," writes one very modern-sounding anxious mother. "Am I doing what is right? Am I doing enough?"[25]

If maternal responsibility was more exacting, it was also more engaging. In the daily care and tutelage of children, for whom mothers were now the primary parents, women developed intense emotions and relational capacities. Expressions of passionate attachment to children replaced the emotional reserve of previous eras. Mothers vicariously experienced self-interest, autonomy, and competition, nurturing husbands and rearing children to their proper place in the world. They tasted "the glory of victory, without suffering the dangers of the battle."[26] In short, women developed self primarily by self-consciously developing moral children. In this context they developed a less differentiated individualism than did men, whose context was contractual relations. Women's individualism tended to emerge communally, and it developed integrally with communal identification and responsibility for others. Their adaptation of individualism blunted themes of autonomy but sharpened those of self-awareness and emotional self-expression.

Women conducted self-exploration in a social world far more homogenous than that of men. Women lived in private worlds popu-

lated by family, kin, neighbors, friends, and fellow parishioners—
people of similar social status whose parallel endeavors built a solidarity of resemblance and whose bonds were explicitly communal.
There is evidence that women's public demeanor in the uneasy
nineteenth century, like men's, revealed a concern for status—for
example, in rigorous customs of dress and speech.[27] Women's daily
lives were, nonetheless, far more private than public. Intimacy in
this homogenous private world required less reserve than intimacy
constructed amid difference, competition, and threat. In accessible intimacy, the elaboration of sentiment also came easier. The
man of sentiment, horrified by cruelty and moved by deep feeling,
was a brief literary vogue that the market culture instantly ridi-
culed. The woman of sentiment was a new social person. Her private world of family and friends welcomed empathy and feeling,
apart from the harsh exigencies of the market. Her sentimental
culture fortified the nineteenth-century woman to carry out a re-
demptive public mission in suffrage, moral reform, and charity.

Collective identifications, the sense of fundamental belonging
and identification within groups, created distinct arenas of self-
awareness for men and women as differences between their social
lives sharpened. Affective individualism flourished amid the social
changes that separated public from private life. Men's individualism involved constructing identities that bridged their public and
private spheres of life. As they individuated, men identified themselves in contrast to other men within the collective identifications
of class and stratum. Gender, for them, was a less complex identification.*

For women, gender emerged as a more important collective
identification. Nancy Cott persuasively argues that for sectors of

---

*This assertion contradicts most other work on the social history of gender,
which treats the nineteenth-century ideology of separate spheres as an era of
changing and intensified gender identification for both men and women (G. J.
Barker-Benfield, *The Horrors of the Half-Known Life* [New York: Harper and
Row, 1976], ch. 19; E. Anthony Rotundo, "Body and Soul: Changing Ideal of
American Middle-Class Manhood, 1770–1920," *Journal of Social History* 16
[Summer 1983]: 23–38). I suggest that the shifts in meaning affected nineteenth-
century men much more as children than as adults. In each separate sphere, the
question for men was of being an individual or a citizen, since both were primarily
male options. The meaning of gender has become much more compelling for men
now that women compete in the public realm.

nineteenth-century American middle-class women, gender was at least as important as class.[28] Women's individualism developed as part of a new ideology of gender. The materials of unique self-definition and expression were drawn from within the sharply etched gender culture of women's sphere, where the possible "others" for adult women were husband and children. In previous eras, women might have perceived the interests of children in competition with those of parents.[29] But under the emerging ideology of a paramount mother-child bond, wherein women's social and moral achievements were largely tied to mothering, women perceived their interests allied with those of their children.

Women's relationships to their husbands were an entirely different story. Although nineteenth-century women's economic interests depended more than ever on those of their husbands, a new female individualism nonetheless evolved. The antipatriarchal impact of Protestant marital values and the increasing secular veneration of women's moral role in the family favored an individualism in which wives defined their collective interests in opposition to their husbands'.[30]

These themes of gender opposition are most evident in nineteenth-century American writing on "true womanhood,"[31] in passages favorably contrasting women's values to men's. "Our men are sufficiently moneymaking. Let us keep our women and children from the contagion as long as possible." Women would counter male mercenary values with "purity of mind, simplicity and frankness of heart, benevolence, . . . forbearance and self-denial."[32]

Women's new moral stature allowed them room for independent judgment and activity. In advocating a negative strategy toward men's sexual demands, they offered female purity as an antidote to male sinfulness. They effected increased birth control by asserting the right to refuse sex. Daniel Scott Smith labels this strategy "domestic feminism"—the flowering of women's individualism in the private sphere.[33] True womanhood themes featured a protofeminist ideology in which the interests of women were defined partly in opposition to those of men. This gender-identified individualism—in which women identified themselves in relation to children and family and in opposition to the interests of men as a gender—shaped the content of the most popular forms of early feminism.

Movements for social purity and temperance, and to expand education for effective motherhood all asserted women's familistic values in the political arena and often attempted to control the public and private behavior of men.[34] (It is not surprising that feminist activity was directed against the public contexts, like the tavern, which had become the main arenas for male friendship and sociability. And even though capitalist urbanization and consumerism were clearly working toward the same effect, and with considerably more force, Christopher Lasch correctly places feminism [more accurately, wives and mothers] among the antagonists of nineteenth-century male public sociality.)

In sum, individualism and democratic ideas did not submerge communal and patriarchal family values. Men and women adapted individualism and democratic ideas differently. In the late nineteenth century, many women who aspired to autonomous public endeavor did not marry.[35] But even in this era, when the number of never-marrying women temporarily increased, most women married and spent most of their adult life rearing children. Once they married, they encountered individualism as mothers. Because eighteenth- and nineteenth-century social developments elevated the moral stature, affective qualities, and domestic influence of mothers, women developed a consciousness of self and of self-interest indissolubly bound to others. Maternal responsibility would thereafter figure in strategies of self-interest in both marriage dynamics and politics. Affective individualism—self-awareness and expression, strivings toward autonomy, and emotional intimacy—would develop for women within the constraints of familial commitment and gender-based consciousness. The ideology of separate spheres and its associated gender identifications limited the scope of women's individualism, but they also provided the cultural materials for constructing individuality.

The History of Marriage Sentiment

The second prominent story about family change identifies the sentimental texture of marriage as the most visible modern family change: marriage became increasingly founded on and characterized by affection. Religious, philosophical, literary, epistolary, and legal evidence of a new emphasis on companionship, love, eroticism, and affection in marriage—from Reformation theology on— prompt confident generalization about the new companionship. In a statement that is now axiomatic in family sociology, Ernest W. Burgess declared that the basis of family life has moved from institutional rules to individual companionship and concluded that "in modern society, the companionship of men and women . . . is upon a plane perhaps never before reached in human existence."[36]

Typically, sociological statements about companionship commingle, collapse, or equate distinct relational characteristics and discrete structures and processes of domestic life. Companionship has variously denoted affection, romantic love, eros, intimacy, similarity of interests, interchangeable division of labor, and joint recreation. Yet these characteristics are not analytically interchangeable. Intimacy does not necessarily evolve with affection, even in long-term affectionate relations such as those among neighbors. Nor does intimacy presuppose mutuality or equality, as the religious confessional and the psychotherapeutic hour demonstrate. Similarly, sociologists have read companionship in patterns of marital affiliation, codes of religious and legal obligation, statements about authority, measures of power, sexual mores, and emotional exchanges. Yet each of these categories refers to discrete marital ideals and actualities.

Constructing ideal-types involves combining concepts. But the loose construction of "companionship marriage" undermines its theoretical and methodological usefulness. Burgess's leap from ideal-type to empirical generalization in describing the actual progress of marital companionship, is an example of the confusion that results from conflation of historical trends with actual fact.* Such assumptions deflect attention from obstacles to change and modern sources of variation. We fail to assess just how companionate marriage has grown and what structures shape variations in marital sentiment. In effect, much twentieth-century family theory adds a coda to nineteenth-century evolutionary theories. Compan-

---

*This fairly common stance led Robert O. Blood and Donald M. Wolfe to classify marriages in their sample as "egalitarian" when husbands and wives were relatively less unequal even though the power scores remained husband-dominant (Blood and Wolfe, *Husbands and Wives* [New York: Free Press, 1960], 23). They are criticized by Dair L. Gillespie in "Who Has the Power: The Marital Struggle," *Journal of Marriage and the Family* 33 (1971): 445–58.

ionate marriage evolves past its full expression in the Victorian family to end with the contemporary egalitarian marriage.

When we look carefully at the story of marriage sentiment, we discover that three sets of changes have definitively shaped marriage: a loosening of familial control of courtship; the emergence of a romantic companionate marital ideal; and the development of a practicable ideal of domesticity, emotionally intensifying the mother-child bond and privatizing family life. Each change was causally linked to other changes in society and family. Let us see how sentiment changed marriage.

Free Courtship and Romance

Seventeenth- and eighteenth-century changes in American and European economy, society, and polity interfered with the coerced marriages that the middle classes often arranged for their kin.[37] Thus, premarital affection became more important in alliance, and initially repellent marriages became less common.[38]

Expressing itself in themes of affection and romance, freer courtship promoted a new individualism.[39] Young people could now pursue their preferences, desires, and personal dramas—the one point in young women's lives when the introspective, individualistic themes of nineteenth-century American courtship coincided with Stone's genderless notion of affective individualism. "Nowhere," wrote Tocqueville, "are young women surrendered so early or so completely to their own independence."[40] The acute self-awareness, liberty, and emotional freedom permitted girls in courtship meant that women experienced, at least briefly, an affective individualism that was somewhat similar to men's in its emphasis on autonomy.[41] Courtship probably represented the starkest experience of individualism that women in these centuries would encounter.[42] The next life stage, sentimental motherhood, obliterated the themes of autonomy and stark individuation in women's culture.

Freer courtship may have improved the distribution of an initial marital companionship that provided admiration, compatibility, and affection. But even the most controlling families of previous eras had likely conceded some role to affectionate consent; these particular companionate qualities probably also developed in marriages (at least to some extent) in precompanionate eras, as the residue of successful interdependence and adaptation.[43] Nonetheless, the affective individualism of freer female courtship likely spurred the creation of a romantic companionate marriage ideal for married women's expectations.

The Rise of the
Romantic Companionate Ideal

In colonial America, Puritan theology emphasized marital companionship and love, but affection was to grow from dutiful marriage—not to unite bride and groom. Furthermore, it was to grow from women's "reverend subjection" to their husbands. "Puritan love," writes Edmund Morgan, "was no romantic passion but a rational love in which the affections were commanded by the will." Indeed, Puritans cautioned against excessive marital affection as well as other "earthly" comforts.[44]

Courtly love had been an adulterous passion, thought to be incompatible with marriage. Puritanism prepared the ground for a marital love ideal by prescribing love in marriage. Drawing upon both traditions, the romantic love ideology resolved the Puritan antagonism between passion and reason.[45] The eighteenth-century novel (a new literary form) adapted the codes of courtly love to courtship and marriage, advertising a new conjugal ideal to the expanding reading publics of the middle classes. Idealized adoration, erotic passion, emotional attachment, enduring commitment, and the practicalities of property, class, childrearing, and conjugal cooperation blended in the new ideal without apparent contradiction. The earthly, the sublime, and the commonplace reconciled in the bourgeois "tender passion." By the late eighteenth century, the romantic conjugal ideal appeared in America and spread rapidly in a nineteenth-century surge of romantic novel reading.[46]

A structural source of the new ideal, Ian Watt proposes, inhered in the changing conditions of courtship in eighteenth- and nineteenth-century England. Single women who were losing economic ground as production moved out of the household faced a marriage crisis; a new emphasis on love offered to shore up marriage chances for these dispossessed (or upwardly mobile) women.[47] Watt's evidence—the letters of wealthy married women and the novels of their literary sympathizers—tells us much more about ascendent cultural ideals than about practices, however. The secular themes of individuality and romance emphasized in free courtship may have stirred imaginations and raised an ideal of romantic marriage among married women who had the leisure to develop their personality and whose economic dependence prompted a search for new marital bonds. But we must not mistake that ideal for actual change in marital relations.

The romance of courtship notwithstanding, nineteenth-century married couples appear not to have realized a romantic companionate ideal. Unless we are to believe that a small sampling of fervid correspondences between spouses or erotic diaries represented the very silent bourgeois majority, scholarship on nineteenth-century Europe and America suggests that marriage became more affectionate before it became romantic, and then more romantic before it became companionate. (I wonder whether a psychoanalytic historian like Peter Gay has considered that torrid correspondences may have represented bursts of romance set off by the obstacle of separation rather than indices of the sentimental texture of marriage.)[48] Even the emotionally intense marriages preserved in correspondence seem to manifest a distance and deference between husbands and wives that must represent a very rudimentary companionship.[49] Domestic sentiment united spouses whose separate lives provided limited bases for engagement, empathy, or joint endeavor. The separation of public and private spheres of life created the needs and possibilities for new emotionalized domestic attachments. Nonetheless, it seems likely that romantic sentiments waned throughout marriage. The attachments women kept to their own families were often more intense than their marriages until as mothers they transferred their attachments to their children.[50]

Even where courtship had become romantic and emotionally intense, writes Ellen Rothman, young women anticipated marriage with "images of confinement, struggle, and loss"; they expressed the belief that the intimacy of courtship could not be sustained in marriage. Steven Stowe infers from his Southern courtship letters that courtship allowed women, who approached marriage with a model of intimacy they had learned from female friendships, to relinquish that ideal as they acknowledged that "the thing is not its vision." Nancy Cott reports evidence of a nineteenth-century pattern of "marriage trauma" among bewildered and disappointed married women.[51]

European visitors of the time noted "a want of entire community of feeling" between husbands and wives. One observer commented on the fidelity of American husbands and also noted their indifference to their wives: "His wife is never the confidante of his intimate and real thoughts."[52] And Tocqueville noted the effects of separate spheres: "All these distinct and compulsory occupations are so many natural barriers, which by keeping the two sexes asunder, render the solicitations of the one less frequent and less ardent—the resistance of the other more easy." He believed men's commercial passions dampened marital feeling—the criticism of American marriage that Frank Furstenberg says foreign observers made most frequently.[53]

Among midwestern farm folk, writes John Faragher, the notion of companionate marriage was "foreign"; and in folk songs of the region, "women's needs for sentiment, passion, and sensuality combined with constancy were nearly always betrayed by masculine incapacity."[54] In urban Los Angeles and Newark, Elaine Tyler May finds no new forms of intimacy in divorce records of nineteenth-century partners who failed to live up to traditional sex roles of masculine provision and feminine purity.[55] Carl Degler, who presents evidence of companionate marriages, also documents widespread complaints by women about their treatment in marriage. In a series of letters to *Good Housekeeping*, women insist that husbands ought to provide the sympathy and support that wives provide husbands.[56]

Whatever the progress of marital sentiment, expectations considerably outdistanced it. The romantic ideal probably affected courtship (and perhaps, early marriage) far more than later married life.* When Christopher Lasch locates a historic apogee of emo-

---

*The literature on companionate marriage often misgeneralizes from the intense romantic passion, reciprocal introspection, withdrawal from social networks—all keynotes of romantic marriage—that characterize these brief early stages better than the later ones. From such erroneous generalizations come Georg Simmel's conclusions that women do not develop friendships because they remain immersed in the sphere of love (*The Sociology of Georg Simmel*, ed. Kurt H. Wolff [New York: Free Press, 1950], 325).

tional intensity in the nineteenth-century bourgeois family, he mistakes lyric celebrations of a new domesticity for conjugal romantic love.[57]

Domesticity: The Sentimental and Private Family

It was the sentiments of domesticity that echoed among the households of the middle classes. As family life became a hallowed repository of private experience and a refuge from the cold, harsh public experience, domestic sentiment celebrated the family's new special comforts.[58]

Edward Shorter, one of the first to sift the chronology and causes of changes in marital sentiment, distinguishes between the sentimental complexes of romance and domesticity. Romance is the sentiment of courtship; domesticity, of marriage. Shorter describes domesticity as "the family's awareness of itself as a precious emotional unit that must be protected with privacy and isolation from outside intrusion." He proposes that the emotional intensification of family life that developed first among the middle classes took form around the mother-infant relationship. This matricentric domesticity then extended its boundaries to include husbands, as households withdrew into privacy and intimacy.[59]

Shorter's logic falters when he explains how husbands entered the sentimental culture of domesticity. Rather than develop his logic of matricentric domesticity, Shorter ignores his own profound doubts about the durability of romance and insists that empathy and equality develop in the intimacy of marriage contracted on romantic love. Empathy, "affective sex," and emotional exchange will equalize sex roles even as the sexual division of labor widens. Voilà, romantic companionate marriage.[60]

Shorter's descriptions of the family in France articulate with nineteenth-century changes in American life that were idealized in the matricentric "cult of domesticity." American domesticity does seem to have intensified family intimacy as the family became a venerated realm of privacy. But even though domestic doctrine asserted the moral equality of wives and husbands, it also cemented gender inequalities in social power and segregated male and female work and sensibility. When Shorter looks to romance for the constituents of domestic companionship, he overlooks the barriers to empathy and mutuality these inequalities represented. Writers like Shorter fail to distinguish among qualities of attachment, engagement, and companionability. Yet a larger problem plagues discussions like Shorter's—they attempt to conceptualize a significant change in marital sentiment with notions of symmetry, empathy, and mutuality. What if these new emotional exchanges involved men and women giving and taking different sentiments and values? Why assume marital sentiments were symmetrical or mutual?

I think it would be useful to analyze nineteenth-century sources to determine if men did more often celebrate nurturance and take consolation in refuge from the cruel world; if women did express emotionalized dependence and attachment and celebrate sympathy, tenderness, and protection. If so, we could describe the new marital sentiment as new *sets* of sentiment, or gender-differentiated individualism, in which autonomous men came home for community and tending and women found emotional self-expression and recognition in interdependent relationship. Men sought a new psychological investment in the one relationship that promised to comfort and compensate them. Women, now entrusted to conserve noncommercial values, found security in greater recognition of their worth and tender gratitude for their new self-conscious role.

Historians of sentiment will probably continue to infer a nineteenth-century elaboration of companionship in marriage. They are likely to agree, nonetheless, that standard interpretations mistake the rise of a newly sentimentalized—but still psychologically and sentimentally differentiated—marital relationship for one built on empathy, mutuality, and equality or symmetry of exchange. The bases for these mutual exchanges were generally missing from marriages, even though social developments favored their inclusion in an avant-garde marital ideal.

Twentieth-century social changes such as women's increasing education and participation in the public sphere shifted tensions between ideals and realities of marriage. These tensions had been muted when preindustrial and then separate-spheres norms of gender difference, deference, and subordination remained dominant. Sentimentalized friendship, which I discuss next, also muted this tension. Twentieth-century realities, however, eroded both patriarchal values and nineteenth-century gender ideals and created new bases for marital companionship. As the divorce rate began its climb in the late nineteenth century, it showed new paths to love and self-development as well as marriage's structural insecurity. As divorce increased, marital companionship accelerated; women correspondingly enlarged the conjugal ideal of emotional interdependence—increasing the role of communication, empathy, mutuality, and sexuality—as the source of marital solidarity.[61] Like nineteenth-century novelists, sociologists responded to this same impulse, heralding a new "exaltation of sympathies" and greater "mental interstimulation and response" in varying prescriptions for companionship. Some emphasized romance; some, clear-headed partnership. Some stressed complementarity; others urged a healthy struggle for communication.[62]

The companionate conjugal ideal always evolved several steps ahead of marital realities. Six decades of empirical research on marriage document women's greater dissatisfaction with many companionate elements of marriage, as well as a consensus among husbands and wives on women's greater self-sacrificing marital "adjustment."[63] During the mid-1920s, when the Lynds found Middletown exceedingly couple-oriented, they also found "little spontaneous community of interests" within couples of all classes. Answering Robert and Helen Lynd's question about what one would do with an extra hour in one's day, no woman of any class wished to spend it with her husband (although some did mention children or friends).[64] By the end of the 1950s, sociologist William Kephart, among others, hopefully postulated a unifying dynamic of "complementarity," since men's and women's interests still appeared too divergent to hope for companionship in marriage. And Lillian Rubin marked the progress of communication and struggle—the prescribed marital agenda of the 1960s and 1970s— as she characterized couples of the 1980s she interviewed as "intimate strangers."[65] It appears that twentieth-century marriages still encounter the limits of companionship.

To summarize, companionate marriage evolved first as an ideal and then slowly, unevenly, and incompletely as a reality. The literature on the development of companionate marriage has tended to imply a mutualism and symmetry in marital sentiment that inaccurately represents the history of marriage. My speculations on the history of family sentiment may now illuminate what has happened to friendship and community.

The Fate of Friendship and Community

The third story tells how the spread of individualism and privatized companionate marriage accelerated a larger process of communal decline. Modernization simultaneously deprived kin, neighbors, and parishioners of bonds of intimacy and emotional depth. Reuben Hill, for example, writes, "Whereas yesterday they derived some affectional satisfactions from neighbors and friends, today adults are dependent on the few intense person-to-person relations found within the family."[66] Where modern friendship exists, moreover, it does not reconstitute community. Louis Wirth writes of the loss of the "spontaneous self-expression, the moral, and the sense of participation" that had been part of traditional community. Friendship, says Robert Nisbet, is characterized by the "growing appeal of pseudo-intimacy with others, a kind of pathetic dependence on the superficial symbols of friendship and association."[67]

Social history in recent decades, however, has assembled considerable evidence that contradicts the simple thesis of devolution. Some historical clues indicate new forms of communal bonds that grew as society industrialized. Particularly for women, these new forms—suffused with values of affective individualism—found fertile grounding in older forms of female interdependence and sociablity that lasted well into the twentieth century. Evidence from feminist historiography and from works by social historians who take little note of the gender differences they document suggests a simultaneous growth of affection in women's relations in family and friendship. Emotion and romance infused elective friendships among women, forming a distinctive culture of friendship that corresponded to the marital changes just reviewed.

A number of historians have challenged assumptions about the intimate and affectionate character of our older ties to kin and community. Traditional community may well have been intimate, as neighbors were party to much familial conduct that is now considered private or personal.[68] But psychological intimacy requires the self-consciousness and sense of individuality that traditional community necessarily restrained in its members. Excessive self-exploration and expressiveness could only disrupt settled communal patterns, which depended upon tradition and identification with kinship and communal roles.

Traditional community was enfolding and solidary. It offered lively patterns of association and stable affiliation and status. Individual isolation occurred only as punishment. But warmth and affection are not synonymous with moral solidarity and stability. Historians show us periods that were rife with discord among neighbors and kin, villages where relations outside economically cooperating groups were hostile and suspicious. At certain life stages, obligations between aging parents and adult children were contractually stipulated rather than left to good faith. Likewise, neighborly responsibility for aid was sometimes minutely stipulated in law, rather than being left to spontaneous communal caring.[69]

Interdependence, solidarity, familiarity, obligation, and authority do not necessarily entail either affection or psychological intimacy. Traditional community offered many values that modern men and women miss; but some of what they experience as loss (a sense of personal authenticity, for example) are retrospective projections of a modern imagination.[70]

Recent historical scholarship has questioned whether industrialism extensively reduced the functional importance of kin. Kin networks continued to be important in migration, resettling, job finding, and transmitting urban values and factory skills.[71] Even this recent literature, however, draws few contrasts between the functions of the kin (or neighborly) bonds of women and men. Histories of the daily lives of women and men in early industrial society suggest that bonds among female kin and neighbors were less affected by encroaching industry than were bonds among males. Indeed, as women continued to exchange child care, sick care, domestic production, and kinship ritual, kinship bonds remained critical through the vicissitudes of daily family survival.[72] Even though the man's new provider role required less daily exchange among kin, the woman's domestic responsibilities continued to rely on—indeed, in periods of market contraction, relied increasingly on—nonmarket exchange among friends and kin. For men of all classes, much of this exchange appears to have been periodic; despite their role in family businesses, kin figured less frequently in men's than in women's exchanges.[73]

Historians have documented a broader sentimentalizing of personal relations—an increasing expression of feelings in friendship and kinship that accompanied the decline of kin authority and paralleled the sentimentalizing of family life in the eighteenth and nineteenth centuries.[74] Once again, Lawrence Stone's history of private life best documents this change in the protean culture of affective individualism: Enlightenment humanism, varieties of individualism and romanticism, increasing choice in association, and new methods of childrearing endowed public as well as private association with warmth and sentiment.[75]

The eighteenth and nineteenth centuries converted kinship to a wider, sentimental, recreational network. Its traditional form rarely extended beyond economically cooperating relatives. The warm and sociable family networks we know as "traditional" consolidated on a broad scale only after state institutions to provide for the poor, the sick, and the elderly allowed us to socialize with relatives without incurring economic obligations. During the same centuries new forms of urban public sociability also appeared.[76] Industrialism and urban growth may have squeezed out vital rituals and forms of public congregation and familiarity typical of preindustrial village life. But contemporary historians document the flourishing sociability and the growth of secondary associations in American and European cities.[77] Fraternal, charitable, and religious organizations provided sociability for city men and women, newcomers as well as old residents.

With the massive urbanization accompanying late-nineteenth-century industrial growth in America, public association in general may have slackened. At the least, secondary associations became weaker at mediating between the family and larger social forces.[78] If so, the arenas of public sociability most stricken were male haunts—tavern, lodge, and fraternal association.[79] The decline of these institutions sent men into the isolation of the conjugal household, where female sociability continued unimpeded, at least during the day, before husbands retreated to these "havens from the heartless world."

Similarly, consumerism may have replaced various sociable patterns but, for many women, shopping remained a sociable pursuit. Gunther Barth maintains that the nineteenth-century department store "made the new phenomenon of a female public possible," as stores transformed downtowns from rough male terrains into areas that respectable women could enter. A department store was perhaps not the "community" Marshall Field declared it to be, but it was a public arena for female sociability.[80] The wider spread of consumerism in the 1930s hastened the retreat of working-class husbands to their new homes, cars, and appliance repairs. Working-class housewives, by contrast, had increasing access to cars to visit family members and to ferry neighbors to market; and they secured a few of the genuinely labor-saving devices (like gas stoves) that could release time for friendship.[81]

Writers like Joseph Folsom, Robert Nisbet, and Christopher Lasch offer male-focused portraits of the modes of family sociability that replaced traditional communal patterns. By overlooking the fact that married women continued to work within a preindustrial mix of labor and sociability and by narrowly focusing on post-working-day socializing, they tend to see an overall decline in friendship. In their narrow purview, they find that only shallow friendliness remains from the patterns of deep, warm, meaningful personal relations of yore. They are referring, of course, to patterns of couple-socializing, the status-building leisure work of the middle classes.[82] By the middle of the twentieth century, family sociability may well have come to dominate the after-work friendly association of middle-class married men but never of women, even of wives relatively isolated in the suburbs; they continued to conduct daytime friendships.[83] (One assumption that blinds writers to new forms of community holds that short-lived relationships are inevitably shallow ones.[84] It concedes, by contrast, depth of feeling and commitment to sudden romantic love—thus love affairs may achieve great moral depth although transitory friendships remain trivial.)

The Rise and Decline of Romantic Friendship

Because women's friendships have generally been conducted in the private sphere, they have been poorly documented, particularly those of working-class women, who often had neither the education nor the leisure to write their own accounts. Letters, diaries, and literary writings of middle- and upper-class girls and women are the sources of most accounts of women's friendships. These, with a few documents on working-class women, reveal patterns of sociability, cooperation, and attachment persisting among women kin and friends.[85] In addition, historians have documented a female culture of romantic friendship that extends from sixteenth-century platonism through eighteenth-century private religious and spiritual experience to the sensual and passionate sorority of Victorian "true womanhood."[86]

Romantic friendship was the idealized, self-conscious, affective-individualistic pattern that women built upon older bonds of material and emotional interdependence among female kin, neighbors, and friends. The most distinctive ideal of women's friendships had its roots in romanticism and the great awakening of religion in the eighteenth and nineteenth centuries. Women's friendly associations had flourished in collective work, worship, and festivities of early modern village life and religious confraternity; and they continued in preindustrial forms that carried into the modern era.[87] But the roots of modern friendship lie more in new forms of self-conscious attachments than in older forms of female interdependence.

The evangelical emphasis on heart and feeling drew women into a self-conscious religious role that historian Barbara Welter considers a feminization of American religion. American religious participation was probably always predominantly female, but the change allotted women a prominent religious role.[88] Nancy Cott documents how this new role became the basis of friendly communion: "'I do not believe that men can ever feel so pure an enthusiasm for women as we can feel for one another,' Catherine Sedgwick recorded in her diary in 1834 after meeting Fanny Kemble, '—ours is nearer to the love of angels.'"[89] The religious redefinition of womanhood in terms of spiritual and moral superiority fed the romantic friendship culture that flourished in middle-class women's narrowed sphere.

Focusing on the republican virtues of true womanhood, secular canons of domesticity paralleled religious themes. Cott explains their logic: "The success of self-government in a nation of diverse characters . . . required 'the culture of the heart, the discipline of the passions, the regulation of the feelings and affections'" that only dedicated self-conscious mothers and wives could provide.[90] The moral elevation of women in evangelical thought and the new emphasis on women's moral responsibility for children and husbands allied women in a sentimentalized sisterhood of religious, maternal, charitable, and moral reform associations that blossomed during the early period of urban growth and private domesticity.[91]

The statements published by women's organizations, the flood of literature on domesticity (including the massive new production by women novelists), and the letters and diaries of women friends document a salient theme of romantic friendship in this period—a glorification of female sensibilities and an explicit hostility to the male (read public) values that domesticity in fact underwrote.[92]

Proponents of domesticity worked to expand girls' schooling to prepare them for women's socially influential domestic responsibilities.[93] The flowering of school friendships both complemented and added adolescent passion to the solidarity of spiritual sisterhood. Carroll Smith-Rosenberg and Nancy Cott illustrate this passionate sorority of educated young women in the late eighteenth century, friends who throughout schooling and courtship relied on each other for spontaneity, emotional expression, and love; they addressed letters to "My Beloved," to "lay our hearts open to each other" and closed, "Imagine yourself kissed a dozen times my darling."[94] Passionate attachments such as these, expressed in public embraces, kisses, and the luxuriant sharing of beds caused no disapproval among elders or suitors.

Spiritual sisterhood was further secularized and sentimentalized in the nineteenth-century adoption of European romantic styles, including the epistolary tradition.[95] Women and girls recorded their ardent feelings for one another in passionate letters, diaries, and novels. Lillian Faderman's history of romantic friendship quotes typical passages from popular literature, such as these turgid verses by Christina Rossetti:

> Golden head by golden head,
> Like two pigeons in one nest,
> Folded in each other's wings,
> They lay down in their curtained bed:
> Cheek to cheek and breast to breast
> Locked together in one nest.[96]

Thus, by the nineteenth century, adult middle-class women had adopted the romantic conventions of friendship that earlier generations of school girls had pioneered.[97] A mature diarist describes her friend: "Time cannot destroy the fascination of her manner . . . her voice is music to the ear."[98] Demonstrating the romantic spur of obstacles, the letters and diaries of nineteenth-century married women who found themselves separated from friends were especially passionate: "Dearest darling—How incessantly have I thought of you these eight days—all today—the entire uncertainty, the distance, the long silence—are all new features in my separation from you, grevious to be borne."[99]

A friend's death presented an obstacle nothing could overcome. One newly married woman whose best friend died, mourned: "To me her loss seems irreparable, I have not a friend on earth, to who [*sic*] I could so freely communicate my feelings, at any time."[100] Even a honeymoon could stimulate romantic yearnings for a friend. From her honeymoon voyage, one bride writes to her friend of having *no one* with whom to share the pleasures of traveling and seals her complaint: "Darling, do you think every day that in my heart, I am close, close by your side?"[101]

Although both Carl Degler and Ellen Rothman question the extent of romantic friendship, all the historians who document its rise consider it an enriched female solidarity—not just an ideal or style.[102] Even though the language of female friendship followed the romantic conventions of an era, those conventions reflected a new sensibility. For women, modern subjectivity unfolded in a gender-identified culture that affirmed their dignity and individuality in a separate sphere of caring that they believed would indirectly influence and enrich all of society.[103]

Romantic women friends shared the heady illusion of that early era of gender consciousness—that women possessed an "almost magic power, which in [their] proper sphere [they] now wield over the destinies of the world."[104] Women's culture ennobled friendships that satisfied deeply felt needs newly defined by the "cult of subjectivity." And by eliciting religious approval and affirmation from their broader culture, women augmented their resources for domestic struggle with men (and for public versions of that struggle).*

---

*Ann Douglas astutely identifies the gender power struggle involved in bringing Victorian sentimentality into the public sphere and points out ways it accom-

Romantic friendship developed parallel to romantic marriage, as its cultural twin. Both ideals centered on themes of affective individualism, mutuality, and romance. The ideal of companionate marriage opposed patriarchal traditions and confronted timeless practices of same-sex socializing. By the nineteenth century, its progress was paradoxically accelerated by a new gender ideology that endorsed the separation of work and home—the segregation of male and female worlds and sensibilities. Thus, romantic expectations of marital companionship spread among middle-class women just as new gender expectations moved them worlds apart from the husbands with whom they hoped to find communion.

Nancy Cott seems to suggest romantic friendship absorbed the tension between the ideals and realities of nineteenth-century marriage.[105] Certainly, romantic friendship fit easily into traditions of female interdependence, sociability, and attachment, whereas romantic marriage contradicted inherited modes of authority, deference, and demeanor between husbands and wives. Romantic friendship thrived on its practicability in a period in which romantic companionate marital ideals were unpracticable.

From the late nineteenth century through the 1920s, various influences undermined romantic friendship; it remained in decline for most of the twentieth century. One set of changes involved male-female companionship, as education (especially coeducation) for women expanded and urban recreation diversifed. Young men and women spent more time in mixed-sex socializing; both in school and with peers, they shared more common interests and endeavors. Dating, which became widespread in the 1920s among high school and college women and men, was an intensive and time-consuming leisure pattern.[106] It isolated couples far more than nineteenth-century courtship or peer activity had, and it preempted the energies of female friendships. In 1920 a woman professor pronounced that "one seldom sees" the kind of women's friendship "that has all the wonderful community of interest one finds in ideal marriage."[107]

---

modated the market and corrupted literary and public values. She nonetheless underestimates its long-term impact on women's identity and domestic authority, and its importance in preparing a transformative public politics of gender (Douglas, *The Feminization of American Culture* [New York: Avon Books, 1977]).

Another influence on friendship was the spread of popular sexology and psychoanalytic ideas. A new belief in the ubiquity of eroticism lifted the mantle of innocence from formerly unclassified romantic and sensual language and behavior. Schools actively condemned romantic friendships among girl students. Those that survived were forced underground.[108] The "lesbian threat" would hereafter shadow the course and culture of female friendships. By 1934 one sociologist, Joseph Folsom, observed fewer girls' "crushes," and less "homosexuality . . . in the form of strong friendships," which, he maintained, had been predominant among women more than men in the preceding fifty years.[109]

In response to a divorce rate that had been rising steadily from the late nineteenth century, sociologists and the up-and-coming professionals of marriage counseling placed more and more prescriptive value on companionship in marriage (strongly emphasizing mutuality), couple socializing, and "togetherness." M. F. Nimkoff observed this new emphasis on "comradeship and understanding" in reviewing family sociology of the 1920s and 1930s.[110] Finally, the burgeoning industry of advertising increasingly sold identity and status through consumption, targeting women and urging them to explore romance and individuality with purchases. Beauty became a commodified individual quest, its products hyped with invidious female comparisons. Advertisers threatened that each failure of a homemaker's acumen or allure could result in loss to her sharper competitor.[111]

These remarks do not indicate the decline of same-sex friendships among women but rather the decline of romantic friendship, a culture of friendship that had been constructed within the ideology and practices of radically separated spheres of gender. Unromantic but intimate friendships among women seem to have survived, filling the gap in marital companionship noted by twentieth-century observers. As the companionate marriage ideal became more popular and more specifically romantic, egalitarian, and empathic, women intensified their emotional investment in marriage. Doing so, they relied increasingly on friendships to manage the emotional strains of marriage and to sustain their commitment to it. The researches of Harvey Locke and Ernest Burgess each concluded that friends were more important for the "marital adjustment" of wives than of husbands.

Sociologists in most eras of this century noted—if not in detail—

both the intimacy of women's friendships and the contrast with the greater distance of men's.[112] The sociologists who restudied Middletown in the 1970s found "overwhelming" evidence that marital communication had improved since the 1920s and offered, without further comment, "a typical example from one housewife": "I feel there is nothing I couldn't go to him and ask . . . I mostly talk to one of my best friends, but I feel that you should look to your own husband for basic communication."[113]

The romantic friendship ideal withered as twentieth-century social changes accelerated the companionship of men and women. They amplified egalitarian and empathic themes in the marriage ideal, stigmatized passionate attachments between women, and replaced material interdependence between women with consumption in the marketplace. The tone of adult women's friendships faded from passionate attachment to affectionate camaraderie. Romantic friendship was not to emerge again among heterosexual women until the 1970s when contemporary feminism opened a new era of gender consciousness and conflict. It emerged once again within a middle-class segment, this time among young, college-educated women. Part of a much narrower class- and age-based stratum, they relied on its countercultural support rather than the larger structures of religion and mass literature that had spread nineteenth-century romantic friendship.

In the 1980s romantic friendship has drawn publicity, particularly from advertisers, who must still exploit autonomous feminist and female cultural themes because women have remained their most important audience. Long-distance telephone commercials, for example, portray the longing and intimacy between separated women friends. For the moment, however, romantic friendship appears to flourish mainly within small feminist circles. Yet if romantic friendship has been in eclipse for most of the twentieth century, intimate friendships among women have continued to thrive in spite of the vicissitudes of geographic mobility, the double day of work within and outside the home, pronatalist and marital revivals, and the feminization of poverty. Intimate friendship among women has not only persisted; it has expanded as affective individualism has affected new sectors of society. In contrast to marriage, the reality of women's friendships has outstripped the ideal.

I have revised the history of friendship and marriage because

my contemporary interviews contradicted so much of what the sociological account of the decline of community and the rise of companionate marriage would predict. I interpreted more than a decade of new social history to suggest that friendship and marriage
evolved intertwined, symbiotic cultures infused with the modern
ethos of affective individualism. The economic forces that separated public and private life, and associated forces of individualism, fostered the change from traditional forms of female interdependence to modern forms of intimacy. Concurrently, intimate
friendship and intimate marriage became social ideals. But for
women the ideals of friendship were generally more practicable
than the ideals of marriage; and so romantic friendship both compensated for and served as a model for romantic companionate
marriage. As husbands and wives became more companionate,
women's friendships became less romantic. Intimate female friendship quietly persisted, unheralded support for women as wives and
mothers.

Chapter Two

Distinctive Values of Friendship

The passionate sentiments of romantic friendship, so evident in nineteenth-century middle-class women's culture, virtually disappeared over the next century as companionate marriage became the focus of middle-class—and then, cross-class—sentimental culture. In the 1980s, the companionate marriage ideal emphasizes equality, psychological intimacy, sexual pleasure, and unfolding process—an ideal of best friendship between spouses. Popular representations of women's friendship, in contrast, evoke recreation rather than emotional life, in a zone of tenuous and ambiguous attachments where private life merges with public.

The companionate ideal pictures marital bonds as unrivaled and sufficient primary attachments, which comparably ardent bonds with kin or friends would presumably subvert. This is the popular belief, echoed in the sociology and anthropology of marriage and kinship.[1] Careful study of marriage and of women's close friendships, however, reveals marriages that diverge from the cultural ideal and intimate friendships so complex that they invite us to analyze their cultural invisibility.

This chapter presents an overview of the evidence I gathered about contemporary women's close friendships and how they relate to women's marriages and family lives. In it, I begin to answer these questions: What kinds of values and exchanges are embodied in elective close relationships outside the nuclear family? How do they correspond to the predictions in theories of companionate marriage? How do they affect marriage? The women's answers to these questions raise issues that the following chapters will examine in depth.

First Glimpses of Husbands and Best Friends

One way to compare friendship and marriage is to compare how women describe their best friends and how they describe their husbands. Early in my interviews, before probing either relationship, I invited open-ended descriptions of husbands and closest friends: Tell me a little about. . . . There were patterned differences between the two characterizations. Descriptions of husbands often sounded like Kay's:

He's a very hard worker. He takes his work seriously. There are disadvantages because he puts in long hours. But he does get paid well. He's very easy-going—doesn't get mad easily. He's a very good father to the kids. He's got some double standards and can be opinionated about what people should and shouldn't do. But basically he's good.

Characterizing their husbands, most women (twelve of seventeen married women) offered a positive personal quality or two—frequently "thoughtful" or "easy-going." Half said something about the husband's work, describing him as hardworking or identifying his occupation. Seven of seventeen described their mates as good fathers. And seven mentioned some negative quality, such as being aloof or moody.

Descriptions of close friends often sounded like Jean's:

She's the nicest person. If my life fell apart right now, I'd probably go to her. She's very nurturing, very understanding, very warm. And she has more integrity—that's one of the main things I think of when I think of her. Just rock-bottom honest with herself and others. She doesn't compromise with her beliefs. She doesn't impose them on others, but her moral code is very important to her.

All but one of the women described their close friends in terms of positive personal qualities. A good sense of humor and nurturance were the qualities they most frequently evoked, but the range of qualities was broader than the one they offered in descriptions of husbands. Women were also more likely to emphasize personal qualities as opposed to roles when describing friends. They rarely described friends by their work, as good friends, or good mothers. Still, the relational qualities they applied to friends are those generally considered to constitute friendship. When asked, What do you like *best* about your best friend? women emphasized amiable qualities like sense of humor, caring, warmth, and moral qualities like honesty.

Because women tended to characterize husbands in terms of roles and close friends in terms of personal and relational qualities, the first glimpses of the two figures revealed sharper individual images of women friends. Their use of different terms to describe husbands and friends was highlighted in women's answers to questions about the distinctive values of each relationship.

Distinctive Values of Close Friendships

Among the most thought-provoking responses to my interview came in reply to two questions: Can you think of things you care about or need from a relationship that only your women friends provide? Can you think of things you care about or need from a relationship that only a husband can provide? An examination of the answers to these questions, individually and in comparison, clarifies the place of women's friendships in their lives.

Looking first at statements about the uniqueness and value of close friendships with women, I found that, indeed, women could think of values that only their women friends provide. Only two respondents were unable to identify values uniquely provided by women friends. Although few had ever considered this question, they answered immediately and affirmatively. Even the women who maintained that "ideally, a man could" satisfy these needs acknowledged, "For me, it's always been women." Although women were apt to trivialize certain values that they exchanged only with women, they granted others their respect.

The responses to this question clustered in one area—an intimacy women most often characterized with the terms *talk, understanding,* and *feeling.*

Women go back and forth, back and forth, just sitting and talking. I need that in a relationship.

I don't know if it's just my husband, but women are more understanding of other women's problems.

Feelings, compassion, because a woman could relate to my problem.

Wives talk to husbands, of course. Since women rarely disparaged this companionship, when they said that "just talking" was what their women friends uniquely provided, they were referring to a particular kind of talk. They especially needed, first of all, a mutually desired exchange:

It's talking to my friends. Could be anything. Otherwise, my basic outlet for talking is my husband. And if he's just come home, he doesn't really want to talk. He'll listen to me, but it sometimes irritates him to do it.

Kay and I will sit and gossip for hours at a time. We'll talk and talk about the kids, for example. George and I would never do that.

Just the gab time. Just to sit and talk about anything and everything. Where a guy would think, "Is she ever going to shut up?"

Husbands and wives talk. According to the women I interviewed, however, husbands are not always pleased to do so, whereas friends usually are. This finding is echoed in recent research on conversation patterns between spouses that shows that even though husbands talk more than wives in conversations, they are less likely to respond to wives' communications than wives are to respond to theirs.[2]

Second, talk between friends is an exchange between individuals with significant common experience, enough to generate a profound understanding. My respondents believed the ultimate basis of this special understanding was "being a woman," a characteristic that varied in their descriptions from an ontological state of being to a sociohistorical construction. Understanding meant the sympathetic knowledge developed in "being a woman" and in occupying gendered roles such as wife, daughter-in-law, and mother. Thus, common experiences (or the natural state) of "being a woman" create a gender consciousness from which women exchange understanding.

The understanding, in turn, establishes a context in which

women can sustain a positive self-orientation. It enables them to avoid exchanges with husbands that would undermine their self-orientation:

There are some things we understand about each other. Like this dizziness I sometimes get. I don't think it's physical—just nerves. Karen's the one I'll talk to on the phone and say, "God, I can't breathe today." And we'll talk about it. If I told Jerry, he'd either say, "Then get your butt to the doctor," or, "You're crazy!"

Annette can understand the feelings of jealousy I have toward my son's girlfriend because she has a son too. She'd be sympathetic where Mike wouldn't—he'd put it off as me being a silly, jealous woman.

I tell Doreen when I start thinking about going places, doing different things with my life. Jesse kind of snorts when I start talking like that.

Empathy is a third characteristic of the talk with friends that women value. Women I interviewed often expressed a belief that women both maintain a more variegated emotionality and exercise a greater capacity and willingness to participate in another's emotional life.

I just think women feel more.

A lot of times my feelings about anything are easier to talk about with June than with Lloyd.

There's a quality of intensity and the ability to focus on what's happening right now that I find in conversation with my women friends alone.

Jack can understand when I'm upset, but a woman can feel the upset. She'll say the right things and contribute to making me feel better. A husband will say, "Oh, quit griping."

Over and over again, women who claimed they had never reflected on their friendships easily described understanding and empathy that they found unmatched in other close relationships, including marriage.

Although they were describing characteristics they cared about or needed in a relationship, nonetheless women often deprecated some of these values. That women repeatedly spoke of valued areas of exchange with women as "gossip" and "girl talk" suggests something of the stigma on women's culture that women themselves accept. They appeared to translate impatience and hostility toward their interests that they attributed to their husbands into self-deprecating assessments of their friendships. They tended to disparage the exchange of news within personal networks, particularly events in primary relationships; and the discussion of physical, psychological, and emotional states. They also belittled a major area of family decision making that is dominated by women—household purchases—even though sociological studies of domestic power often interpret this decision making as evidence of women's marital power.[3]

Women rarely disparaged certain other exclusive topics of feminine friendship. They were straightforward in describing discussions about children, and personal problems in marriage and motherhood, even though these topics also might have been slighted by husbands or the larger culture. In general, they seemed to enjoy participating in an exclusive women's culture, bracketing some of it with stigmatized terms and defending other aspects of it against social devaluation.

Women's Culture Defended: Women Friends as Mothers

Among mothers, the most frequent answer to the question of the unique value of women friends was talking about children or about being a mother. Twelve of fourteen mothers with children at home mentioned this valued exchange. Women friends, they said, had a different way of talking about children than women and their husbands do. The uniqueness and importance of this exchange emerged over and over in their answers to general questions about friendship that did not explicitly refer to children. Women said they talked to friends about the individuality and the moral and psychological development of their children and about the parent-child relations they saw as crucial to these areas. They believed their husbands were not as minutely interested in these questions and were less helpful in approaching them than other mothers were. The unique value of husbands as partners in parenthood lay elsewhere—most often summarized as the bond of a long-term commitment and its legacy in daily relations with children.

Women of varied classes and educational backgrounds noted friends' interest in discussing the moral and psychological individuality and development of children, although their language for discussing these concerns varied. Frances, for example, is not a highly educated consumer of childrearing expertise; nonetheless she felt it important to answer her young daughter's questions about sex with delicacy and sensitivity: "I've been real concerned that I tell her the right way—that I've said the right thing to her. So I tell my friends about our conversations. Women are more understanding of these problems. Jack wouldn't understand it, quite. A woman is more tuned in to it."

Louise explained why she could talk about "parenting things" more easily to her best friend than to her husband, whom she considered a good father:

Somehow I take it more seriously than Gary does. Deep down, I think he looks on it as my job and my problem. If the kids are doing something that worries me, he won't let it worry him. He looks at it as something she's doing this second. He doesn't look at it over a long-run scale of the reasons why they're doing it. So, a lot of stuff Jan and I discuss among ourselves.

Both Frances and Louise appreciated their husbands as fathers and valued them as partners in childrearing. Still, like other mothers, they found their husbands not as willing and not as effective in "figuring out the kids," placing their behavior in a "long-run scale of the reasons why they're doing it," or evaluating their own responses in light of this sense of the child's individuality.

These childrearing concerns, which Louise enunciated so simply and elegantly, form what may now be a cross-class culture of child socialization. Both Frances and Louise come from classically defined working-class households. Yet their emphasis on the child's individuality and motivations and on the delicacy of their maternal role is the same childrearing ethos that their affluent college-educated sisters have. And the women's beliefs that husbands were unpracticed at these intricate aspects of childrearing were also cross-class. Debby and Thea are affluent, educated women married to men they view as loving and "involved" fathers. They described why they needed close friends to discuss children:

My husband is very devoted to the kids, but there are just some things he just doesn't feel and I do. . . . It's not just because so much more of my time is devoted. . . . It's just some kind of tug. I'd have to explain myself so much more talking with Jay than I do with Joanne.

Most of the husbands I know are very involved with their kids. But it's the mother who—my husband just doesn't empathize with them.

This exchange of childrearing problems among close women friends opens a moral discourse about childrearing. Stressing caution and delicacy, women said they discussed childrearing values with friends and attempted to influence each other in this area.

Talking generally about moral influence, constraint, and obligation among friends, women first mentioned the needs and interests of children as appropriate terrain for moral constraint. By and large, the women I spoke with thought it rarely appropriate to attempt to change a friend's attituces or beliefs or ways of doing things. But when asked to imagine occasions in which such influence would be right, they thought most often of situations in which a child's interests were at stake. Weighing a friend's obligation in situations clearly involving a child's welfare—when a parent is too ill to care for a child or when a child is being abused, for instance—women answered unambiguously that a friend was obligated to intervene. "Always," they responded to such questions of obligation; "children always come first."

These unparalleled discussions about children, framed by shared moral beliefs about the obligations of friends toward each other's children, forge unique bonds between close friends. Women also construct and symbolize these bonds by the exchange of children in child care. In answering questions about trust in close friendship, women spontaneously referred to the solidarizing effects of exchange of child care.

"Do you trust Anne?"——"I'd trust her with my kids, which is all I have." Another woman answered more explicitly: "Did anything ever happen to make you especially trust Doreen?"—— "She'd leave her daughter with me. I'd pick her up at school and take her home with me when Doreen couldn't be there. That's how we became really close."

Over and over again, women brought up children when talking about the construction and meaning of trust in close friendships. They frequently referred to favors with child care when explaining how friends helped them out when they had difficulties in their marriages: "She'll take the kids so Ed and I can go out and talk."

Some referred to exchange of child care with a close friend that helped keep marriages together. Exchanging loving care of the people women most love and for whom they feel most responsible, in a context of shared values of care, women construct bonds of material and emotional reliance and moral constraint.

Understanding and Women's Sphere

Women are most likely to want the unique understanding and empathy of women friends for those aspects of life that are both important to and characteristic of women. As we might expect, the more distinct the lives of husbands and wives, the more women emphasized how uniquely women understood "being a woman." Women who stayed home with young children were particularly likely to value the understanding and empathy of someone in the same circumstances. "I think you definitely need a woman to talk about how you're feeling, being home with the kids. Just that kind of antsy feeling that a man, I don't think, understands."

The birth of a child, for whom a woman will be the primary nurturer, creates a new sphere of responsibility, interests, and problems. And it may require companionship and help from someone who has experienced a similar transition. Most women find a lack of empathy and engagement in their husbands, whose child-rearing role differs significantly from theirs.[4] This lack particularly strikes women whose lives before childbirth were more similar to their husbands', perhaps in education and work commitments:

We had been each other's best friends. But when I suddenly found myself with a baby, it was something he could share in only a limited way. He could understand some of the problems, but he couldn't understand what it meant to spend every waking moment devoted to this baby who was really a handful.

At the same time, the ability of mothers of young children to cultivate or maintain friendships may be hampered by a lack of time, decreased physical mobility, exhaustion, and the constant presence of an infant. Several women recalled this as a time when they had no close women friends and suffered from that absence.[5] One woman explained, "I was confined at home with small children, I didn't have any close friends, and it was a really difficult time. I was lonely. I was isolated. I felt I was the only person doing what I was doing. I felt so totally cut off."

Frequently, the transition to parenthood follows immediately on a honeymoon phase of "libidinal withdrawal," in which a newly married couple withdraws from old friends to explore the marital intimacy promised in courtship.[6] The time just after marriage was the second most frequently mentioned period when women lacked close friendships. In contrast with the period after childbirth, however, it was one when women rarely reported the absence of friendship, presumably because they shared more of their absorbing interests with their husbands and dwelt less in their separate sphere: "Andrew and I were extremely good companions. I don't remember needing somebody else then."

Arlene and her husband, Jeff, were students together when they married; and later both worked at full-time careers. When their first child was born, Arlene quit work for several years of full-time motherhood, while her husband continued in his occupation. She felt satisfied with her choice but found herself newly aware of a need for the empathy of other mothers.

I think my women friends have a different attitude toward children and toward the activities that mothers are bound up in that, certainly, my husband doesn't understand—I've never met a man who did. Jeff thinks I sit around and eat bonbons all day. He doesn't understand why I'm tired, how taxing my life can be. And my friends do, because they're going through the same thing.

"My husband certainly does not appreciate what it's like being a woman now," said Arlene, expressing a conviction that had been growing in the years since she became a mother. Her conviction was probably influenced by the wide cultural diffusion of feminist ideas; but feminism had been popular in her premotherhood days as well without arousing her deep sense of gender difference. "He wouldn't know what I was talking about if I said, 'This is the situation I find myself in as a thirty-four-year-old, soon-to-be-mother-of-two in a changing world.' Only my women friends can appreciate that, and it's very much a part of our conversations."

Housework and shopping continue to be tasks that wives perform. Time-budget studies over the last three decades show little significant change in husbands' participation in housework, even when wives have full-time jobs.[7] Both spouses tend to view husbands' ventures into domestic labor as "helping out the wife." Thus, shopping and housework are activities that women view as distinctive experience to share with women friends. Reflecting the low social prestige of this unpaid work, women discounted their conversations with friends about housework and their joint shopping ventures: "We talk about what we do—like cooking, sewing—things my husband would say are trivia. He just really doesn't have an interest in it."

Sylvia recounted her husband's attitude toward her daily work without the slightest irritation. Like others, she described the companionship of homemakers as valuable but trivial. These women know, although they did not mention it, that the quality of their household care is an important measure of their wifely role, within and outside the family. And the quality of their domestic display is a public measure of their family status-building effectiveness. To husbands and to the world, the effort of homemaking is generally invisible. But women know how much work is involved, and what judgments are balanced on its outcome.

"Can you think of some kinds of things you care about or need from a relationship that only your women friends provide?"—— "There's things you just don't talk about with your husband. It's just household things. But they think it's nonexistent."

It seems ironic that women acknowledge that advice and help in shopping and keeping house are exchanges they want and need in a relationship and, at the same time, that these are just "small stuff" and "girl talk."

Personal appearance is another area of concern in which women find their lives distinct from men and which they recognize as important, although not morally comparable to motherhood. Maintaining an attractive appearance is important to women's social well-being. Like homemaking, cultivating appearance is family status-building work. It is a pursuit that husbands approve of, even demand; but according to the women I questioned, it is one that men are rarely willing to abet. Husbands tend to expect that in appearance making, as in homemaking, the sweat and artifice should be concealed.

Women friends share in this labor. Seriously, they help each other in appearance making. And in accepting the limits of their ability to be beautiful. Thus, when Lee, a young single woman, responded that "standing in front of a mirror together and looking at each other's flab" was the kind of thing she values most in a relationship with a woman, she was not being facetious. She was talking about an intimacy and empathy that felt crucial to a young woman who lived in a society whose values she did not create. Similarly, Frances placed among important values her friend's considered opinion on a prospective purchase: "If I went shopping with my husband to buy a new pair of pants, they could be halfway up to my knees and he'd say, 'That's just fine.' Carol would know how she'd feel in my spot and give a better opinion."

Motherhood, housework, and cultivating appearance are three activities so regularly exclusive to women that they exaggerate the experience of gender and heighten the distinctiveness of women's culture of friendship. Moreover, in its own way each activity figures prominently in the marital power balance, making it a difficult subject for communication and confrontation with husbands. The clearest example is that of motherhood, which research shows to signal major decreases in women's power in marriage.[8] The decrease in power that follows childbirth also discourages the communication and confrontation with husbands that might elicit understanding.

If Not Unique, Preferred

The values I have been describing are the ones that women believed women friends alone could provide. Throughout the interviews, respondents identified other important values for which they *preferred* to turn to friends, even though husbands or others could also provide them. Once again, most of these values circulated in communication rather than material exchange. I asked women specifically for subjects they could talk about better with close friends than with husbands. Thirteen of seventeen married women identified such subjects (seven further identified some they could talk about *only* with friends). Since I assume that the preference for talking with friends tells something about the distinctiveness of the bond of close friendship, I shall explore these subjects here.

"Him, mainly—I can talk about *him* better to Jan," was a typical answer to my question. This answer tended to have two main subtopics: figuring him out and solving problems with him. The women who preferred talking about "him" with friends to talking to "him" in person generally believed that conversations with good friends were more likely to help them understand husbands' attitudes and motivations than were probing conversations with taciturn mates. Chapter 6 looks more closely at this collaborative "marriage work," in which friends discuss their husbands and marital problems.

Another group of topics that women preferred to discuss with other women includes topics that husbands concede, or perhaps delegate, to friendships. This group includes the subjects women described as gossip, like news in personal networks; and those they elevated, like detailed discussions of children. Although women sometimes reported that husbands complained when they revealed personal details of the marriage to friends, they reported few jealousies of the sharing of personal problems that did not implicate their mates.

I don't usually talk to Jeff about problems. My husband believes when you've got problems, you can solve your own. I learned early on in marriage that he's not a good choice. I'm not sure if it's a lack of sympathy or empathy—but it's sure a lack of patience. He'd rather I tried someone else, so I do.

A third category of topics women preferred to discuss with friends includes areas of contention between husband and wife in which a woman wishes to preserve or defend her method or perspective. One such area is emotionality and emotional dependence. Several women said they relied on friends in expressing emotion, both to reveal emotional states and to use an emotionalized mode of expression.

Feelings. For example, I can talk about experiencing sorrow far easier with a friend.

Women are allowed an emotional freedom that men are just not allowed. They can really express how they feel to other women. I really enjoy that warmth I get in friendships with women. It's totally different from the warmth I get from my husband or any other man I know. It's a unique shared experience.

Women friends are comfortable with and encourage emotional revelation; husbands are often less at ease with this mode. Even sympathetic husbands, their wives said, often responded to emotional discourse with hostility, withdrawal, or an attempt to "help" modulate feeling.

A husband will say, "Oh, quit griping!" . . . My husband is not reassuring like my friend is.

He can't understand me, but he cares. It worries him [when I'm upset]. He wishes he could do something, but he doesn't know what.

Mike would be less sympathetic that I'm feeling jealous [of my son's attention]. I feel intimidated by it.

Related to this reliance on friends for emotional discourse is an accepting recognition between friends of emotional dependence. The women I spoke to believed their husbands needed them; yet they found when their husbands acknowledged this need, the men were uncomfortable. They said that husbands were especially loathe to admit dependence on anyone other than their spouse and that husbands could not comprehend their wives' emotional dependence on óthers. One woman described this contrast: "Catherine understands needing other people. Andrew sees himself as a loner, not needing others. He pooh-poohs that need."

Women also reported turning to friends to defend differences of opinion with their husbands.

Dennis always said he respected me intellectually and trusted my opinions, but if he disagreed with me on something that was really crucial to him, he would put down my opinion. With my women friends there was more respect. Even if they disagreed with me, they wouldn't tell me "somebody's been trying to put ideas in your head." Even if there was a disagreement, there wouldn't be a put-down that came with it.

In this exchange Jean, talking about her former husband, illustrates a pattern of talking to friends to protect areas of belief, opinion, or practice under contention in the marriage. Chapter 6 explores how this pattern of confiding in friends may be construed as marital problem solving that adds to the wife's power in marriage.

Jean's account of her former husband's contempt for her differing opinion illustrates another situation in which women turn to friends to protect their methods or beliefs: women seem to prefer talking to their close friends about thoughts, plans, or fantasies of autonomy.

I can talk about wanting more independence better with June. I act it out more with Lloyd, rather than talk about it.

I talk to Doreen about thoughts of other things . . . different walks of life. Maybe other men . . . doing things with my life.

Once you're a mother, you don't have such a mind of your own as you did before. That's one of the qualities Jerry used to like in me. But now, if I talk about that change to him, either he turns it into a fight, or he thinks I'm being ridiculous. It's easier to talk about it with Karen.

When I thought I was pregnant and would need an abortion, I couldn't speak about it to Les. I didn't want the confrontation of him wanting me to have a baby. I knew Brenda would urge me to change my mind, but I could say "no" to her and know she'd still be with me.

This last statement, about keeping an abortion decision secret from a partner, is Lee's. A single woman, she confided in a close friend rather than her boyfriend. One might think that this would rarely happen in a marriage. Informal discussion with health clinic workers discourages such a conclusion, however. On the abortion decision, as on less momentous issues of individual autonomy, women often feel too powerless to hold their own in debate with their husbands. The finding that women avoid discussing issues concerning autonomy with their husbands—and that they prefer to engage these issues with friends—is one of the strongest patterns that emerge in this research.

Friends' special exchange of thoughts about autonomy or individuality is indicated also among the responses to questions probing various personal exchanges. The question, Is there anyone who encourages you to try new experiences or activities?, elicited the names of close friends or kin—but not of husbands—from over half of the married women. Women included their husbands in answering most of the other thirty-three questions of this kind. I pick up this issue of friendship and autonomy again in chapter 4.

As unique values of close friendship, then, women described intimacy in self-disclosure and a mutual validation of individual activity and inner self through understanding and deep affection. Such descriptions of intimacy and emotional depth are worlds apart from Robert Nisbet's depiction of modern friendship as "pseudo-intimacy with others, a kind of pathetic dependence on the superficial symbols of friendship."[9] In fact, they are close to Ernest Burgess's transports on companionate marriage.

Unique Values of Marriage

If women's close friendships contain many of the elements generally attributed to companionate romantic love, what then do
women find irreplaceable in marriage? And there values they want
and need in a relationship that only a husband can provide? Immediately, as when I asked about friends, women answered affirmatively. But in interesting contrast to the earlier occasion, this
time they found the values difficult to articulate. Women described
more easily how women friends uniquely satisfied their needs than
how husbands did. The details of what only a husband could provide took more time to think of, were more abstractly phrased, and
were more likely to be retracted: "Oh, I guess a good friend provides that too."

This pattern paralleled the responses to a long series of name-
eliciting questions asking who provided (or received) various emotional or psychological exchanges. I phrased the questions to discover a woman's strongest attachments. Surveying the responses
to each question, I rarely found a response (and never more than
one) that listed the husband alone as the provider (or receiver) of
the significant exchange. Responses nearly always listed close
friends or kin. An earlier question produced a similar pattern:
among those to whom they would talk personally all the women
who listed husbands listed a friend or relative as well; the reverse
was not true.

Ultimately, however, each woman was able to describe values
unique to marriage. Kay's answer includes most of the frequently
mentioned elements: "Love, a deep commitment. He's always
there. Companionship. Planning together. Sex (I would hope that
would only come from your husband). Just the security of knowing
things are going a certain way and knowing that next week things
will probably be that way."

Most of the women specified love, affection, and companionship
as values unique to marriage. A few said they were more likely to
use the word "love" to describe their feelings about family than
friends. But they, too, admitted to deep affection, dependence,
intimacy, and a sense of bonding in friendships. When women
used terms like love and companionship to describe a *unique* relation of marriage, they situated these feelings in the context of per-

manent commitment and daily cooperation. Commitment, physical intimacy, and domestic sharing seem to define the unique experience of love, companionship, and security that women feel only with their husbands.

Maybe it's just that you're loved in the way that a man loves a woman. Not necessarily physically—it's just that you're there with him. . . . Just depending on him in a different way than you can depend on your friends.

Intimacy. There's a bonding with someone who you've lived with as many years as we've lived together, that you can't share with someone you don't live with. It's more irreplaceable than love.

Women who did not pinpoint the qualities of commitment and domesticity were more likely to find themselves confused by the contradiction of their sense of uniqueness and their inability to find a unique emotional exchange. Lisa provided an example of this: "I wouldn't say strong emotional feelings because I've felt like that for Doreen. I'd hate to limit it to sex—I know there's something else."

Women who regarded their marriage as very companionate were inclined to look for unique values generated in their individual marriages rather than in formal elements of marriage, like commitment and domesticity. These formal elements they sometimes ignored, thinking about their own husbands rather than husbands in general. Having just answered the parallel question about women friends that focused on dynamic aspects of their friendships, women often sought and had difficulty finding unique dynamic qualities in their marriages. They laughed sheepishly—"I know I must be letting a lot of important things go by. . . ." The sheepishness suggests their sense of deviating from the companionate conjugal ideal, which emphasizes individual relational qualities.

Another set of responses to the question of a husband's unique values described the satisfaction of having realized an ideal:

Maybe it's what I really wanted to do with my life—to be with a man.

Identity—I know I feel stronger to go out into the world because I'm part of a couple.

I like being married. It's what I want to be. I like depending on a husband. That's why I don't like women's lib—I like being taken care of.

Perhaps the singular force of these statements stands out clearest from the context of the last one: ironically, it comes from a woman who finds her own marriage spiritually and emotionally empty, who is economically more independent than most, and whose emotional needs are met almost entirely by friends. In practical terms, she is less "taken care of" by her husband than most women. "Being taken care of" is thus for her more a matter of social status than a personal exchange. The preceding words convey one sentiment I heard frequently: one thing women want and need that only a husband can provide is marriage itself. Being married marks the achievement of a most valued social status; it is both socially approved and materially critical to a woman's economic well-being; for these and other reasons, being married brings something of psychological value to many women.

Other frequent responses to the question of uniqueness referred similarly to achieving and fulfilling marital roles. Husbands were uniquely valued as men, as fathers, and as economic providers. One of the values of being married was being with a man, most often described as being able to see the world from a man's point of view. "They do think differently from women. You have a man's point of view." Exploring this thought, another woman says, "I like the view of living in this society as a male. I learn from it. Sometimes I enjoy the vicarious experience."

Other wives phrased the experience more abstractly: "I like having the male figure in the home—male companionship." Still others mentioned the security they derived from a sense of male protection: "I don't like to be alone at night. At night when he's home, and I hear noises, I think 'Oh, macho man will take care of you.'"

Women—married, divorced, or single—spoke of appreciating the public social identity in being associated with a man: "There's times when you go out, that you don't want to go with women—you want to be escorted by a man."

"He's the only one who can be the father," answered Nancy, summing up the views of others who also acknowledged that a male parent was unique. The same women who said they needed a woman friend with whom to talk in depth about children expressed the need for a husband who shared a history with and "stake" in the child.

Our interest in the children is different from anybody else's. . . . Our commitment to them—I don't share that commitment with my friends.

You're the only two people who care about them as much as you do.

It's the feeling of shared responsibility having to do with children. It's sort of a lightening of the load.

A few women stated that economic support was one of the values that husbands alone provided. But many, including those who clearly relied on such support, were reluctant to describe it as a value. Sometimes they began to say so and then retracted, as Karen did: "That he'll provide—or rather, that we'll take care of each other in different ways." If valuing economic support as something they "needed in a relationship" seemed too mercenary to women who believed in companionate marriage, they generally acknowledged lack of money as one of the most serious problems they would encounter if the marriage ended. All but three married women answered immediately that finances would be their biggest problem. Of the three exceptions, one earns a high income, one is the sole wage earner because her husband is unemployed, and the last is a young, childless working woman.

One final value unique to marriage recurred in women's descriptions, a paradoxical ability to "be alone together."

I can get space from Lloyd. I can go to the other end of the house and be involved in what I'm doing and still we have a relationship.

You can be totally yourself with friends, too, but I find myself a little more "up" with friends than I feel I have to be with him. It's nice to have somebody who I don't necessarily have to sit and talk with, but I can still feel real comfortable and close just to be in the same house. With my friends, I feel real comfortable and close, but I think "maybe we should be talking about something." I like being able to be sort of separate together.

At first, I thought these responses referred to the authenticity of marital relations versus others—that husbands are sole co-residents of what Goffman calls the "back stage" of sociability. Yet, surveying what women said about the uniqueness of close women friends, I found repeated comments on authenticity there also. Indeed, women are frequently admitted to a "back stage" to which men are barred; one example Nancy described in the post-party debriefings she and Annette loved to stage: "We laugh and joke about what our husbands did at the party, about our designs on other men there, and that sort of thing that we'd never tell our husbands." Being separate together, however, is distinct. It is a kind of authenticity that women did feel they shared only with those they live with. It is not the authenticity of active sharing so much as the authenticity constituted by intimately living out daily life alongside another person.

As they described what they wanted and needed in a relationship that husbands alone could provide, women focused on the formal dimensions of marriage rather than unique attributes of their partner or relationship. They noted the special character that commitment and domesticity gave to love and companionship. And they emphasized the gratifications of fulfilling marital and parental roles over individual companionate values.

Comparing Close Friendship and Marriage

Set against the voluntary exchanges of women's friendships are the contrasting benefits of the compact of marriage. Most of the values women attributed uniquely to marriage are its constitutive, formal characteristics rather than emergent or dynamic qualities of a companionate relationship. Women valued the state of marriage and savored their realization of this socially rewarded ideal, which is intertwined with a social recognition of womanhood. They enjoyed sharing the intimacy and history that, in some form or extent, are the product of any conjugal coresidence. Women prized the sense of stability and security that results from a formally permanent commitment and were gratified by the confident planning for the future that such a commitment allows. And they valued the physical intimacy that is accessible in marriage and socially proscribed in extramarital relations.

What seems noteworthy about these values is that they distinguished the nineteenth-century marital ideal rather than the egalitarian, romantic companionate ideal that unfolded in the twentieth century. This is not to say that the modern ideal lacks values like commitment; but the values that best distinguish this contemporary ideal are not salient in the women's accounts of unique attributes of their marriages.

Dynamic companionate values—such as empathy, mutuality, multifaceted engagement, and evolving common interests—are much more often invoked as unique aspects of close friendships. Although time and commitment enrich these attributes, companionate bonds often develop among women friends independently of time and commitment and are intrinsically gratifying. In this sense, companionate values are less time-bound—they can gel quickly—and are less contractual or covenantal. They seem to develop from qualities or capacities of the participants and from dynamic qualities of the relationship rather than from fulfilling a role. Unique friendship values emerge in voluntary exchanges of friendship, in contrast to unique marriage values, which result from fulfilling the general marriage compact.

The companionate conjugal ideal is nurtured by the ideal of romantic love, whose powerful feeling transforms capacities, transcends distances and limitations, and establishes a spiritual communion between lovers. Contemporary culture extols a companionate romantic love that extends beyond the souls' companionship celebrated by nineteenth-century poets. To be sure, partners are to be spiritual companions; but within this communion (or perhaps prompting it) an unparalleled intimate friendship develops. Husbands and wives are to be each other's best friend.

To an extent my research confirms the idea of contemporary marriage as intimate friendship. Certainly in comparison with nineteenth-century marriages whose partners dwelt in essentially separate spheres, the marriages described here were both intimate and friendly. But they involved one set of meanings, and friendships an overlapping but partly distinct set. The intimacy of marriage was born of sharing and daily cooperation in the context of physical intimacy and permanent commitment. The intimacy of friendship was made of mutual self-disclosure and empathic understanding in the context of voluntary support and contingent commitment. The friendship of marriage affectionately appreciated difference, uniquely experienced an intertwined history, and valued fidelity. The friendship of women friends attracted engaged and empathic others who share a gender consciousness; it valued the shared experiences of womanhood and motherhood and the relation between self and others that is characteristic of contemporary women's culture.

This situation leaves us with a puzzle. We have accounts of deep and vital friendships, but no cultural ideal. We have accounts of deep and meaningful marriages, but an unacknowledged contradiction to the cultural ideal. How do we assess these two patterns and their respective sets of contradictions? Furthermore, if close friendships illustrate values that are prominent in (or exclusive to) the cultural ideal of marriage, might not friendships compete with and undermine marriage? The following chapters address these puzzles. Here, I present women's own testimony on the questions, which I posed after each woman recounted the unique values of her close friendship.

Do Values of Friendship Interfere with Marriage?

Do the values unique to a woman's close friendship help her marriage work more smoothly; do they interfere; do they do both, or neither? Answering my question, half the women stated that friends' special understanding, empathy, and companionship in shared interests made the marriage work more smoothly. None believed the effects were only negative. One quarter called the effects both bad and good; and the last quarter said there were no real effects on their marriage (this last group frequently listed positive effects, however, when I asked, How has your close friend helped when you've had difficulties in your marriage?).

The positive effects that women specified included garnering personal resources that enrich a woman's contribution to marriage; satisfying needs that marriage did not meet; and developing the model for a good relationship. In the first category, women reported that they improved their marriages by bringing to them a self-regard enhanced by friendship, by developing their talents and interests, or by learning how to resolve marriage problems.

I'm happier and not dwelling on my problems. So, that improves the marriage.

Talking about problems with her gives me a chance to sift through and get to what I want to talk about with him.

I figure there must be an easier way to do this than arguments. She helps me come up with a better alternative.

Explaining the compensatory effects of friendship, women stressed that they could take the strain of their own dissatisfactions off their marriages by turning to a friend rather than their husbands for engagement, mutuality, and empathy. "I'd probably be at my poor husband's throat all the time," remarked one. Sylvia, who had described her husband's desire to avoid conversation ("He'll listen to me, but it sometimes irritates him to do it"), managed this rejection with equanimity because she can talk to friends: "If I'm able to talk to someone besides my husband, I'm able to give him that quiet time."

Similarly, Jean, now divorced, believes friendship helped her endure an unhappy marriage: "I think [friends] made it work more smoothly because I was getting what I needed there. So my life was acceptable."

Betty said that because her close friend satisfied important needs, she could refrain from overwhelming her husband with them. "I'd probably be putting too many demands on him. I'd be pressuring him for everything I needed and that would suffocate him."

Although one might imagine that a gratifying relationship would make women more dissatisfied with others they find lacking in comparison, this is not the effect women reported. These wives seemed to believe that marriages rarely approached the companionate ideal; surviving in their own marriages was more appealing than either looking for one that worked better or setting out alone with their children. They said their friends' companionship buttressed marriage, meeting needs for empathy and understanding that husbands could not satisfy and allowing them to free husbands of demands that might antagonize them.

Relatively few women suggested that friendship values served as a model for successfully changing marriages. Yet this category is a promising one, for it suggests a potential effect of friendship on marriages once women have gathered the social power to risk more assertive domestic influence: "I think they make my marriage work better. If I've had a good experience that's important in my life, then I work to get some of it—at least, some of it—in my relationship with Lloyd." I am certain that the two women who noted this effect of marriage had been emboldened to ask more of their husbands because both had recently improved their social options with education, employment, and the construction of friendship networks.

Paradoxically, the same women who had been emboldened by supportive friends to demand more in their marriages were among those who reported that friends' help had also made their married life rockier. Rita, just quoted on striving to build friendship values into marriage, continued to reveal the paradox: "He may not think it improves the marriage, but I do." Similarly, Louise took friendship as a model of give-and-take in a marriage where she had mostly given: "I guess Gary and I would have hit fewer bumps if I hadn't become friends with Jan. Because for him, things were running more smoothly before. He's had to learn to make some compromises in the marriage." And assessing her feelings, Nancy experienced both exhilaration and guilt after talks with Annette inspired her to assert her needs in the marriage: "Lots of times [such assertion] is real contradictory to the way you've been brought up."

Other questions, reviewing times when women lacked women friends and other times when they forged new friendships, corroborated their accounts of the effect of friendship on marriage. Except during the honeymoon period following marriage, being without close friends often left women lonely, depressed, and feeling they "could not survive on [marriage] alone."

I was down and depressed and jealous that he had his friends if he wanted to get out.

It was the first time in my life that I ever used tranquilizers. . . . When he had to travel, I'd say "Don't leave me." I think now if I'd had someone to talk to, all that might not have happened.

They reported that during such times they felt more boredom and dissatisfaction with their marriage, more jealousy of husbands' friends, and more "suffocated" reactions from husbands who felt that their wives "asked too much."

It was a stagnant time. If it had continued, it would have hurt the marriage. Any time we've had friends, we get along fine together.

I think I was too dependent on my husband then. I'd get easily disappointed. Then angry. You know the cycle.

I was afraid to let him do anything without me. I felt trapped and blamed
him, even though it was my fault. I wasn't happy any of the time, not
even when I was with him.

The stories of first budding friendships after these times heralded improved personal and marital well-being. One woman ex-
claimed, "I began feeling good about myself for the first time in a
long time, which of course was very positive for my marriage. Oh,
it was just a panacea for all my ills!" A few accounts of the evolution
of new friendships suggest another provocative comparison with
companionate marriage and hint at one way new friendships enhance marriage satisfaction. These accounts often portrayed the
beginning of a new friendship in terms of excitement, heightened
energies, frequent thoughts about the other, invigorated self-
regard—in short, in terms of the ardent sensibilities of romantic
love.

I spent a lot of the time on the phone with her. A lot of time thinking
about her and about things I wanted to tell her.

It was a catharsis. To release all that was pent up. . . . That hour [spent
together] was so exceptional in my life. It certainly turned me around.

The respondents themselves did not offer this analogy with romance. Yet their descriptions of the joys of new friendship often
sounded much more like courtship than familiar routines of friendship or marital love. My research with Claude Fischer, which compared the friendships of men and women through the life cycle,
indicates that women form new friendships regularly throughout
their lives, whereas men do not. Men are more likely to rely on
older friendships; and their store of close friendships significantly
declines as they approach old age.[10] Zick Rubin, who measured
liking and loving elements in various relationships, found that
women, more often than men, express love as well as liking for
their same-sex friends.[11] All this research suggests that when
couples remain faithfully married, wives are more likely than their
husbands to have ardent relationships throughout their lives. It
also suggests a nonsexual motive for men's apparently greater marital infidelity. If men do not seek intimate friendships with other

men, sexual affairs with women may be men's route to ardent and intimate friendship.

Community, Power, and Love

In our first glimpse of women friends and of husbands, a few issues stand out in relief. They bear on friendships and also on modern community, gender power, and ideals of modern marriage.

Evidence of a moral discourse among women friends on motherhood and childrearing touches upon the theory of the decline of community, which holds that the historic decline of kinship, neighborhood, and parish leaves individuals without a community of moral interchange and constraint. My research reveals a significant area of personal life—childrearing—where women's close networks weave a moral community that observes, influences, and sanctions mothering responsibility. I cannot say how widespread this moral discourse is or how it works. Since its effectiveness is limited by the voluntary association among friends, it could certainly not approach the level of social control found in traditional settings. Still, this flexibly woven fabric of constraint constitutes a much more authoritative moral community than most "decline" theorists concede to modern life.

Furthermore, this moral discourse on motherhood and family obligation may well undercut the tyranny of expertise that "decline" writers see working within women's isolation in families.[12] I have not gathered evidence on my respondents' dealings with health and family experts. Listening to the language in which they talk about childrearing, though, I can clearly distinguish echoes of expert voices that have reached these women through media and education. Still, the women's reports of extensive discussion with close friends on children and childrearing suggest that among mothers, there remain funds of traditions, practical knowledge, and communal resistance to egoistic, individualistic solutions. Expert advice appears to be discussed, reworked, perhaps rejected— in short, significantly mediated by dialogue among friends.

A second issue turns on how the compensations of best friendship contribute to relations of gender power. Does the unique companionship among women friends, which fills the gap between marital ideals and realities, affect women's marital or social power? In choosing friends who provide what husbands do not, women may gain power in marriage; this adaptive response to power asymmetry may well establish women's resources of power. The "principle of least interest" formulated by Willard Waller in his writing on marriage holds that the partner who is less invested in continuing the relationship has power on that account.[13] Although wives' economic dependence constitutes a considerable investment in marriage, their emotional alternatives in friendships—for which men apparently have no parallel—may well augment women's marital power. If men lack the intimate friendships women sustain, their meager possibilities for achieving personal integration outside marriage may limit their power. Intimacy validates the inner self; without intimacy, there remain only the solutions of solipsism.

What then is the place of the twentieth-century ideal of companionate marriage in the lives of the women I interviewed? What of the touted themes of equality, engagement, and mutual understanding that have amplified the nineteenth-century companionate vision? My research suggests that the ideal of companionate marriage remains an ideal—imperfectly practiced and not seriously anticipated as possible. The women I spoke to professed a desire for the relations that make up the new ideal. But most did not expect husbands to provide those relations.

Among the women I interviewed, the practical standard for marriage seems to be a fairly minimal one in terms of the companionate vision. Its components are compatibility, affection, and economic support of children. In contrast to the supposed hegemonic vision of engagement and struggle for perfection, a survival standard appears most prominent. Success means keeping a marriage together while countless others fall apart. Women are willing to credit men as husbands and fathers if they are caring, faithful, and good providers. If their men are "not big discussers," if they withdraw from emotional engagement, if they somewhat distantly regard the inner lives of their wives and children, and if they disparage their wives' desires for autonomy and accomplishment, these terms are tolerable. The remainder of this study explores the ways close relations with friends work with this stance toward marriage.

Chapter Three

Close Friendship
as an Institution

The women I spoke with claimed that friendship helped their marriages. But could they be mistaken? Given their strong attachments to close friends, my respondents might be ignoring subtle ways friendship tended to undermine marriage. They admitted they were unaccustomed to reflecting on friendship. Perhaps a distanced analysis of the interviews would be more telling. Examining friendship as an institution, this chapter and the next pursue such an analysis of friendship patterns and their connection to marriage.

Examining friendship as an institution runs counter to much modern work on friendship. A good many social scientists regard modern friendship as the most individualized and unregulated social relation.[1] Recognizing the latitude friendship grants to individual preference and strategy, some even hesitate to call it an institution. Because friendships are unregimented by kinship-type rules and free of formal role expectations, many view them as unique "interstitial" relations of individuality and freedom.[2] One anthropologist, Robert Paine, reflects the ambiguity in the institutional view of friendship when he dubs it an "institutionalized noninstitution."[3]

As distinctively voluntary relations—begun and continued by choice—friendships are based upon autonomous activity and individual gratification.[4] Compared with other more institutional relations, they are private, mutable, and terminable. Because they are affectionate and personal, formed without regard to collective

60

identity or interest, literature often presents close friendships as relations expressing in purest form both personal capacities and culturally elevated virtues such as honesty and faithfulness.[5] Whatever its contribution to social integration, solidarity in friendship is nonetheless interlaced with themes of individuality and autonomy.[6]

Emphasizing the individualistic character of modern friendship, social scientists have also advocated studying the social and cultural relations that influence friendship. Georg Simmel paved the way by positing a relation among differentiated market economies, individuated personality, and revelation, concealment, and attachment in friendship. Participating in complex societies, Simmel maintained, individuals become differentiated; they form bonds based on one or another element of their personalities or interests and conceal other aspects of their lives and minds.[7] Cora DuBois, an anthropologist who conducted a seminar on the topic in the 1950s, called attention to influences on friendship of cultural variations in definitions of self and sexual identity.[8] Paul Lazarsfeld and Robert Merton—and, following them, a long line of empirically oriented scholars of interpersonal dynamics and social networks— have attempted to specify how social position or personal attributes shape the process of friendship.[9] All these writers treat forces institutionalizing friendship, recognizing that the character of institution may be more implicit or tacit in friendship than in other social relations. I continue this theme.

I use the term *institutionalization* to denote the formation of regular patterns of friendship and shared expectations about its conduct and content. Institutions have both structural and cultural dimensions, which take shape within a larger institutional configuration. Institutional regularities can be more or less normative and more or less recognized by participants. Shared values and expectations may govern much or little conduct. Friendship patterns may also be regularized by the values and workings of surrounding institutions, like family, work, politics, or kinship. Thus some friendship patterns are regular, in the sense of being governed by explicit or implicit friendship rules; and some are ordered by practices and beliefs in other spheres. The latter are probably best characterized as residual patterns.

The rules and ethics of contemporary women's friendships are

not discernible in laws, rituals, or well-known codes. To uncover
the structure and ethics of women's friendship, I examined the
patterns, rhythms, correspondences, and rationales in twenty-one
accounts of close friendship. I considered the bounds of frequency,
time, place, and permissible content of exchange within these associations. From these bounds, I inferred their ordering principles
and hierarchy of commitments. I paid very close attention to the
relations between close friendships, marriage, and family, looking
at hierarchies of obligations and other beliefs and patterns that reveal the orientation of each institution to the others.

I approached this project with two analytical concepts suggested
by Robert Paine. First, *rules of relevance* (Paine uses "relevancy")
are the indices of or discourses about "what is permissible and/or
desirable" in the relationship. Paine stresses the private or idiosyncratic character of rules of relevance; he believes that friendship
does not have rules imposed upon it.[10] I treated this question empirically, seeking sources for rules of permissible conduct outside
or preceding the friendship.

Paine defines his second concept, "standards of equivalency,"
simply as "the nature of the exchanges" between friends. As Graham Allan points out, this formulation is a subconcept of rules of
relevance, since exchanges are permissible or desirable content
and conduct.[11] Nonetheless, one aspect of Paine's concept seemed
discrete enough to treat separately. I use the term *standards of
commitment* to indicate an exchange that establishes stable mutual
trust, investment, and satisfaction in a relationship. Since this category rests on psychological orientations to a very personal and
private relationship, I am more sympathetic to Paine's assumption
that standards of commitment tend to be specific to each relationship;[12] they may thus be more individual than rules of relevance.
Still, my ultimate theoretical interests directed me to seek sources
for standards of commitment in a particular sphere external to
friendship—in marriage. As with rules of relevance, I focused on
patterned personal concerns that generalize individual strategies.

To Paine's norm-based analytical framework, I added a third category, *residual patterns*. They develop around normative practices
of friendship as well as superordinate commitments in other
spheres. For example, work patterns or a political climate may
shape particular friendship modes though they may not structure

the principles of friendship. But they are regular, and they may give friendship much of its recognizable form. Over time, residual patterns may take on the symbolic weight of custom.

I propose that standards of commitment (the exchanges that make up friendship), rules of relevance (the normative realm), and residual patterns (the customary realm) all derive from general cultural values and practices that are mediated by the distinctive social positions, experiences, and needs of contemporary women.

Standards of Commitment

In some cultures, friendships are formally institutionalized through blood brotherhood or ritual kinship, culturally specified standards of exchange.[13] In a culture where friendship is unritualized and individually established, individuals make their own standards of mutual commitment, and only the most general virtues, such as honesty, apply a priori.[14] Although writers like Paine have stressed the idiosyncratic strategies that result, DuBois and others have advocated looking at the ways that standards are patterned by cultural or subcultural themes.[15] Following DuBois's lead, I sought evidence of general standards of commitment among women or groups of women—standards that clarify the link between women's social position and their strategies in friendship. In the interviews, I found those standards in responses to questions about the sources of trust, conflict, satisfaction, and disappointment.

The women I interviewed perceived friendships as the most voluntary and contingent of close relationships. They rarely noted explicit rights and obligations, rituals of solidarity, or firm expectations of permanence. They did not necessarily expect even the closest friendships to be permanent or long-term. When asked for the names of the people they expected to "still be close to ten or twenty years from now," all but two women named current close friends. Yet only occasionally did someone identify long-term commitment as a pivotal value of friendship. This contrasted with their frequent emphasis on the centrality of commitment in marriage: women often cited long-term commitment as a unique and valued attribute of marriage. Even though they hoped to sustain their relationships with best friends and expected to do so, barring unforeseen conflicts or relocations—they seemed to view long-term relationships as a reward of successful friendship rather than as a defining expectation.[16]

According to the standard of commitment most evident in my interviews, a close friendship rests upon mutually satisfying companionship and reciprocal exchanges of intimacy and emotional support; these exchanges generate trust, investment, and stability. Only in relationships that have endured over time or distance are shared sentiment and history sufficient for stability and trust; there, mutuality is not contingent upon other contemporaneous exchange. In the lives of the women I interviewed, relationships that did not develop over time and distance took their shape through the kinds of engagement, revelation, and mutuality I discussed in the last chapter.

If friends do not generally pledge long-term commitment, if they frequently exchange nothing material or concrete, if they have no ritual to express solidarity or formal status to confer upon each other, what then expresses their trust and solidarity? The answer is once again the exchange of intimacy, of self-disclosure, and of empathic understanding. When asked why they liked a particular close friend, women specified a friend's personal characteristics. When asked why they trusted a close friend, they most often said that they had exchanged confidences:

I guess it's just the telling of confidential things you'd never tell anyone else.

We've shared so much that's intimate. It's almost that we know too much about each other not to trust each other.

We've expressed our friendship for each other in a way that is special—I mean, we've exposed our deepest selves.

When you've told somebody something, and you realize it's been kept in confidence. And then it weaves its way back through conversations—you know, I've told her things I've never been able to tell anybody before. That's what creates the trust.

All the women (including four who listed their sisters as best friends) mentioned close friends in responses to questions about who shared important confidences. Sharing intimacy was the reply women gave most frequently to the question about what generates trust. Other answers mentioned common values: "She considers a friendship sacred, and so do I." "It's her Christian attitude about a lot of things. Our religions are different, but her outlook begins with a definite belief in the Lord." All but three of the women included close friends among those who shared their most important values.

A third frequent response was that care for each other's children cemented the trust. "I've trusted her with my kids, which is the most important thing I have." Counting not only answers to the question about trust but also spontaneous descriptions of the meaning of exchanging the care of children, mothers of young children commented on the significance of this exchange nearly as often as they emphasized exchange of intimacy. Women whose local kin helped with babysitting and those with the means to purchase child care or babysitting services were loathe to undertake routine exchanges of child care; they saw such exchanges as a burden upon themselves and their friends and as a likely encroachment upon exclusive family time. Yet in general the willingness to provide loving care for a friend's children when this favor was necessary women considered an important and binding exchange.

Exchanging intimacy and shared values over a time long enough to build trust brings a close relationship that women may call on in emergencies for more than the usual fund of help and support. A few women described such emergencies, when friends proved their devotion through sacrifice.

Jan had to go back into the hospital shortly after the baby was born, and Eddie would have had to take off work to take care of him. So I brought the baby home with me until she came out. It was hard on my family, but I know she'd do it for me.

The night my husband got put in jail, she came and sat with me there. I'd never been through anything like that, and I was a mess. It really meant a lot.

Such sacrifices among friends seemed to build exceptionally strong bonds and trust; but relatively few of the women I spoke with tested that trust by asking or making a great sacrifice. The *projection* of ultimate availability and obligation seemed by itself to seal the trust. Many were careful to stress the need to avoid such demands: "You have to have your friend's best interests at heart—it's easy to take advantage of a friend." Still, every one of the women named close friends (or sister-best friends) among those they would make sacrifices to help. The quality of the emotional relationship or intimacy—rather than an actual sacrifice—seems to be the basis of a conviction that both friends would make sacrifices if called upon. Intimacy is the essential ingredient of friends' commitment.

The exchange of intimacy covers a variety of modes of revelation and recognition. Thea and Catherine shared the intensity of lives that perilously wove career ambition and family devotion. They used the languages of philosophy, psychology, and literature. Kay and Linda shyly but eagerly explored emotions and wishes neither had put into words before their friendship. Penny and Fern rarely placed self-conscious terms around the knowledge they had exchanged since they were youngsters. Silences, glances, jokes, and daily companionship communicated an immense understanding between them. Each woman described this unique understanding as the foundation of the relationship and of her confidence that it would endure.

Are these standards of exchange unique to women? Studies of men's intimate self-disclosure to friends (which I summarize in chapter 5), and my respondents' descriptions of their husbands' friendships, strongly suggest that these standards of commitment are a distinctive attribute of women's culture. Although men's friendships surely involve meaningful self-disclosure, men do not appear to bind friendships with mutual revelation of personal life and empathic validation of inner selves as women do. Barry Wellman's data on men's and women's friendships show that married men exchange primarily task-oriented help with close friends; Lillian Rubin's study confirms this distinction.[17] Camaraderie and sociable pursuits seem to be the exchanges that create trust and investment and bind men's friendships over time.

Given these distinctions, women develop more practices of attentiveness, disclosure, and empathy. Gender stratification and gender personality may account both for this development and for the particular balance of psychological and emotional resources in women's standards of mutuality. Gender stratification allows women to exchange generously only those values they control or possess. Most married women own few material resources they dispose of at will. Arlene, whose marriage fits the sociological model of a companionate middle-class couple was asked, Who would be more likely to lend money to a friend? "Men," she answered. "Because it's easier to lend your own money. Women don't make much. And I think my friends pretty much see a husband's money as his own." Those women who perceived a gender difference rated men, seven to one, more likely to lend money to a friend, although a majority thought there was no difference. Of the two dozen general characteristics contrasting the friendships of men and women, this was the only positive quality on which a number of women rated men higher than women. Even their own services, like child care for a friend's children, they often viewed as a drain on family resources. Frances took care of Jill's children from time to time when her friend, a single working mother, needed her. "My family feels put out, though. Jack says, 'Why do you have to have all these kids around?' But he wants me at home, just with our kids. Thank goodness she doesn't ask often."

Carol Stack's ethnography of poor urban blacks documents the destabilization of marriage commitments when extended kin and close friends pool scarce material resources. In the families she studied, the survival strategies of kin networks made leaving these networks on marriage risky, given the economic uncertainty facing poor women. If they withdrew from kin networks of economic exchange to put resources in the individual nuclear family, after a divorce or an economic catastrophe they could find themselves without a network to fall back on.[18]

Economic hardship and its corrosive effects on marriage are among the more predictable currents of daily life for the urban poor. The women Stack observed, who may have been exceptionally integrated into stable survival networks, often could not risk honoring the interests of their nuclear family at the expense of kin exchange. With one exception (Cass, whose family had chased away her abusive husband and taken her back home), the women I interviewed, even the most unprivileged, all lived beyond the economic borderline of that risk or else lacked available kin networks of material exchange. Their interests clearly lay with the nuclear family.

Poor people who exchange the simplest means of survival cannot escape the attendant possibility of exploitation among friends. As Stack notes, themes of distrust and exploitation combine with trust and friendship in the fiction and lore of black culture.[19] The women I spoke with wished to avoid that danger, particularly where their families as well as they themselves would register exploitation. By giving of themselves, they believed that they could strike friendship terms without exploitation and that they could gauge and bear costs autonomously.

Another ultimately structural explanation of why women friends' standards of commitment differ from men's lies in what Nancy Chodorow calls the development from "oedipal asymmetries" to "heterosexual knots." Her argument of gender personality begins with a division of labor in which men are primary breadwinners and women are primary parents. Chodorow maintains that forming gender personality and identity in a stratified society where only women care for children produces asymmetries between boys and girls, men and women, in their capacities and needs for intimacy and attachment. Men develop stronger needs for separation and suppress desires for intimacy; women keep stronger needs for intimacy and attachment. These asymmetries strain heterosexual relationships, impelling women to rely on kin, friends, and children for emotional engagement they do not receive in marriage.[20] Chodorow's argument places what others perceive as natural, biological, or learned gender differences in intimacy into a structural framework of gender stratification: differences between men's and women's standards of commitment in friendship may reside partly in differences in gender personality that come from social structure. Chodorow summarizes these gender differences as deep differences in capacities of masculine and feminine personality. One interesting empirical study, however, suggests that preferences rather than capacities explain gender differences in intimacy.[21] Although we might view preferences as variables in gender personality, we might also examine them as attitudes that correspond more directly to power differences.[22]

Rules of Relevance

Moving from the essential to the desirable or permissible content of friendship, I looked for some exchanges women friends approved of or valued but did not require in making best friendships.

I noted a few rules of relevance in the last chapter, where I sum-marized the values unique to friendships among women and the topics women especially preferred to discuss with women friends. Here, I turn again to the themes of permissible talk and moral obligations among friends in order to discover explicit and tacit rules of relevance.

To uncover these rules, I asked about topics that women felt they could and would discuss with close friends. Other questions concerned obligations. I asked about the appropriateness of vari-ous demands that friends might make of each other, the obligations friends should feel for each other's welfare and for the welfare of each other's children, and the responsibility friends should take for influencing each other's behavior and beliefs. In another strategy for identifying unformalized rules, I asked about instances in which friends had overstepped the bounds of friendship by asking too much, involving the friend inappropriately in concerns or conver-sations, or otherwise making a woman feel that she had "just had enough." In this way, I sought tacit rules through their violation.

Permissible Talk

One series of forced-choice questions asked women to estimate how often they would discuss a particular topic with a friend, if the topic were "on your mind." (Sixteen women responded to this se-ries, which I added to the interview after conducting the first five. Forced-choice questions provide a range of answers from which respondents choose one.) The questions probed their willingness to discuss different areas rather than frequency of discussion. The topics ranged from political or religious beliefs through emotional states to work or family problems. In general, the women would discuss any given topic with a friend "Some of the time" or "A lot of the time" rather than "Once in a while" or "Never." The main exception was marital sex—that is, a woman's own sex life, not sex in general—which nine out of fifteen women said they would never discuss.

Financial problems also presented a sensitive topic, although not as private as marital sex. Nine of sixteen would discuss financial problems, if they were on their minds, only once in a while. Given that sex and money are quintessential items of family privacy, however, it is perhaps more appropriate to focus on the complements of these fractions: all the women said they would talk to a friend about money problems at least once in a while. And over a quarter would discuss their marital sex lives once in a while. In open-ended questions a few women volunteered that they preferred discussing financial matters with a close friend rather than husbands ("because she isn't as close to it"). It is obvious that some women do discuss such sensitive areas with friends: even though just over half of the women interviewed considered their sex lives and money problems too private to discuss, over a third confided them to their friends.

Problems with other friends fell in the intermediate range of sensitivity or privacy. Answers to whether women friends would discuss problems with other friends were fairly evenly distributed over the four categories of inclination. My respondents described themselves as more likely to confide marital problems than those involving friendship.

For the rest of the questions in this series, at least two-thirds of the women would talk to friends, sometimes or a lot, if they were thinking about problems with husband or children or household, moral or religious beliefs, or husband's work problems. At least three-quarters of them would discuss feelings of love or of anger, their own problems involving work, news or politics, and future dreams and ambitions. Considering all the topics, the problems women felt they were most likely to discuss were ones dealing with their own work and future dreams and ambitions. Nine of sixteen said they would discuss these a lot of the time. I say more about these items in the next chapter when I consider friendship and individuality.

Asked about subjects or areas of life a woman would *never* discuss, two-thirds of the women said there were none. Even more women said their best friend had never even tried to broach issues or problems they did not wish to discuss. One category of discourse they seemed to avoid, however: issues that generated conflict between the friends. Yet not all combustible topics were easy to avoid. Women did try to resolve childrearing differences that made it difficult to socialize when children were around. Friends did feel compelled to address disagreements about how much of a friend's time is available for friendship. However, they more easily suppressed other issues of disagreement or conflict of values. Take, for example, this rather significant difference of belief between Sylvia and Pat: "When we were first getting to know each other, I didn't see how we could be friends, because our views aren't close at all. She believes in women's lib, which is completely opposite of my views."

But Sylvia and Pat built upon their common ground and avoided tangles over feminism. Sylvia showed little sign of infection by her friend's belief system; I suspect the noninfluence was mutual. The same appeared to be the case with Karen and Marla: "She's a Republican and I'm a third-generation Democrat. You can imagine why we never discuss politics."

Others revealed more frustration with their chosen mode of suppressing differences:

We disagree about work habits. She's big on shortcuts. I'm a stickler for doing it right, down to the last detail. Sometimes it kills me to watch her doing sloppy work. I get frustrated, but I'd never say anything. It wouldn't do any good.

She's a born-again Christian. We don't discuss religion, because we're in such different worlds in our beliefs. Maybe it's just that I don't understand her complete dependence and devotion. But I'm concerned that it keeps her from having any belief in herself. It feels like something strange between us.

It disappoints me that she doesn't share certain feelings about what's right, about the way the world should be. . . . It's a difference in ethics . . . in a feeling for other people. It's hard to let things she says pass. But it's too frustrating to try and make her see how I feel. I try not to be angry.

Each of these women felt that suppressing conflict was the way to preserve harmony in a friendship, although for some it nonetheless left troubled feelings. Their sense of the destructive potential in unrestrained conflict seems accurate: sustaining relationships surely depends on partners' ability to express and restrain conflict. But I was surprised at the extent to which the women seemed to have avoided expressing disagreement and conflict. Given the extent to which they revealed to each other their beliefs and opinions and their emphasis on the value of honesty, I would have expected a greater willingness to disagree openly. Studies show that conflict occurs more in marriage than in friendship, and that conflict in marriage does not necessarily correlate with dissatisfaction.[23] Why then do rules of relevance for women's friendship appear to proscribe virtually all conflict?

I have no evidence that addresses this question, but I have a few ideas. For one, a relationship of contingent commitment may feel (and be) considerably more vulnerable to the destructive effects of conflict than one whose conventional bonds help assure the relationship will survive periods of distress. It is far easier, for example, to stoke anger in self-imposed isolation when the requirements of daily life do not bring a pair together at meals or in bed. On the other side of the coin, a relationship of contingent commitment may not build in primordial or irrational conflicts as marriage does, with its cornerstone issues of sex and identity. In other words, friendship may be less subject to uncontrollable conflict than marriage is. A further explanation for women's suppressing conflict in friendship may lie in the relationship's dynamics of empathy and identification. Women's exchanges in friendship strongly emphasize the projection of similarity. By contrast, the experience of difference may threaten the capacity to empathize. The sense of separation and distance created by disagreement and conflict may appear to women to menace the intimate and mutualistic bonds of their friendships. Avoiding conflict does not necessarily avoid stress, however.[24] The frustration evident in the remarks describing conflicts smoothed over may affect the relationships in ways the friends fail to grasp.

Whatever the actual cause, women not only avoided conflict with friends, they believed friends in general should do so. And two to one, they believed that women friends avoid conflict better than men friends. To one question from a series on beliefs about gender differences in patterns of friendship, a majority of women agreed that men are "more likely" to argue with friends than women are—the only characteristic of friendship, out of twenty-three, that a majority credited to men over women. (On two others—jealousy of a spouse's friend and being likely to lend money to a friend—women credited men more often than women, although a majority believed there was no gender difference. On another seven items, including loyalty and breaking up friendships more easily, a majority of respondents pronounced no gender difference; but here women received more votes than men. And on thirteen items—most centering on closeness, emotionality, and disclosure—women overwhelmingly acknowledged their greater inclination.)

These responses suggest some of the rules of relevance for friendship talk. The desirable topics, as chapter 2 revealed, are feelings, childrearing, husband problems, the deprecated daily tasks of homemaking, news in social networks, and thoughts of individual achievements. The range of permissible talk is vastly inclusive, but most women felt that it excluded money problems and marital sex as well as issues of conflict between friends.

Moral Obligations

Moral obligations also create rules of relevance. The women I spoke with held similar ideas about the moral obligations of friendship, which may be summarized in three categories: personal relational virtues; respect for personal liberty; and communal responsibility in warranted circumstances.

Although I did not ask directly, I listened in my interviews for beliefs about the virtues that qualify a friend. Women's first descriptions of their best friend and what they "liked best" about their friend repeatedly specified honesty, caring and concern for others, trustworthiness, and generosity; and they frequently mentioned constancy and strength of character (my terms). Their language was concrete rather than abstract, avoiding terms like loyalty or fidelity or devotion, which represent formal virtues of other institutions.

When I raised the subject of loyalty, the women tended to abandon the female chauvinism they usually applied to gender comparisons of friendship: this is one of the few friendship virtues that they attributed equally to men and women. One possible interpretation of this pattern involves the status of loyalty as a public institutional virtue as well as a private one. Public institutions are the traditional "male sphere." Since organizations of men developed the public virtues of loyalty, comradeship, collegiality, and union "brotherhood," women are not likely to claim superiority on masculine turf. A second explanation may lie in the widespread assimilation of moral philosophy's emphasis on the disinterested motivations required to establish a virtue. For example, some say altruism cannot be defined by emotional attachment but only by selfless concern for the good of another.[25] Women, however, are likely to recognize their own emotional investment in relationship as well as the web of dependencies relationships establish. They may not perceive their loyalties as selfless. The women I interviewed were very likely to describe important relationships in these terms of attachment and to substitute them for terms like loyalty or fidelity.

A series of questions about rights and obligations among friends uniformly evoked circumspect libertarian themes. Do friends have a right to try to change a woman's attitudes or beliefs or way of doing things? No, responded a majority of respondents, "Hardly ever." Asked to specify occasions when such influence would be appropriate, most invoked times when a woman was being self-destructive or harming others, especially children. Those who believed that "trying" was acceptable spoke of the need to approach with delicacy and respect for the integrity of the other. "'Try' to change her, no. But one should be able to 'offer' change." And another said, "I'd be careful about making judgments. I might say 'If it were me. . . .'"

Do friends have a right to tell a woman her behavior is immoral and wrong? Because this question posed a sharper moral dilemma, answers were less negative and more deliberate. They upheld the value of moral engagement between friends, even at the risk of disharmony. Answers cautioned against moralism and disrespectful judgment. They aimed at preserving a space for individual differences. Again, the interests of children were preeminent considerations, as were the preservation of a woman's integrity and self-esteem and (implicitly or explicitly) her esteem in a community.

If you're a friend, yes, you should [tell her she is wrong.] But you should know when to keep your mouth closed too.

If she's doing something that's really making her look bad in the community—a friend should make her aware. She can still do what she wants.

If you could save her from a future of disillusionment, dismay, and unhappiness, you should.

A friend can say she believes a behavior is immoral, but I don't believe in judging. If a friend were doing something harmful to herself or her kids, I would tell her. If I thought an affair was immoral, I'd keep it to myself.

The first response to questions about obligations among friends always involved a concern for the welfare of the woman or her children. This value always superseded the values of liberty and autonomy for either partner in the friendship. When questions moved from a friend's rights of intervention to a friend's obligation to intervene or sacrifice, the answers became unambiguous when grave issues of welfare were posed. Two-thirds or more of the women answered a firm "Always" (as opposed to "Sometimes" or "Hardly ever") to these questions:

————If a friend seemed to be in trouble emotionally—having a break-down—do her friends have a responsibility to try to get help for her?

————If a woman were being beaten by her husband, do her friends have a responsibility to take her in if she asks?

————If a friend were ill or somehow unable to care for her children, do her friends have a responsibility to care for them?

————If a friend was beating or abusing her children, do her friends have a responsibility to stop it?

————In this same case, if all else failed, would they have a responsibility to call police or some outside agency?

Respondents who hesitated to answer "Always" to these questions generally specified that others, such as kin, might be the ones who should intervene; but unquestionably friends should if more appropriate others did not.

Spontaneous accounts of real-life moral dilemmas also confirmed the strength of this set of values. Many accounts also forcefully demonstrated the crosscutting obligations that made honoring these values difficult. Several women had taken their friends' children into their homes or had friends take theirs, in two cases for fairly extended stays. All were certain they were right in having done so, even though they had subjected their own families to discomfort. Three women had taken in friends in the process of divorce, although these situations proved very troubling to husbands, even the cooperative ones. Hilda's husband, who was not one of the cooperative ones, forced her friend to return home. Hilda reflected, "Maybe she was intruding; but at the time, all I could think of was that I was there." Many years after the incident, Hilda still recalls with regret and bitterness that she failed a friend.

Finally, several women talked about criticizing or being criticized by friends on childrearing issues.

I've tried to get Trish to change her lifestyle to a healthier one for her kids—and for her. Then, I go round and round on whether I'm right. I usually end up feeling it's not my place to change her.

Sometimes when I've let my kids go out of line, Gwen will let me know. If I wasn't paying enough attention, just letting it slide, I'll look at it a little harder.

These responses suggest that the rules of relevance in women's best friendships permit vast familiarity with private personal and family matters in each other's lives. This extensive disclosure, in turn, permits a moral discourse between friends—one that combines a tolerance of individual liberty and a concern for family responsibility. Women friends viewed the welfare of a friend's children and of the friend herself as the signal issue for applying constraint. Despite considerable intimacy and moral interchange, the women I interviewed meticulously avoided conflict with friends. This suppression of conflict was only one tacit rule of relevance I inferred from women's testimony. I pursue other tacit rules in the next chapter when I examine the reasons women gave for withdrawing from friendships.

Customary and Residual Practices of Friendship
Networks of Close Friends and Kin

The titles "friend," "close friend," or "best friend" mark the only statuses in the institution of friendship. I wished to learn how women chose the status of close or best friend. Who were the people to whom they felt closest? I asked this question a few different ways. Very early in each interview, before mentioning friends or kin, I asked, Who are the people you would describe as most a part of your life? Every one of the twenty-one women answered this ambiguous question by first listing husbands and children. Thirteen added kin, mostly parents and siblings. Thirteen also listed nonkin friends. Only two listed nuclear family members alone.

Every woman resubmitted all these names when I asked for information on those to whom she feels closest, whether nearby or far away. Women who had listed only nuclear family members for the former question now added close kin and close friends. Those who had listed these earlier usually named a few more of each. Members of both groups added far-away kin and friends, closer-by immediate kin whom they saw infrequently, and husbands of close friends or kin.[26]

The average size of these close networks, counting only adult, nonhousehold names, was seven (corresponding to Fischer's finding in his much larger data set).[27] The smallest close network belonged to Cass, who listed only a sister, and her own children, although she frequently visited her many local relatives. Kay claimed the largest close network, listing fourteen outside her nuclear family. Kay listed more couple-friends than most and fewer kin.

Kay's close network was one of seven—a third of my sample— in which friends outnumbered kin; in these networks women did not always list more friends but included fewer kin. Most of these women had fewer kin in the area than the eleven women whose kin dominated close networks. The last three close networks were evenly divided between friends and kin, even though all three women had many relatives nearby; thus these networks differ from a pattern in Fischer's data, which associated larger kin networks with smaller friendship networks.[28]

Just over half the members of most close networks were nearby friends and kin—local people or people living within an hour's drive. A majority of the women listed three or more local close friends and kin and at least some others who lived within an hour's drive. True to the stereotype of mobile Californians, these women frequently commuted the distance of an hour's drive—or further— to visit kin and friends they listed as close.

Close networks numbered mostly women. Six networks were entirely female. Only Lee, who is single, listed a network where fewer than three-quarters of the members were women. Men named were almost always fathers, brothers, in-laws, or husbands of close women friends. Only two women, Lee and Lynn (Lynn was newly married), listed men who were not relatives or couple-friends. Moreover, although most of the women I interviewed had jobs, only seven placed co-workers in their close network (usually one co-worker). And although a majority considered some neighbors friends, only five included neighbors among their closest friends (again, usually one neighbor).

With my third question about the people to whom women felt closest, I sought the name of one "closest" or "best" friend, to focus later questions. I asked, Is there *one* person you feel closest to? From the total of twenty-one women, six named friends; four named sisters; one named her mother; one her sweetheart. Of the seventeen married women, nine named their husbands or children in their answer. I am intrigued by the fact that only half of the married women named their husbands. Yet I hesitate to interpret it, given the possibility—suggested in another study—that many women forget to list their husbands.[29] (To avoid the dilemma, I began a later series of questions by reminding women that they might name husbands and then proceeded through my long list.)

Continuing to seek the name of a closest woman friend, I repeated the question when necessary, asking if there were one person other than husband, child, or parent to whom a woman felt closest. At the first repeated question, several women who had named either husband or children then listed either children or husband; three listed parents, including one woman who said her mother was her best friend. The question finally yielded these results: seventeen women listed nonkin friends, and four listed sisters (one woman who named a nonkin friend added, "also, my sister"; I perhaps arbitrarily counted her among the seventeen).

When I asked if the friend or sister they listed was a best friend, twelve of the seventeen who had named friends affirmed the label, as did all four who listed sisters. I accepted sisters as best friends because preliminary and later interviews all suggested that women who list sisters as best friends describe the relationships in terms similar to those others apply to best friends. And they distinguish relationships with these sisters from the generally close relationships with sisters they do not consider best friends. Of course sister-best friendships also differ from other best friendships: they have longer histories and are more often perceived as eternal.

They tend to feature the kind of senior-junior themes that only some nonsororal best friendships have.

Five women declined to describe as a "best friend" the one person outside the household they felt "closest to." Since all five had listed these friends earlier among people they felt closest to, I know they did not randomly offer the names to comply with what they perceived as my wish to hear about a best friend. Nevertheless, a few said they did not feel appreciably closer to "one person." In four of these five cases, the women later described the friendships as somewhat less intimate and attached than those other women willingly labeled "best"; even though they appear less close, I included them in the following discussions of closest friendships (occasionally referring to them as "best friends" along with the others).

Contrary to my expectations, the term *best friend* seemed to be used similarly across classes and subcultures. Those women who hesitated to give that title to a close friend often described only their husbands as "best friends." Yet their marriages were not more companionate than those of women who named women best friends. In fact, women with women best friends were also likely to call their husbands best friends. Companionate marriage, defined by women's references to symmetry, amity, joint activity, and couple socializing, does not seem to impede women's close attachments to women friends. Characteristics of personality appeared to account for attachments, casting women who do not form best friendships into more dependent, but not more companionate, marital roles.

How Closest Friends Met

Women establish close friendships in contexts that introduce them to attractive people and allow them to begin the exchange of self-disclosure that opens a close friendship. That statement fits what I found. Best friends generally met in contexts that made self-disclosure easier and minimized its risks.

High school and college friendships unfold during years in which girls have considerable time for building relationships and in which psychological needs and social pressures invest friendships with enormous value. Every woman I spoke with described high school friendships as having been extremely important: "They were my whole life." "Everything was staked on friends." Separations and partings of ways had broken many women's ties to high school friends. Yet several had kept these friendships over considerable obstacles. Kay, for example, still regularly corresponded with four high school friends, although she had not seen any of them in years. One of them was socially mobile: "Jeanette's in a whole different social realm. She's got a couple of degrees, a lot of money, and all. You'd think we'd grow apart. When she came out here, we hadn't seen each other for ten years. But we hadn't changed a bit. We're both still crazy. We got along as if it were yesterday." A large number of high school attachments similarly promised to endure.

Frances and Carol met in grade school and have been best friends ever since; both still live in the community where they were born. Lisa and Jean each met closest friends in high school, moved away from home, and yet kept up intense friendships long distance. Jean developed other very close friendships in the decades since high school but continues to regard Ellen as her very closest friend: "It just doesn't depend on seeing each other a lot." Lisa, who is in her midtwenties, recently moved out of state and away from Doreen, her best friend since high school. Being in a new relationship with Jesse and working full-time, she has not developed a comparably close friendship in her new town: "I've got a lot of good friends back home. Here, I've met quite a few people, but I don't have very many friends."

Other women had also kept up friendships from school days. Five listed high school friends on their close network lists. Most of these women added newer "best friends," whom they had met in more immediate contexts such as spheres of voluntary participation or, for mothers, arenas of participation with children. Three women met their best friends in classes at community college, the context that—along with mothers' groups—sparked the most ardent friendships among married women. Others met in church or in independent socializing.

Friendships set in contexts where women communicated deeply felt personal adult experience were especially likely to be ardent ones. Some of the warmth reflected the newness of adult-made

friendships. But much of it was clearly the mutuality and the recognition of developing aspects of self.

The women who met in community college classes had all married and borne children after high school before they returned to
school. Each of the four became attracted to her friend in the
moral-intellectual engagement of this setting. Jean described the
tight-knit group that formed in one class.

We were all married suburban housewives who were going back to
school. We'd start talking about things in class, and we'd continue afterward in the cafeteria. Then we'd start coming an hour early. It was almost
like being at camp. It was such a close experience—that sharing of ideas,
thinking in new ways about our lives. Most of us hadn't had that experience. We all had neighborhood friends, but it wasn't the same.

Two women had had similarly galvanic introductions to friends
in groups where women talked about being mothers. Arlene remembered the pleasure of a spontaneous meeting of mothers at a
nursery school, which turned into a year-long group, prompting
friendships that lasted for years. "It was such an experience! . . .
To discover other women going through the exact same things.
From an accidental discussion, we ended up revealing the most
intimate details of our relationships with husbands and children. . . . Now, after not seeing one of them for years, we can pick
up where we left off." Arlene described Heidi, whom she encountered in that group and continued to see outside it, as her "spiritual
sister" because they thought out so many contemporary issues together.

Work is a context that provides common interests, challenges,
and problems. It brings people together regularly and offers them
varying opportunities and incentives to get to know each other
very well. But this and other studies show that people are unlikely
to recruit close friends at work, although the likelihood varies with
work settings and cultures. Probing the circumstances that favor
friendship at work, Fischer found that "years on the job, hours
worked, working unusual hours, and [for men] moving for the job
promote involvement with co-workers at and away from the workplace."[30]

It may be that people hesitate to recruit close friends at work because the voluntary character of friendship is at risk in this fixed setting; or perhaps here competition or stratification of roles impedes trust. For whatever reason, only five of the women I interviewed listed co-workers or former co-workers as members of their close network, although many more reported friendly relations with co-workers, with whom they discussed problems at work. Four of the five with co-worker close friends considered a co-worker a "best" or "closest" friend. Because the women I interviewed all worked in traditional women's jobs and their patterns of employment were typical of this sector (for example, interrupted rather than long stretches of employment), the four women with co-worker best friends did not fit the categories Fischer found most likely to encourage friendships at work. Personal characteristics, not professional ones, distinguish this group from others in my sample. The four women who formed close friendships with co-workers are among the five women I spoke to who spontaneously described themselves in terms of uncertain self-image or of self-chosen or inflicted social isolation.

Hilda traced the work-influenced origins of one of her older close friendships. Hilda and Rose met nearly forty years ago working a factory shift that let out when the rest of the world was still asleep. "We were on the same awful shift. We got off in the morning with no place to go. So we'd stop for breakfast, and we just started gravitating toward each other." Their close friendship weathered their marriages, divorces, jobs, and childrearing; for thirty years, it survived a separation of half a continent. The friends speak regularly by phone and visit every year, although both are far from wealthy.

Hilda met her closest local friend, Emma, at work as well. They have the same occupation, although they no longer work at the same site. Both work full-time. Having ended her marriage long ago when divorce was rarer, Hilda enjoyed neighborly help but little sociable companionship in her off-work hours. Emma, who is widowed, became Hilda's first sociable companion in decades. With children grown, they evolved a routine of get-togethers and joint recreations.

Karen and Marla also met at work. Daily contact allowed Karen, who described herself as "a bit of a loner," to form an interest in and attachment to a friend in a setting that demanded little initiative. The couples began socializing on weekends. This was the first close friendship Karen developed since she married David two years ago. In what was one of the smallest close networks in my interviews, Karen included Marla, with her own husband, and her mother. Sylvia, who described herself as "until recently, almost a hermit," is the only respondent who met her closest friend through her husband—in a joint business the two couples now conduct.

All these women had used the routine exposure and civility of the workplace to build friendship slowly without initially risking great initiative and self-revelation. Although each eventually expanded the rules of relevance of her relationship from workplace civility to sociable and then intimate friendship, all maintained a greater reserve in their friendships than the more extroverted members of the sample did.

Few women had met best friends in the neighborhood, even though a fair majority had sociable visiting relations with a few neighbors. Friendships with neighbors tended to be a residual pattern; that is, neighborhood friendships were generally undertaken by those with economic or other constraints upon friendship choices.[31] With the women I interviewed, economic constraints influenced friendly relations with neighbors in contrasting ways, depending on whether a woman perceived her neighbors as "similar"—largely, but not simply, a matter of race. Penny and Hilda, both white, lived in low-income, racially integrated, single-family neighborhoods. Neither developed visiting relations with neighbors. Cass, also white, lived for years in a poor, white, ethnically mixed neighborhood but avoided neighbors because her kin were close by. Janine, who is black, cultivated many friendly relations and recruited all of her nonkin close friends among black neighbors in a neighborhood to which she was a relative newcomer. Mothers of young children, whatever their locality, were most likely to establish close friendships in the neighborhood.[32] The close networks of several women included the names of former neighbors who had become close friends when they were both home with young children.

In sum, most best friendships formed in situations where women had an opportunity to choose an attractive friend and to build a relationship through self-disclosure. Contexts that constrained free entry or exit from close friendship were avoided by all but those whose personalities or material circumstances encouraged them to recruit friends in the accessible areas of workplace or neighborhood.

Are Friends Similar?

Given the importance of empathy and identification in women friends' standards of commitment, we would expect certain similarities among best friends. Studies have shown friends to be similar along most dimensions, whether socioeconomic, value-oriented, or personal.[33] Generally, they explain, people like people who are like them and thus choose similar friends when they can. This suggests that close women friends' emphasis on disclosure and empathy as standards of commitment encourages homogeneity between best friends, since it might be easier to understand and participate in the feelings of someone who seems like oneself.

How were closest friends similar? All were very similar in race, age, marital status, and life-cycle stage, less similar in household income and religion. All but one of the closest friendships were between women of the same race; fourteen were between women of the same marital status; all were between women. Seventeen of the twenty-one women were similar in age, within six years. Sixteen were at the same stage of childrearing (both friends with children who were either young, older, or grown). I did not inquire about friends' education, but accounts indicated rough similarity there too.

The strongest similarity between closest friends, after gender and race, was in work status. Eighteen of twenty-one women had closest friends who also either worked at jobs or at home. The full-time paid workers were most likely to have closest friends whose jobs took up the same percentage of their time. Eight of nine of their closest friends also worked full-time (the one exception was a sister-friend).

By contrast, only seven believed their friends' households were at about the same income level (although I suspect that most were noting fairly small income differences). Half had closest friends of the same religion. When we exclude the sister-friendships, however, only six of the seventeen remaining closest friendships were between women of the same religion, even though a majority of the respondents mentioned that they regularly practiced their religion.

Social segregation is probably the ultimate explanation of the racial similarity among best friends. White women and women of color rarely even engage in acquaintances in the contexts in which close friendships grow. The one cross-race best friendship, between Rita and June, grew out of work in a community service program. Their joint project encouraged them to think and talk about racism and cultural differences, and their personal relationship developed in this sensitizing climate.

The other dimensions of similarity among women underline the importance of empathy and mutuality in their close friendships. Similarities in age, marital status, and childrearing stage suggest that women draw closest to others who are sharing central identity-defining experiences. Between single women and married women, childless women and those with children, a gulf separates their interests, priorities, and problems.

Several women spoke of abrupt and inevitable changes in friendships when they or their friends married. Sometimes the change was provoked by a husband who disapproved of continued friendships with single friends or who wanted his wife to alter the terms of an old friendship to ones more consonant with a new primary commitment. Usually, women located the problem between the friends themselves.

After you're married, you're more tied down. I didn't think of it that way at the time, but Chris sure did.

We were still friends, but they weren't able to tear around the way we were used to—didn't have the money or the time. They had an interest in the marriage and the house.

I think friendships change because you have different expectations about someone who is married. That you won't see them as much alone. I didn't want to depend on her as much.

They didn't call me as often once I got married. They were out looking for boyfriends, and we had less and less in common. They looked at me differently.

Another recalled the pain of adjusting to newly diverging needs in the friendship when her friend remarried:

I missed her, even though she was still here. It seemed that when she was in need, I was always there. But when I was in need. . . . She didn't want to lose the friendship, but we couldn't stop it. If I were to call her up and say, Let's do something, chances are she'd have plans. They had their own set of friends—couples. I'd understand that, but I got my feelings kind of hurt at times.

Most of the friends who occupied different marital statuses met when their marital status was similar. Single and divorced women, most of whom worked, also often socialized during times married women identified as couple time or family time. Meeting now, single and married women would experience asymmetries like the impediments to mutuality just described. A husband's relationship to his wife's single friend would become a factor in the successful continuation of a friendship; at most, it might mean that socializing time is completely usurped.

Similar differences separated new mothers from their more footloose childless friends. Arlene described the decline of a college friendship that had held despite differences in marital status but dissolved when Arlene's first child was born: "There had always been a real chasm in our experiences, but we really clicked intellectually. When Tim was born, the chasm expanded. I was going through something she just could not comprehend. And I was so involved with him, I didn't have the room left in my life for her."

Arlene, and others, allowed close friendships to fade as they drew closer to friends who also had children. Other pairs of friends seemed to anticipate the problem. Whether or not they did so consciously, several avoided the strain by synchronizing their childbearing. More than a few respondents echoed Nancy's response to a question about how close friendships fared once her first child was born. "All three of us were first pregnant together. We went along together from school to marriage to first babies. We still got together just as much, only now we had our kids."

Preschool, school-age, and teenage children each present a world of issues and problems to their primary caretakers. It is not surprising then to hear the mother of a teenage girl or the mother of several boys exclaim over the special camaraderie of a close friend whose parallel experience helped her interpret a very important one of her own. "It's so reassuring to commiserate on what it's like to have teenage daughters screaming about what horrible mothers we are." Another, more restrained comment: "We both live in an all-male household. She knows that having boys in the house is not always bliss."

Similarities in employment seem to aim at symmetry of time available for friendship, which symbolically represents an equality of need. I interviewed only a few permanently full-time housewives. They preferred to visit friends during the day, when husbands were at work. Nonemployed women were likely to constitute their pool of potential friends, because employed women posed scheduling difficulties that were onerous to accommodate. Nancy, for example, who does very part-time work at home, was adjusting to her close friend Annette's return to a full-time job. "Annie just called me this morning while her boss was out. I'd been waiting to hear about her weekend. She didn't even get to finish the story. I miss our leisurely coffees." When asked what she wished was different about her friendships, Nancy said wistfully: "I guess everyone wishes to see more of her close friends than is necessary. I just wish we had more time to laugh together." Nancy's children were increasingly independent; and most of her friends who had stayed home with young children had returned to jobs. "It's difficult to meet friends. I think most of my friends work now. Those I'd like to be with or get acquainted with, they don't really have the time. It seems to be more difficult to meet people."

Housewives want friends who are available when they themselves are most available. Women who have jobs outside the home, raise children, and keep house—the universal triple role of employed mothers—need friends who are prepared to compromise with their severe time constraints. Women who labor under the same pressures are most likely to be amenable to the compromises working a double day exacts. Few of the employed women spoke directly of this motive. Thea is one who did. "Even at the time I met Catherine, she had zero time for anything outside her family. . . . Both of us are so busy, and so intense and driven. It's really nice to have someone who understands that in me. We can relax together with that."

As Thea found disappointing but familiar, Catherine's demanding professional schedule interfered with her friendship commitments many times.

She has a tendency to do what I also do—to promise to do things that, in fact, she's too busy to do.

I'll feel, "Sure, she's doing it again." And then I realize that I often have to do the same kind of thing. I just remind myself that I shouldn't depend too heavily on Catherine for some things.

Other employed women are also likely to understand work problems, even if they perform different work. Because women are concentrated in very few kinds of work, they are especially likely to grasp others' work predicaments. All seventeen of the employed women said they would discuss work problems with their friends. All but three regularly talked with friends about work. Another reason employed women have employed friends may be that friends lead one another into the workforce. At a time when more women are financially compelled to hold jobs and when more women wish to find them,[34] the path from housewife to employed worker may be cleared by an exemplary friend.

Popular literature portrays a mutual resentment between full-time housewives and employed mothers. My interviews picked up only faint echoes of this resentment, which is purportedly rooted in conflicting values. The most apparent explanation for the strains I detected, however, is the difficulty of achieving mutuality and symmetry of exchange when different kinds of work generate different sets of needs. Mutuality and symmetry are important standards of commitment among best friends. In relationships less intense than best friendships, even those within the close network, there was less similarity in work status. I believe this is, in part, because the standards of mutuality are more relaxed here.

Sociological analyses of similarities in friendship have argued that structural constraints like poverty and lack of physical mobility limit people's ability to achieve desirable homogeneous relationships.[35] The constraints that employed mothers' triple role put on their time, however, do not appear to decrease their chance of finding friends in similar situations; employed women probably have a balancing advantage in broader spheres for recruiting friends. Finding friends with compatible time constraints, and the issue of equality this represents, may be important enough that, although their jobs limit the time women spend with friends, women still strive to find friends with the qualities they consider important.

Best friends met only occasionally in voluntary organizations. As mothers of youngsters, most of the women I interviewed had little time for organized activity. And although some socialized with other women and couples they met at church, in children's recreation, or in the few voluntary organizations that they belonged to, they did not often do so. Several friends had joined each other in independent hobbies; several shopped together. But the women themselves attached little importance to this camaraderie. Best friendship centers on intimate talk; the women often cited joint activity as a vehicle for "just sitting and talking." They believed coparticipation in sports and clubs was much more integral to husbands' friendships than to their own, as studies of men's friendships confirm.[36]

Pairs of women friends are very similar. The demographic results here parallel other friendship studies. Yet if these women correctly assessed friends' household income—and because women are consumers, they are excellent readers of economic indicators— they may be less similar in this respect than men friends are.[37] Best friends may also have a lower rate of religious similarity than friends in general. As women's comments here showed, only some differences in beliefs and values inhibited their friendship; others they effectively ignored.

If indeed women friends are more similar in working hours and life cycle than in economic status and religion, this similarity may correspond to standards of commitment that very strongly emphasize psychological identification and empathy. Women best friends —more than women friends in general or men best friends—may select each other because of similar characteristics, such as marital status, that powerfully shape the experiences of personal life that women best friends talk about. Other similarities that figure less prominently in intimate disclosure may be less important.

Frequency of Contact

Do the standards of commitment in women's best friendships require more frequent association than friendships based on shared sociability or exchanges of services? My data suggest they do. The close friendships I learned about were extremely active. A majority of the women I spoke to saw their closest friend at least a few times

a week. Even those with best friends who lived out of town frequently visited with them at least once each week. Of the thirteen
women whose best friends lived in the same town, six saw their
friend nearly every day (two of them at work), and five saw their
friend two to four times a week. Women who had part-time jobs or
who did not work outside the home dominated the former group
of most frequent visitors; those with full-time jobs dominated the
latter.

Friends also frequently phoned each other. All but one of the
women whose closest friends were local spoke to each other at least
a few times a week. Five of the thirteen spoke to their closest
friend nearly every day. Even the women whose closest friends
lived out of town spoke frequently by phone. All but two spoke at
least once each week. And these two, whose closest friends lived
at a considerable distance, phoned their friends every few months.
Because the central medium of exchange between best friends is
talk, for women in particular the phone company's advertisements
may be correct—telephoning may be nearly as good as being
there. Given the effectiveness of telephone communication for the
constitutive exchanges of women's close friendships, close women
friends should be considered to sustain an enormous rate of binding association.

The women I interviewed, especially those who were not employed full-time, frequently visited with and telephoned others in
their close network as well. Immediate kin—parents, grown children, sisters and brothers (and their spouses)—were predominant
among the kin women felt closest to and frequently contacted.[38]
Friends in this category had been friends for at least a few years.

Frequent face-to-face contact with close network members was
pervasive among the women I interviewed, even though they did
not see all their friends often. Nineteen of the twenty-one women
saw at least one close friend or relative once a week. A majority
saw at least three close friends or kin each week. The two who did
not often see close friends or kin were both in the first year of
living-together relationships: one was new to the region she lived
in and was very attached to faraway friends and kin; the other had
retreated from an active friendship network of many close friends
when she entered a love relationship. All but one of the women
also phoned members of their close networks; a majority had four
or more close associates they called at least once each week. The

sizes and compositions of their friendship networks varied. By far most, however, had someone close—at least a few woman friends or relatives—whom they often visited and telephoned and at least a few others whom they visited less frequently but telephoned often.

Women regularly drove an hour or two to visit kin and close friends, often couples who had moved away. Traveling to visit close friends is a family activity that takes place during "family time," such as weekends or vacations. Social norms favoring contact with immediate kin seem to make it easier to use family time to visit a woman's relatives than her exclusive friends. Thus more "elective" close friends selected for routine visiting tend to be those both husband and wife feel close to. Women visited less regularly with distant women friends who were not such couple friends, even those who lived at comparable distances. Women often offered husbands' hesitations as explanations for why intense high school or college friendships had faded once either friend married and moved away.

Network scholars remind us that quantities of friends and rates of contact do not necessarily indicate social support. Conflict and stress also circulate through social networks within the same relationships that exchange support.[39] Similarly, frequency of association can be meaningful only when we also consider the content of the exchange. I have suggested that much of the fundamental exchange between women best friends takes place by telephone; so in figuring rate of association we must weight phone contact as nearly equal to personal contact. I would not, however, advise this equation in friendships that have other standards of commitment. If men's friendships use solidifying exchanges like joint activity and help in tasks, telephone contact would not substitute for them. Indeed, men do not appear to use the telephone as a medium of friendship. Lillian Rubin, for example, vividly describes her male respondents' aversion to telephone conversation and their bafflement at wives' opposite inclinations.[40]

Configurations of Association

Women see some of their close network in the company of others, some alone. Close kin often convene in groups, so the group configuration is more typical of relationships with kin. Best friends, on the other hand, are more likely to visit independently of others. Although best friendships are embedded in larger networks of friends, much that is crucial to the friendship takes place in pairs of friends. This pattern appears to hold as well for best friends who are sisters, even though they meet in group contexts more often than unrelated friends do. Mothers, however, frequently have their young children with them when they meet, and the dynamics of these visits are clearly more of groups than pairs.

Close friends also get together as couples, that is, with their husbands. Over three-quarters of the married women saw some of their larger close network in this socializing; some were introduced by husbands. Although best friends rarely became acquainted through their husbands, about half later associated as couples. Nine of the fifteen women who socialized in couples got together with their best friends and the husbands. Women see virtually all the men in their close network in groups or couples. The most intimate exchanges among friends take place among pairs of women friends, but these conversations may well be private moments taken aside in gatherings of kin or couples.

I never asked why women incorporated best friends into socializing as couples, but some of the reasons seem apparent. This socializing opens new activities and time periods to women friends. Since nearly all the married women save evenings and weekends for husband and family, socializing in couples admits women friends into these leisure hours. Because mothers, particularly poorer ones, are likely to hire babysitters only for special evening activities, socializing with couples offers some women their only chance to be with best friends without their children present.

Nancy liked the familial sense of integrating her close friends with her family: "We're very family oriented, and I really enjoy friendships among families." Louise found that successfully introducing her husband into the friendship made Gary less jealous of her friendship with Jan. "I try to involve him in the friendship a little, so that he doesn't feel left out. We've started doing things as couples. He found out they were O.K. people and he's been around Jan enough to like her. Before, he didn't even want to meet her." Louise was also thrilled to be socializing with people she really liked. She had been unenthusiastic when the couples were all Gary's friends and their wives. Arlene expressed similar relief: "When we finally became friends as a couple [with Les and Richard], it was the first time in years we'd found a couple we *both* liked to socialize with."

Looking at all the couples with whom women and their husbands socialized, I noted that both spouses successfully inducted friends. In the aggregate, husbands had introduced more friends; but their majority in my sample was slim. Other studies show a greater skew favoring husbands.[41] Even in my sample, the apparent parity between husbands and wives may mask a disparity privileging men if wives are correct in judging that husbands have smaller and more kin-dominated close networks.[42] These husbands then were considerably more successful at recruiting—that is, they incorporated a larger portion of their close networks into socializing as couples.

Mothers Are More Constrained

In the customary realm of close friendship, we can easily see the impact on friendship patterns of higher commitments to marriage, family, and work. The Northern California Community Study shows that marriage and parenthood constrain friendship patterns of women more than men. Mothers of young children have fewer friends and are especially likely to be socially isolated.[43] In the last chapter, I summarized the more obvious impediments to sociability for young mothers and cited my respondents' testimony of their felt need for friendship. Here, I look at some subtler ways that responsibility for young children influences patterns in friendship.

Although few best friends met through husbands, many met through children. Best friends with young children were particularly similar in life-cycle stage. When women emphasized common values as an important basis for friendship, childrearing values were those they most often specified. And although closest friends tended to socialize in pairs, those with young children generally conducted their friendships in the presence of children.

Several reasons explain why close friendships so frequently began through children. One is the importance to women of confidantes who share the experience of mothering (see chapter 2). Child-centered activities are excellent places to meet other mothers. Even simpler is the fact that children are participants in friendships. Women visit their friends in the company of children, so meeting friends through children allows women to judge how these crowded friendships will work out. Sylvia, whose children are all under six, saw this distinction between men's and women's friendships as the fundamental gender difference in friendship. "Men's friendships are men only. They can go out to the club, play cards, whatever. When women go out, they have their kids along. That affects what they do and where they go."

That friendships among best friends are ideally autonomous and dyadic, yet practiced in the company of children, has much effect on friendships. If the children do not get along, there is no peaceful terrain for the friendship. In child-centered contexts, a mother can note how the children fare together and assess the possibilities of peaceful association with another mother. Differing values and styles of childrearing frequently attend these friendships. When mothers talked about "common values" as important bonds among friends, they most frequently stressed childrearing values. Their reasons for this emphasis were largely instrumental, as the following examples should make clear.

Kay and Linda met in a class on child development at the community college. They were attracted to each other's ideas about childrearing. Kay said: "I could see when she answered questions the teacher brought up, that she feels the same way I do about things." Their friendship developed slowly, finally blossoming over a summer of afternoons spent minding the children and talking. According to Kay: "Just last summer we started doing things with the kids, and we got along real well. Sometimes we get them all together outside and just come inside and play cards and talk. We have the same perverse outlook with kids. We joke around about them, just to get through the day." Kay and Linda, along with their youngsters, saw each other nearly every day, even though Linda had a part-time job.

Things just jell when we're together. We can tell each other's kids to "knock it off," or whatever. You know, with some people, anything goes with their kids. Maybe they don't have a bedtime, or maybe they don't have to mind. That just causes dissension with your own kids. With Linda, I'm at ease with her and the kids. We think alike in all the important areas.

Kay had become close to another friend, Trish, before Kay's children were born. Kay perceived Trish as her "absolute opposite" in every way and, most problematically, in childrearing style. "I don't disapprove that she does things differently. But we can't 'blend' our differences in the house. If she doesn't put her kids to bed at a regular time, that's fine. But she used to come over at my kids' naptime or bedtime and wake up my kids to play with hers. And that used to drive me nuts!" Kay said "used to" because she tried to visit less often with Trish, whom she still listed among those she felt closest to. Kay befriended her "disorganized" friend for years, defending Trish to other friends and to her own disapproving husband. She felt surprised at how "blending" childrearing styles disrupted a rapport that withstood a great deal of personal differences in values and style. "It's hard to explain how important these small differences are. Her kids can walk around the house with a bag of cookies, eating as much as they want. My kids think they've died and gone to heaven. It always causes tension in my stomach. If I try to deal with my kids, they'll be crying. Linda and I don't have any of this."

Kay's relationship with another, newer friend, whom she liked a lot, did not develop very far because of childrearing differences. "We believe in a lot of discipline and they don't. It's funny how little differences add up, though. I can't wait till the kids get older and those things aren't such a problem."

Sylvia pursued her friendship with Pat in spite of considerable childrearing differences mostly, it seems, because their husbands—close business associates—encouraged their connection. Yet Sylvia complained:

I'm often really disappointed when our childrearing differences come up. They're not as strict with their children. For example, our children have to ask before they leave the yard. Last week, [my daughter] Cathy came in crying because Pat's kids left her behind before she could ask permission to go. Then Pat made matters worse by telling her to "shut up."

I felt very angry, but that's the way she raises her kids. It's irritating to her when the kids cry. Whereas her children irritate me when they're outspoken or disrespectful. I just try to rationalize it out so it won't affect the friendship.

But it does affect the friendship. Sylvia frequently noted differences in childrearing values and styles that impeded the development of ease and trust in her friendship with Pat.

Mothers are constrained in their friendship choices in many ways. It is not just that primary responsibilities for home and children—and, job responsibilities as well—leave little time and energy for socializing in friendship or that women who are home with young children frequently have no easy access to transportation. Mothers who have day-long charge of children bring a third (and a fourth and a fifth) participant to friendships that, in other circumstances, are contracted between two friends alone. Mothers must construct an intimate relationship in a collective context.

Friendships may be personal and private and relatively free of procedural rules and rituals, but they are not endlessly varying free relationships. In charting the essential practices of best friendship, surveying the normative realm, and noting residual and customary uniformities, we note the ordering influence of marriage, family, and work. Family commitments shape constellations of values and practices in friendship. Marital status and stage of childrearing become salient characteristics for recruiting friends. Among desirable subjects of conversation are those dimensions of wifehood and motherhood that women friends protect from devaluation, if only by mutually acknowledging their interest in them. Among moral obligations between friends, ultimate responsibility for each other's children figures prominently. The companionate values of self-disclosure, intimacy, and empathy that women find distinctive to friendship rather than marriage become friendship's standards of commitment. Contemporary close friendship thus responds to needs engendered in the nuclear family, incorporated in a companionate marriage ideal, but not fully satisfied in marital love and companionship.

It is easy to imagine that changing family patterns could shift or change the core of friendship's standards of commitment. New patterns of moral discourse, sociability, or conflict among friends might respond to changes in marital power or division of labor. Under some circumstances, friendship patterns might develop more autonomously of marriage and family commitments. At present, however, despite the very personal and private character of close friendship, it remains in the orbit of family commitments.

Chapter Four

Friendship and Individuality

In friendships, theorists have proposed, we best express our individual identity. Between friends obligations rest on fulfilling general human virtues—all else we negotiate individually, privately. Our mutual self-expression forms friendship and determines its solidarity. Because friendship is perpetually voluntary and relatively free of institutional obligations, it can be a terrain of moral excellence, spiritual growth, and psychological expression.[1] Georg Simmel selected friendship as the relationship par excellence of individuation, the best example of a relationship ungoverned by the "super-individual elements" of larger institutional orders. Individual freedom to construct a mutually gratifying relationship has "much more play" in modern friendship than in marriage, according to Simmel. Modern marriage, based on free choice and love, remains lodged within "traditional forms . . . social rules . . . and real interests" that do not favor "the most pointed individuation."[2] Even theorists who view the family as the crucible of adult identity generally concede that we consolidate our individuality in the more autonomous realms of modern experience.[3]

I have questioned the view that the nuclear family bounds the relations of intimacy, attachment, affection, and altruism—the primary relations of identity and commitment. Women's close friendships extend the bounds of emotional and moral investment beyond the family. Now I look at friendship and individuality, scanning my interviews to see how individuation and autonomy are engendered and reinforced in women's close friendships. I con-

97

sider how ideals of friendship and practices of individuality intersect with women's commitments to marriage and family.

I define *individuation* as autonomous activity and the experience of self as both distinct and complex.[4] Simmel treats the historical, structural, and interactional dynamics of individuation;
friendship is often his example. In his structural social psychology
of friendship, Simmel causally links segmented participation in
market society to the individualized personality to "differentiated
friendships" in which people share only certain aspects of themselves with others. Modern friendships, says Simmel, restrict "absolute psychological intimacy" and access to individuals' total personalities; friends share various but limited sentiments, interests,
and aspects of life and mind. "Modern man, possibly, has too much
to hide to sustain a friendship in the ancient sense. . . . Personalities are perhaps too uniquely individualized to allow full reciprocity of understanding and receptivity, which always, after all, requires much creative imagination and much divination which is
oriented only toward the other."[5]

The distinguishing mark of Simmel's analysis of modern friendships is not, however, his recognition that they are specialized and
restricted. It is rather his view that such relationships may yet be
morally and affectively rich, personally and socially integrative,
that distinguishes Simmel among nineteenth-century writers. Simmel believed that although modern friendships were typically "sur-
rounded by discretions" regarding access to whole knowledge of
the other, "they may yet stem from the center of the total personality" and involve "the same affective depth and the same readiness
for sacrifice, which less differentiated epochs and persons connect
only with a common total sphere of life."[6] In spite of Simmel's dim
view of the drift in metropolitan life toward "tendentious individuation," a positive valuation of individualism is implicit in his writing. His modernist ideal might be characterized as an organic solidarity binding autonomous individuals in a network community of
friendship pairs.

Simmel's depiction of modern friendship has aged well. Following Louis Wirth and others who elaborated only the negative side
of Simmel's portrayal of metropolitan individualism were those like
Claude Fischer and Barry Wellman who revived the positive vision
in his analysis. But Simmel's social psychology is most persua-

sive when we read it, as he intended, to apply to the social and private worlds of men.

Now women are the less individualized sex; variation of individual women from the general class type is less great than is true, in general, of men. This explains the very widespread opinion that, ordinarily, women are less susceptible to friendship than men. For friendship is a relation entirely based on the individualities of its elements.[7]

Simmel's gender distinction in individuation appears to rest on nineteenth-century men's greater social participation. He does, however, envision an eventual inclusion of women in the modernizing logic of friendship, as prefigured in the "modern, highly differentiated woman [who] shows a strikingly increased capacity for friendship and an inclination toward it."[8]

The increased incorporation of women into public roles over the twentieth century lets us reexamine Simmel's analysis, which still appears to hold up a mirror to men's friendships. Our examination, in this chapter and in others, does not corroborate Simmel's structural logic. Women who occupy differentiated social roles do not form only specialized friendships that conceal broad areas of personal experience. Evidence here and elsewhere that men are more likely than women to limit self-revelation in friendships suggests that Simmel's conception needs two kinds of refinement. Simmel considers only the structure of public life and its effect on personality; but that effect is mediated by the practices of private life. To understand differences in the friendships of modern women and men, we must consider how the division of labor in the family affects the relations between the structures of public life and practices of friendship. Thus, the first refinement is a structural analysis that expands to include private life and gender stratification in private and public institutions. The second is a more complex social psychology of self.

I have already presented several examples of how a more inclusive structural analysis could explain gender differences in intimate styles. In the last chapter I argued that a woman's resources shape her friendship exchanges; women friends prefer to give of themselves because they have relatively little autonomous control over material resources. Chapter 2 offered another gender power analysis: women friends reveal more of their private life to one another because some of their significant private experience is ignored, de-valued, or rejected by husbands. Wives, on the other hand, are more likely to attend upon their husbands, just as any subordinates asymmetrically do with their superiors.[9] This argument suggests that husbands are less impelled to make themselves vulnerable to friends through intimate self-disclosure. It may also be, because men have more power, that they have fewer marital troubles to disclose.[10]

To explain intimate styles, structural analyses need a social psy-chology of self. Yet Simmel's analysis lacks a psychological exten-sion that could explain the various patterns of discretion and re-serve, individuality and dependence that have developed among contemporary men and women. Specialization and the division of labor do shape modern personality, individuality, and intimacy, just as Simmel says. But structures not only operate immediately and directly on mind and self through adult experience in differen-tiated social roles; they also operate developmentally through their internalization in personality. The division of labor in private life, including childrearing, shapes gender-differentiated person-ality and individuality in children, who as adults develop differing modes of intimacy. Simmel's narrowly structural analysis misses such personality differences, which may lead to gender differences in friendship practices of "creative imagination and . . . divination . . . toward the other."[11] Such differences may substantially influ-ence friendship cultures.

In the following pages, I explore how women's culture of friend-ship both promotes individuality and subordinates it to family re-sponsibility and how this culture sustains an autonomous realm of friendship and submits its claims to those of family. I propose that individuality and autonomy are practiced in a variety of modes. Understanding specific practices of individuality and autonomy in close friendships can clarify the connections between friendship and other social structures like marriage. It can also suggest hy-potheses about gender-based cultures of community.

Autonomy in Friendship

The ideal of autonomy poses friendship as an independent and pri-vate relationship—independent even of marriage. It suggests why individuals rarely choose best friends from contexts, like work or church groups, that they do not enter or leave easily or often (see the last chapter). And it explains why they regularly choose best friends from contexts separate from marriage. Among the women I interviewed, only one had a closest friend whom she met through her husband (hers was the most distant of the close friendships described). All of the others drew closest to women they knew independently of their husbands.

I have already noted how responsibility for young children limits autonomous choice in friendships. For example, the mothers of young children chose friends whose childrearing practices were consonant with their own, to ensure a peaceful ground for sociability that necessarily included children. Poverty, long work hours, educational disadvantage, old age, and disability are also likely to limit choice in friendship.[12] So, of course, are individual differences in needs and capacities for forming friendship; they may, in part, be gender-related.

I saw all of these constraints operate in my interviews. Poverty, for example, narrows the contexts from which one can choose friends as well as the resources one can exchange in friendship. Of the four women in my sample whose sisters remained their best friends, three had the lowest incomes and educations. There is more in their stories than disadvantage, however, to explain their choices. All three came from ethnic cultures that emphasized ideals of family solidarity; they also came from families with many daughters, so each chose among several potential sister-best friends. All three lived in family networks and economic circumstances that limited the "flowering out of rules of relevance" in their other relationships.[13] That is, their values and poverty discouraged them from turning social contacts into friendships involving variegated exchanges of personal and material resources.

Whatever their circumstances, virtually all the women chose best friends independently of their husbands. Note, in the above examples, that family of origin—not marriage—appeared to narrow the choice of friends. Indeed, all three women with sister-best friends significantly defied husbands to help kin or accept support by kin. Like others in the sample, they perceived their best friendships as autonomous.

Best friendships emphasize autonomy from marriage more than

other friendships, even those in the close network. Thus, I expected that more "second circle" close friends and more sociable friends would have been acquainted through husbands. That is precisely the case with the women I interviewed. Moreover, couples often carry on friendships that are more sociable than intimate. Their relative power may easily influence how they recruit friends and socialize. Unless we assume that couples are of one mind and inclination, we must assume that one member's preference will prevail. And since husbands tend to have more marital power, I would expect more couples to be inducted by husbands than through wives. This was true in my sample, although the differences were not large. According to the wives, husbands periodically exercised a veto power over wives' choices of sociable couples. In many cases, this power seemed to leave the husbands happy to delegate the arrangement of the couples' social lives to the wives. Other, larger scale studies suggest the same: husbands recruit more couples as friends, and wives coordinate contacts within kin and couples.[14]

A second indication of the ideal of autonomy appears in women's descriptions of their husbands' attitudes toward their women friends. All the women believed their husbands "approve of" their closest friendships. All but one believed their husbands "like" their closest friend (the exception said her husband "doesn't feel either way"). Contradicting these forced-choice responses, however, spontaneous comments occasionally revealed more than a few instances of husbands' hostility toward closest friends.

He'll ask, "Who'd she go to bed with last night?" But he won't discourage the friendship.

He's made little remarks about me and Jan, like "You guys are so close, you must be lesbians or something." He says it jokingly, but. . . . Now I tell him, if he's worried about that, it's his problem.

Women may have emphasized their husbands' positive attitudes toward best friends because there is a norm of benignity toward a spouse's close same-sex friends. Its rationale is the liberty to choose one's friends. This interpretation is supported by responses to questions about whether husbands had "ever disapproved" of a friendship and whether they had "ever discouraged" one. Thirteen of twenty women said husbands (or former husbands) had at some time disapproved of a friendship. But only six of these thirteen believed their husbands had actually discouraged the relationship.

He would never say, "Don't see her." It was more an intellectual put-down. Her ideas weren't sound, the feelings she had were laughable, or whatever.

He never tried to discourage it. But we'd talk about her and he'd tell me he just couldn't see how I could have anything in common with her. But he never tried to stop me.

He wouldn't have much to say when she was around; or he just wouldn't be there [be engaged]; or he'd try to set it up so he could disappear. But he'd never tell me I couldn't do things with her.

As the foregoing quotations hint, in most cases where apparent disapproval or outright discouragement had overridden the norm of benignity, the husband believed the friend to be morally suspect, a bad influence, or in some manner threatening to him or the marriage. This was Louise's conclusion when she recounted her husband's remark that she and her best friend must be lesbians. "I guess he feels threatened—because we *are* so close. Sometimes he feels I like her better than him. It's like what happened when I first went to work. He felt I wouldn't need him."

The friends who aroused disapproval were frequently single, divorced, or bad housekeepers. Dwight, Janine's husband, put a stop to her socializing with single girlfriends. "He thought I'd be messing—doing the same things they do. He figures they're single, and I'm married, and I shouldn't be around them." Betty's husband forbade her to associate with a woman in the neighborhood who was rumored to be "wild and irresponsible." Nancy's husband, Mike, and Kay's husband, George, were hostile to those of their wives' friends who neglected their housekeeping and paid too little attention to family. Nancy described Vi: "She was more interested in her clothes, herself, and her work. But I still liked her. Mike couldn't understand how we could be friends." Kay conceded that Trish was "disorganized," but she liked her for her "basic goodness." However,

George doesn't even want me to take the kids over there, because her house is such a mess. He gets disgusted because he thinks it would be easy for her to get things more together. He doesn't want to do much with Trish and Jim. He gets all tensed up around them, and I get nervous and talk too much, trying to cover up what's happening. But I wouldn't say he discourages the friendship.

Frances first attributed Jack's hostility to her divorced friend, April, to a "bit of jealousy." Then she amended it: "Not jealousy, maybe a fear: 'I hope she doesn't decide to pick up April's bad habits.' She *is* loose, but she loves her kids. She's really O.K." Hilda's former husband had jealously crushed one friendship after another, insisting each was breaking up the marriage. She recalled his statements: "He never said why. But they could never come back."

Had the women found their husbands' disapproval discouraging to the relationship? The fact that most of the disapproved friendships are now defunct suggests that they had. Yet the women described the decline of their friendships as motivated by their own disenchantment. "I ended up feeling the way he did about her."

Because most of these women were not hesitant to admit elsewhere that they had complied with their husbands' demands against their own desires, it was not egalitarian marital ideology that caused them to deny their husbands' negative influence on friendships. Rather, I suspect, they wished to see their practices consistent with their belief that close friendships are a very individual matter and should begin and end independently. As we shall see, women expected friendships to respect marriage as a highest priority. But the friendships themselves were to be personal.

Friendships were also to be private. The protection of confidences was a clearly specified friendship norm and the foundation of mutual trust. All but two of the married women named friends as those "to whom you've told things you've never told anyone else." I initially concluded this meant a friend's confidences were secret, even from one's spouse. Yet when I asked a hypothetical question about confidentiality to gauge how each woman actually constructed the boundaries between friendship and marriage, some answers were conditional. I asked, If your best friend asked you to keep secret something you really wanted to share with your husband, how would you deal with that? Two-thirds answered firmly, "I'd keep the secret." The remaining third answered conditionally:

I probably would keep it secret. If it were really personal, like something about her marriage, I wouldn't tell. Some other things I might tell.

If I thought I had to tell him, I'd tell her then. Most things, fine, I wouldn't tell.

If she really didn't want anyone to know—if it would hurt her in any way, I wouldn't tell him. Some things I think she wouldn't mind. And I know it wouldn't go further.

For these women, breaking a friend's trust to share a confidence with one's husband was conceivable, although hardly routine. Comments like this suggest that most women regard close friendship as an autonomous relationship with its own firm rules of closure.

Friendship and Individuality

Evidence that friendship encourages individuality and autonomy appears in its exchanges or content. As evidence of support for individuality I took statements that emphasized a close friend's contribution to self-awareness or understanding; a friend's approving recognition of individual effort, achievement, or self-development; or a friend's privileged access to a woman's authenticity (that is, her perceived "real self").

These exchanges are only part of what we might consider relations of autonomy and individuality. There were aspects of an ethic of autonomy that I did not find in my interviews—specifically, support for unfettered individualism, for a severely differentiated sense of self, or for individuality as a supreme value that should override responsibility and commitment. I believe I might have found an ethic emphasizing more autonomous aspects of individuality had I interviewed more younger women, more unmarried women, more women who had jobs but did not parent. In my sample of mostly married mothers over thirty, themes of individualism were distinct but constrained.

In strikingly similar ways the women emphasized how well close friends knew women's true selves and how friends contributed to their self-understanding. Chapter 2 illustrated the pervasive reliance on close friends for empathy and companionship in self-examination. Here are more examples from two large sets of questions—one, a set of name-eliciting questions, the other a set of probability-of-exchange questions. The latter set showed women very likely to involve friends in solving personal problems and in discussing love, pride, anger, unhappiness, and self-doubt. For each kind of intimate exchange, no more than three respondents—usually just one—said they would exclude friends. *All* the women said they would talk with a friend about moral or religious beliefs, all but one about news or politics.

Thirty-four name-eliciting questions sought to identify the people with whom the respondent exchanged intimacy, genuine response, and emotional support. On these questions, eighteen of twenty-one women named women friends (including sister-best friends) among those to whom they would confide very personal problems; all included friends among those whose personal problems they would "take to heart" (although six of the seventeen married women did not include their husbands on this item). About three-quarters listed friends among those "to whom you've told things that you've never told anyone else" and among those "to whom you can confide something you're ashamed of."

Two-thirds of the twenty-one women talked to close friends about their most important beliefs. Seventeen felt that close friends shared their most important values. All but two listed close friends among those who "know and like the real you." The same number placed friends among those who made them feel good about themselves (although six of the seventeen married women omitted their husbands from this answer). Seventeen named friends among those who like to share their moments of pride.

Exploring one connection between friendship and individuality—the mutual recognition of individual striving and self-development—I uncovered some interesting contrasts between friendship and marriage. I found a unique specialization of friendship was discussing autonomous activity and experimentation, as well as the fantasies, ambitions, and plans they generate. Specialization is not entirely surprising: married women might prefer not to confide to their husbands their fantasies about romances with other men. Wishes and plans about work, schooling, and civic participation, however, seem an appropriate subject in a companionate marriage. Certainly, the image of a young husband thrilling his wife with his grandest vision of future achievements is a staple of companionate marriage's image in literature and the media.

If this image in fact reflects actual husband-to-wife communication, my interviews testify to an asymmetry in this supported self-development. Women not only talk to close friends about such ambitions or strivings; many say they discuss these topics with friends more than with husbands. In the series of questions on how often one would discuss a subject with friends if it were on one's mind, women most frequently answered "A lot of the time" to questions about discussing future dreams and ambitions, work problems, and opinions about news or politics. Each is a theme of individuality or autonomy. Individual aspirations, endeavors, and beliefs are clearly appropriate topics in friendships.

The thirty-four name-eliciting questions allowed me to compare exchanges with friends and with husbands. Women were to name anyone who came to mind for sharing specific kinds of exchanges. In name-eliciting surveys other researchers found that respondents sometimes forgot to list husbands.[15] To avoid this, I reminded my respondents that they should list husbands, children—anyone—who fitted the description. Moreover, since I asked many consecutive name-eliciting questions, I assumed that husbands would be mistakenly overlooked in some regular way. But there was no regular pattern of husband-absent responses; the rate of husband-absent responses varied by the question. The differences are provocative.

Seventeen married women answered the thirty-four questions asking with whom they exchange intimacy, genuine response, trust, and affection. For fifteen of the thirty-four questions, one to three women did not list their husbands, although most listed friends or kin. For fourteen, four to six did not list their husbands. For four questions, seven or eight did not name them. And for one question—Who encourages you to try out new experiences or things?—ten of seventeen women failed to list their husbands. This last figure contrasts with a total of four married women who did not list friends for this question.

The exceptional absence of husbands from those who encouraged new experiences, with the strong presence of friends among those who discussed future dreams and ambitions, marks women's

perception that friends more than husbands recognize their strivings for individual autonomy. It suggests that a woman friend (and
less often a kinswoman) may play a unique role in supporting these
individual aspirations.

Responses to other questions in the name-eliciting series supported this conclusion, although much less powerfully. In answer
to the question, Who recognizes your talents or abilities?, only two
of seventeen married women failed to name friends, whereas four
did not name husbands. Only one married woman did not include
friends in her answer on mutual respect; four did not name husbands.

It is difficult to interpret these contrasts without more probing
investigation; I did not explicitly pitch my interview to this topic.
The subject of friends as better support for individual aspiration
emerged spontaneously a few times, however, in responses to
other questions—for example, in comments on areas that women
could discuss with best friends but not with husbands. Rita talked
about "my own independence" with June, preferring not to touch
the subject directly with her husband. "I act it out more with
Lloyd, rather than talking about it." Debby, who repeatedly spoke
of her husband, Jay, as her "best friend and advocate," still preferred to talk with Joanne about "problems of deciding what to do
from here on in—knowing there's something better out there, job-
wise—wondering what to do about it." Thea, whose marriage is
among the most companionate, also preferred to talk to her best
friend, Catherine, about "what I personally would like to do with
my life." Arlene conferred with Sally when she began "getting involved in new things," like taking on the presidency of a civic organization: "Jeff felt it would be overwhelming for me, which of
course it was. He didn't want to hear about it, and I didn't want to
talk to him about it." Lisa, one of the youngest in the group I interviewed, summed up the area she explored better with Doreen:
"It's different walks of life. Maybe other men. Going other places
and seeing new things. Doing other things with my life."

Lisa's comment hints at one reason women may avoid this general subject with husbands: certain ambitions and fantasies may
hint at alternatives to marriage. That is why Nancy, like Lisa, confided thoughts of other men to Annette, although she said the topic
was entirely fanciful. But Rita, who returned to college in her late

fifties, was content to imagine a future with her husband. It was in work, ideas, and friendships that she wished to expand her autonomy. Rita said that her husband, Lloyd, for all his pride in her accomplishment, found this kind of independence inexplicably disturbing.

Likewise, Arlene was not thinking about leaving Jeff. She simply wished to avoid being discouraged from accepting challenges that might unsettle her life (and Jeff's). Similarly, Kay talked to friends rather than George about her desire for more schooling and then returning to work. "George and I have been on a good ride since I quit my job and stayed home with the kids." Kay was intent on going back to work the day her youngest was old enough for day care. She was postponing the conflict her working raised in her marriage by keeping her plans among friends. Debby, by contrast, never hinted that planning to change jobs was a tense subject at home. Yet the topic came to mind as one she could discuss better with her friend than her husband, simply, she said, because Joanne was thinking about the same thing.

There is some sociological evidence that associates working wives with marital conflict and discusses the advantages in power that wives derive from organizational participation, education, and income.[16] We might guess that women learned from experience that by doing the planning elsewhere they could at least postpone the tremors in marriage that independent achievements can create.

My theoretical guide for interpreting these patterns is an essay by Jessica Benjamin. Benjamin conceives of individuality as *recognized* independence, autonomy, and selfhood. Individuals who suppress their awareness of depending on recognition by others— who cannot openly recognize relationships in which selfhood is defined—develop not individuality but "false differentiation."[17] Benjamin uses object-relations psychoanalysis (and a rather unparsimonious array of philosophy and social psychology) to construct an alternative to the classical psychoanalytic model of individuality. She aims to replace psychoanalytic views that individuation begins in oedipal relations of authority and must repress awareness of dependence and attachment to others.

In Benjamin's view, autonomy and individuality are established through recognition by others. Mutuality is a condition of independence, in that "true differentation involves not only the awareness of the separation between self and other but the appreciation of the other's independent existence as an equivalent center."[18] Only a person who is an independent subject can recognize the other. And only a person who can simultaneously acknowledge depending on the other for recognition can achieve independence. Dependence and independence, recognition and autonomy, exist in this reciprocal and paradoxical but inevitable relation. Benjamin contrasts this "related" individuality with a widespread "one-sided" defensive individuality that eschews depending on and indentifying with the other and exists through instrumentalism and domination.

Benjamin's work poses an ideal that must be seen as two separate ideals in contemporary gender arrangements. Benjamin joins other object-relations theorists of gender—notably Chodorow—who maintain that the division of labor and authority in the modern family creates gendered personality. Men and women divide the internalized capacities: separation, differentiation, and activity on the one hand (masculine); and dependence, mutuality, and nurturance on the other (feminine). Only men, in this ideal-type, reach the available form of individuality—a falsely separated independence. Men are likely to fear attachment; women separation and independence. This dynamic leaves women with more complex internalized object-relations and a greater capacity and need to sustain intimate relations alongside heterosexual love.

The work of Benjamin, Chodorow, and others in the tradition[19] suggests how the structure of family dynamics and the psychology of self might be interposed into the causal relation Simmel draws between social organization and friendship culture. The gender structure of family life and its impact on gender personality help to explain how the larger social structure affects friendship culture. These psychodynamics also suggest another basis for my argument that close relationships among women exhibit mutual support for a communally situated and constrained individuality, similar to Benjamin's nonauthoritarian ideal: within the family, women may be structurally inclined toward interdependent individuality and psychologically disposed to favor it as well.

My interviews suggest that women's close friendships, more than their marriages, engender a mode of individuality that acknowledges interdependence as a condition of and constraint on independent striving. I am proposing that there are two strands of unique influence in friendship. The first is support for individuation and autonomy, which marriage suppresses more through asymmetries of power between men and women. Women's economic dependence on men and the "oedipal asymmetries" of gender personality corrupt the possibilities of mutually recognized subjectivity within marriage. Husbands less often than friends support independent ambitions or endeavors. (The reverse is also true: if wives cannot be autonomous subjects when they support— or mirror—their husbands, then men cannot confirm their individuality in marriage.[20] This lack of confirmation may be another structural explanation for men's lesser interest in marital self-disclosure.)

The second strand of influence in this scheme is the practice of constraint in friendship. A communal ethic of interdependence is evident in friends' recognition of women's dependence on and responsibility for both friends and family. We shall see in the next section and again in the next chapter that friends help each other to emphasize family responsibility over individual autonomy; they do so by muting the claims of independent friendship and by advocating accommodation in marital problem solving. The communal authority of friendship operates in standards of commitment that place vast areas of personal life within the scope of friends' observation and intervention. As in traditional communities, communal constraint is possible because of mutual knowledge and familiarity.

In the friendship, however, the tension between dependence and autonomy pulls women toward the pole of individualism. As I have shown, friends are most often equals in status with symmetry in relational need and capacity. Their standards of commitment center on the mutual intimacy that highlights individuality and admits dependence. And their rules of relevance strongly enforce both personal liberty and ultimate communal responsibility.

In their closest friendships, women may well create a unique moral voice of community. The dependency friends establish in intimate exchange encourages mutual responsibility, mutual independence, and individual agency. Friends reinforce each other's independence within the context of familial and friendship commitments; they do not develop the stark individualism popularly attributed to modern culture. Neither themes of individuality nor communal obligations predominate, although their balance can certainly vary. Friends know they depend on and have obligations to family. By extending both friends' communal responsibility outside marriage and by invigorating their subjectivity that is easily submerged within marriage, friendship builds and strengthens a communally rooted individuality. Within such bounds, friendship's intimacy, autonomy, mutability, and terminability allow individuation considerable play.

Subordinating Friendship to Marriage

The higher obligations of marriage, family, and work constrain patterns of friendship even though its norms stress autonomy from these institutions. Although it adapts to other institutional commitments, friendship shows little strain of adjustment. Women's close friendships appear to be crucial ingredients of their wellbeing and satisfaction and an important support for their marital and familial commitments. Given the importance and distinctive character of these friendships, and considering the expectations that generally accompany such important relationships, we might expect contention between family and friends. We might look for conflicting demands on women's time, jealousy of attachments, and competing loyalties, like those that occur when women are heavily involved with close kin as well as family.[21] In fact, I turned up little evidence of conflict. Women reported few antagonisms between husbands and friends. They rarely experienced difficulties in balancing their obligations in these two arenas; friendship and marriage appeared effortlessly harmonized. How do women operate in two different spheres of strong emotional attachments without feeling torn between them? What orderings of obligations and expectations underlie this apparently peaceful arrangement?

This section explores these questions, attending to the explicit and tacit ways friends adjust to each other's marriage obligations. I summarize this material with Simmel's work on discretion in mind and extend the notion of discretion beyond his focus on revelation and concealment to clarify the relation between social struc-

ture and the culture of friendship. The discussion should also illuminate the particular individuality practiced and promoted in
women's friendship.

Just over half of the women I interviewed reported they had to
"choose" between their friends and their husbands or families; but
they said this conflict occurred only once in awhile. All but one of
the currently married women rarely experienced conflicts between
their alliances with friends and with family (although the divorced
women were more apt to recall conflicts). When asked what they
did to keep obligations to friends from competing with obligations
to husband and family, most women had to stop and think. "That's
the most difficult question you've asked," Thea responded. Then
she continued: "But it has the simplest answer: it's just realizing
that my family always comes first. Period. Any friends I have know
that."

I heard versions of that answer over and over:

I don't think it's ever been a question. Sally and I are both aware that our
families come first.

My obligations to my family come first. Keeping a home, providing for
my husband and children, making sure there's a meal and that they have
clean clothes—all that comes first. After that it's a priority list of what's
most important at the time. If it's more important that Helen is upset
about something, then I talk to her, and the kids will have to wait.

Women so much take for granted that obligations to family come
first that they rarely remember ever explicitly negotiating those
obligations with friends:

It just kind of falls into place.

There's never any question that something Sally and I might want to do
would come before our kids or our husbands.

All I have to say is, "Oh, I just have to go home and make dinner." I may
have to do what I don't want to do. But I've got this obligation first.
[——Do friends ever have difficulty understanding your obligations?]
No, not my friends—never.

Some, however, were aware that they had worked out methods of
balancing the two sets of obligations, even though most friends had
not discussed these arrangements.

I divide my time. I go to visit Lily in the morning, when Dwight is at work. We've got an understanding—when Dwight comes in from work, I'd rather not have any company. When her husband comes home, I leave too. We just do our spare time together when the kids are at school. And we just resume the next day.

I would say timing—when I go out. I'll try to do it when he's at work. And frequently—not just *when* I go, but how often. I try to work it out between me and him.

There's an understanding that my weekends are pretty dear. Sometimes I'll have to say, "That's Lloyd and my night for ourselves—can't we make it a daytime plan?"

Martin and I are flexible about finding family time that fits our schedules. But I don't usually plan outside things on weekends. When I'm not working, it's easier to do things with friends strictly during the day, avoiding time when husbands are home.

I try to limit calls in the evenings. We all do.

I'll try to do things that bring people to my house, so I don't have to be away. Or I try to find ways to include families.

Some of the arrangements women friends worked out involved very contingent commitments to joint plans.

We're good enough friends that she would know that if we had plans and then Jerry wanted to do something, we'd just postpone. She wouldn't get upset with me. She understands that he would come before her as far as doing something social.

It used to be if Gwen and I had plans and Fred decided he wanted to go out together, I'd say, "I just agreed to go out with Gwen." He didn't like that. Then I thought, "Wait, the husband comes first." So, now I just tell Gwen, "Fred just called about going out," and she understands.

I just try not to commit myself too much. I'll say, "Yea, probably, we'll see." Then I have a way out if I need it.

If Jay and the kids came up with something to do and I'd made plans to go out with a friend, I'd probably change that arrangement.

Yet, in spite of their precautions and reservations, women occasionally found themselves explicitly choosing friends.

One time Lily was upset about something with her husband. She asked if I'd come down and visit her and talk to her. Dwight said, "No, you can't go now." But if I see that she's really upset, I'll just have to go on and see her. I feel he's wrong to say no. Because if I were in her place, I know she'd come to me. It just troubles me to have to choose like that.

Like Janine, above, others had made the choice of friends' needs over family wishes; and all had found the decision stressful. Several said husbands felt "hurt" or "left" by their choice; some said husbands or children objected or became angry. Unexpectedly, Betty found herself upset at her husband's cooperativeness when she anticipated an objection to putting her friend first. "I didn't expect it. I thought, 'Hell, this means he just doesn't care.'"

Some of the women volunteered strategies they used to reallocate time peacefully from family to friends. Three strategies cropped up a few times. The first involved "brownie points" or "buying time":

I do my home work. I live up to my role here. Even if I'm going to go out, I'll have dinner ready for him. Then he feels taken care of and that cuts down on the static.

The three of us would say, "Let's get together in two weeks." Then someone would say, "Well, I'll spend this weekend with my husband." That meant she could get to join us. There would be some consulting of calendars: if we're going to take a night out, what do we have to do to buy that time. But it wasn't something we really talked about. It was more subterranean.

The second strategy involved simple justice:

I just say, "You're not home that much either. Or when you are, you're drinking. If you go your way, I'll go mine."

If I'm going to do something at night, I'll ask way ahead. But if it comes down to an out-and-out negotiation, I'll say, "Well, how many times did you play baseball this month?" But it doesn't usually come down to that. I don't ask much, so he doesn't often say no. I've never said, "I'm going somewhere and that's it!"

A third strategy involved the telephone. Friends stole brief visits during family time, sometimes extending phone conversations "until somebody complains." Debby laughed sheepishly when she revealed her sense of deprivation when that strategy is not available: "The main problem [in keeping obligations from competing] is the telephone, especially in the evenings because we try to save that kind of time for family. I should really limit my calls more. We often unplug the phone in the evenings. But I find it really hard to cut ourselves off—we might miss something."

Women take as their obligation to one another the responsibility for learning the subtleties of a friend's familial constraints. An example of this attention to subtleties is Lynn's account of how her friend Donna sensed the appropriateness of her presence when Lynn's husband was home. "She could figure out if it's O.K. to visit just by walking in and seeing what's going on between Jerry and me. She'd just read her cue to exit if she sensed something was going on between us. It doesn't happen that often, but she could tell if we were in the middle of a fight or something."

Lynn and her friend extended permissible visiting time into what, for many of the women I spoke to, was time for family alone or for socializing as couples. The price of extending the friendship's time boundaries was a delicate sensitivity to relations between Lynn and her husband and a willingness to defer immediately to a signal of desire for privacy. Lynn and Donna never talked about how and when to undertake these mutual adjustments. They "just know." Others noted the same tacit agreement: "I can just hear Leslie saying, 'We didn't even include you in these plans because I know you have family then.' Or 'I'm sorry to call you now because I know this is your family time.'" Underlining the general rule, another said, "With Sarah, I just know not to call at night."

The expectation that friends recognize and adjust to each other's primary commitments to family is observed so meticulously that one only becomes aware of rules in their violation. But, when a rule is violated, women seem quite disposed to making it explicit.

Gloria's husband was always out with friends at night. She'd get lonely and drop in over here. I finally told her what I felt about friends dropping in like that. I thought she understood, but she kept it up. I was furious. So this time I made it clearer. She was hurt, but she stopped. And we're still good friends.

A lot of the women in my [volunteer] group are younger and single. A lot of things they'd like to do together are easy for them, but hard for me because of my home obligations. I try to get them to understand my situation and I ask them not to put the pressure on.

The acknowledgement of the priority of family obligations was not simply descriptive; it was normative. In answering questions about how friends generally *should* behave, women underlined their convictions that friends should accord family first place. A majority (ten of seventeen women) answered "Always" to the question, Should friends expect each other's first loyalty to be to a husband? The remainder, those who answered "Sometimes," offered only circumstances of extreme need to justify contravening what they saw as the general rule. The answers were similar for the question, Does a friend have the right to ask an important favor that is likely to create conflicts or problems at home for the woman from whom she's asking help? A third of the women selected the most negative of their three choices, "Hardly ever." The remainder, nearly all of whom chose "Sometimes," explained that an "important favor" should indeed be critically important to justify such an intrusion. "I would hope I wouldn't have to ask."

Although few of the women I spoke to found it easy to identify the kind of limitations they placed on friendships, those who did stressed placing family first and avoiding "excessive demands" on friends. I asked, Are there things you'd never ask of a friend? One woman put the contrast in absolute terms: "I'd never ask her to make decisions about her and her family versus me. I'd never make any of my friends choose." Another generalized: "I wouldn't do anything that would greatly inconvenience her, if I could help it." A third woman stated specifically, "I'd never ask for financial assistance, although I could."

In general, women wished to avoid entering into the exchange of resources over which they did not have sole jurisdiction. These included family time, family territory, and money. These limitations on the exchange of friendship were the form of discretion I heard most about in women's descriptions of friendship.

Certain characters appeared over and over in the women's accounts, those friends who failed to get the message about the priority of husband and family. There were the husband's pals, who continued to "hang around" after the couple married; the single women friends, who did not have similar obligations; the occasional married friend whose husband "doesn't always come first"; and close kin—often aging parents—who asserted kinship obligations. Women tended to see such asymmetries in expectations as structurally determined but still amenable to reform; they generally attacked the problem directly, with good results. Kay's story about the friend who dropped in late at night is one example. Another is Rita's account of her attempt to educate single friends about the demands marriage made on her free time. Rita was less successful in limiting the demands of one of her younger friends: "She had tremendous expectations of my being available to her at all times. She wanted me to be more like a mother to her than a friend. At first I was very gentle; then I began to say no; and finally I withdrew altogether."

The women I spoke to had tolerated differences of opinion with friends, distaste for friends' life-styles, friends' distaste for their husbands, and various disappointments and disagreements. They did not tolerate "unreasonable" demands on their time. The few accounts I heard of deliberate withdrawal from friendships all involved a friend who wanted more of a woman's time than she could give. Respect for constraints on a woman's time emerged as a primary rule of friendship—uncodified but clearly recognizable in reports of its transgression.

Parents, close kin, and husbands' pals presented problems more difficult to solve. The reform of husbands' friends was the responsibility of husbands, who frequently viewed things differently. Parents and close kin presented ambiguous problems because the priority of family over kin obligations is not as clear as the priority of family over friends; kin networks, closer-knit, do not allow people to withdraw as easily as do looser networks of friends. I heard many more accounts of recurring disagreements between spouses about a women's attentions to kin than disagreements involving friends. Women capitulated to husbands' disapproval or jealousy of friends—resentfully perhaps, but more frequently than when the object was close kin.

Another mechanism that subordinates friendship to family is that friends do not discuss the relationship itself among themselves. Friends may recognize each other through a self-conscious conferral of the status "best friend," but they do not otherwise make the relationship a topic of discussion (or even, it appears, contemplate it privately). Friends do not assess friendships in the way couples often assess marriages. They do not identify problems in the relationship and discuss ways to solve them (indeed, as the last chapter showed, friends actively suppress conflict). They do not often mention problems in their close friendships to spouses or other friends. Eight of sixteen said they would rarely, if ever, talk with friends about problems with other friends. Only a few volunteered that they talked about their best friends with their husbands.

Inexperience with reflection on friendship caused most of the women to express surprised satisfaction at the end of the interview. They had never thought so clearly about their friendships before— what they shared, how they felt, what they wished. They were often moved by what they had just told themselves aloud. Although many had exposed deep feelings and complex arrangements, sometimes giving them eloquent expression, little of this kind of language had ever passed between the friends. Of course, many women rarely discussed their assessments of their marriages with their husbands. Even these women, however, had assessed or critically reflected upon their marriages privately; and many had done so with close friends.

This silence about the relationship does not mute emotions but deflects evaluation that could interfere with a woman's commitment to putting family first. It is particularly eloquent in a period which increasingly applies voluntarist ideals of mutual gratification and good companionate relations to all close relationships, including marriage and kinship.

In sum, by explicit or tacit agreement and by unreflective but regular arrangement, women friends subordinate the claims of the most valued friendships to the claims of marriage and family. To find a framework for interpreting this coexistence of deep attachment and psychological intimacy with fairly rigid constraints and explicit second-priority status, I return to Simmel's work on invasion and reserve in friendship.

Simmel argues that the ideal of modern friendship, which developed in a romantic spirit, aims at absolute psychological intimacy.[22] But modern men (and, increasingly, women) are too "differentiated" and "individualized" to engage in friendships of such full reciprocity. Friends practice discretion regarding invasion and reserve, revelation and concealment; they respect the vast unfamiliar and unknowable regions of each other's life and mind. Discretion, according to Simmel, allows friends to avoid the painful experience of the structurally induced "limits of their mutual understanding."

My interviews with women, including those in the most modern social and economic sectors, revealed that women do not extensively practice this form of discretion. Rather, women's close friendships achieve the affective depth embodied in Simmel's ideal by striving toward full reciprocity in knowledge of the other. In contrast to relations in traditional society, private regions of modern experience may be less knowable and familiar to close friends. Yet women friends exercise the "creative imagination and . . . divination . . . oriented only toward the other" that allows them empathic access to a considerable breadth of each other's private experience.[23] Occupying specialized social roles does not seem to lessen their ability or willingness to engage in mutual understanding with their closest friends.

The women I interviewed do practice another form of discretion, however. They scrupulously distinguish arenas of individual liberty from those of communal responsibility, and they deliberately practice reserve in the former. Now it may be that men practice this form of discretion as well. The women I spoke to, however, believed that their husbands, and men in general, do not develop many nonkin ties that would elicit the same degree of communal responsibility. And however close or attached their friendships may be, if men practice more concealment—more discretion, in Simmel's sense of the term—they have a narrower terrain of moral exchange and fewer opportunities for commitment and constraint.

A second form of discretion these women practice, with great subtlety and delicacy, is prudence regarding the higher commitments of marriage and family. Again, it is likely that men also practice this form of discretion. Yet the women I interviewed believed that their husbands, and men in general, do not share ardency and intimacy with friends or acknowledge a need for close friendship. If this is so, the task of prudence regarding a friend's obligations is likely to be more formulaic: men are not foregoing relations they deeply need or putting someone so important in second place. Prudence for men friends may require the sacrifice of self-interest but perhaps not deeply felt need. Moreover, if men's time together is more child-free, they are less consistently called upon to practice this form of discretion.

This chapter has presented women's close friendships as singular relations of individuation. The interviews offered persuasive evidence that women friends uniquely support individual aspirations and efforts, that friendships enhance self-development, and that the values of friendship favor individual liberty. Both the autonomy of friendship and its mutual support for individuality are, however, constrained by communal obligations within friendships and by communal values that oftentimes supersede individual ones. Women friends construct and enhance individual identities that are both individuated and interdependent.

The dynamics of constraint in contemporary friendships are not as systematic or effective as those in traditional community. Individuality is a much stronger theme. Yet women's entrenched social position strengthens an ideology that subordinates obligations of friendship to those of family, and individualism to family responsibility. Friends accept and attempt to realize this ideal, harmonizing friendship and family commitments to a degree that seems astonishing when we consider women's emotional investment in both spheres. Yet women's culture of friendship—the quality and content of relationships, the manifest ideals of individuality and interdependence—holds the possibility of an expanded role for both community and autonomy as women's social position advances.

Chapter Five

Women Friends and
Marriage Work

"If he knew some of the things I talk about with her, he'd have a fit!" When the women I interviewed laughingly made comments like this, they were usually recounting how they talked to friends about problems with their partner. My questions about confiding in best friends gave me another angle on women's friendships in relation to their commitments to marriage. My object was to learn how women exposed problems in the supposedly private sphere of marriage to close friends, with what aims in mind, and with what effects on the marriage and the friendship.

We might plausibly predict—given the partisan nature of friendship and the concerns of friends for each other's happiness and well-being—that friends who confer on problems in marriage would find strong support for their grievances and strong encouragement for strategies advancing their interests over those of their spouse. That is not what I found. To explain the actual involvement of women friends in each other's marital problems, I must explain how women defined their friends' (and their own) interests and well-being and consider how these definitions shaped marriage work.

All the women said they talked about their marriages or romances to close women friends. All but two routinely talked about problems in marriage or romance as they occurred. Seventeen (of twenty-one) easily specified ways friends had helped them when they had difficulties with their husbands or boyfriends. Of the married women one-half even specified ways they believed friends had helped them keep their marriages together; over three-quarters at least occasionally discussed a marital disagreement first with a friend before raising it with a partner; the same proportion talked to a friend about how to talk about a problem with a partner. Four of the thirteen women I asked had talked over their most recent marital disagreement with a friend before they talked it over with their husbands. Clearly, these close women friends are involved with each other's marriage.

Marriage Work

A useful way to examine the active involvement of friends in each other's marriage is in a process I call marriage work, building on Arlie Hochschild's concept of "emotion work."[1] *Marriage work* refers to reflection and action to achieve or sustain the stability of a marriage or a sense of its adequacy. I see marriage work as a voluntary and individually improvised effort rather than one institutionally specified. The term *work* is not a synonym for role. Rather, work indicates the purposive and exertive quality of the activity and connotes a sense of craft; it is purposive because it is intentional. Within this component I might include unconsciously destructive motives and marriage work that proves ultimately subversive of marriage.

Marriage work may intend to influence or accommodate. Influence-oriented marriage work uses power to produce effects on marriage. Its strategies may be coercive, combative, manipulative, or based on bargaining. Accommodative strategies aim to adjust oneself to a situation or capitulate to the demands of another. I consider accommodation a strategy in this discussion because the object of action is commitment, not power. A strategy of accommodation may sustain one's marriage commitment. Moreover, marriage work may aim at oneself or at one's situation, which includes others.

Emotion Work

There is a type of self-oriented marriage work that Arlie Hochschild has labeled "emotion management." Emotion management (or emotion work) refers to "the act of trying to change in degree or quality an emotion or feeling." Hochschild identifies emotion work in acts upon nonreflective primary emotion, attempts to comply with "feeling rules" that are implicit in authoritative ideologies;[2] an example is the attempt not to be angry when one believes one has "no right" to be. I depart from Hochschild's schema to reserve the term *emotion work* for work upon the self; I include emotion work upon others in my second category, situation management (my reasons for doing so should become clear by the end of this chapter).

Among Hochschild's techniques of emotion work, I focus on cognitive techniques: "the attempt to change images, ideas, or thoughts in the service of changing feelings associated with them."[3] In women's accounts of discussions among friends we can identify their cooperation in cognitive emotion work. Every woman I spoke to said that talking to a friend had changed her attitude or feelings about her husband or about a disagreement with him. All but one easily produced examples. The most frequent first description of a friend's help with emotion work was *just listening,* although something more than passive listening was often implied.

I think it helps just to freely say it out loud to someone you can trust.

I can let out things that have been pent up inside me. I can let them out and forget them.

The best thing is just having someone else to hear it, so that I know I'm not really nuts.

[My friend] just being there if I need to talk to somebody. That kind of emotional support. . . . Sometimes it puts it into perspective just to hear it out loud. Or to hear what someone unbiased thinks about it.

Several women said that the opportunity to think aloud, without getting advice or guidance, allowed them to explore their own minds at some distance from the emotion, confusion, or conflict they felt when examining a marital problem. But whatever the value of "just listening," most of the women added, as did Kay above, that they engaged in a more extensive give-and-take on the subject of each other's marriage problems. "There are times when it's appropriate to listen to someone bitch, and there are times when it's appropriate to give some constructive criticism. Sally and

I have done both for each other. Nowadays, she tends to come to me for advice and I tend to go to her to listen."

The advice and "constructive criticism" is the end product of a process that involves a woman in actively examining and analyzing her friend's situation, behavior, and emotions. Gail explained: "They showed me ways I hadn't seen before of looking at a situation. They've given me different viewpoints from the ones I was taking. And their views made sense. I'd take Gwen's viewpoint and look at it and think, 'Yeah, this really could be happening for that reason. I hadn't even thought of it!'" The result, Gail went on to explain, is "a better evaluation of a situation," "relief" from anger— new bases of tolerance. Exploring the aims, contents, and effects of emotion-oriented exchanges will take us further into the nature of marriage work among friends.

One mode of emotion work for which friends are frequently credited aims to generate *empathy* for a woman's husband.

So much of the time I only see my side—I've got blinders on. And June will say, "You know, he's probably feeling real insecure and angry." And for the first time I'll realize there's another human being mixed up in this, instead of just me and my own passions.

Vera could see Hal's problems. She had a brother who was an awful lot like him. She would try to understand him and to help me understand him.

Marla is very positive in her thinking. I might go to her and complain that David did this and I'll have made my mind up why he did it. My explanation will be pretty negative and angry. She'll listen and say, "Maybe he did it because of . . . ," and her explanation will be something I never even considered. It's something else for me to think about, and it makes my anger subside.

Emotion work evoking empathy can be followed by situation-changing marriage work. Lynn described how Donna helped her empathize with her husband so that Lynn could improve relations between him and her daughters by a former marriage: "There would be times I'm thinking, 'Poor me, I can't take this,' and blaming it all on Jerry. And Donna will remind me, 'Well, you know, he's never had any children. You have to. . . .' And my feelings about it will really change. . . . I can help them work it out."

Generating empathy to subdue anger or frustration is an example of what Hochschild calls a "frame change," a recodification of a situation that brings (or frees one to adopt) an appropriate emotional response.[4] As women recounted these frame changes, their voices carried awe and appreciation for a friend who moved them through unyielding anger and negativity to affection and hope and set them on a calmer, problem-solving course.

A similar but not identical frame-changing strategy is *ennobling the adversary.* The pacifying change in perspective occurs here when a friend reveals some brilliant facets of what until then appeared to be a rough, heavy stone.

A lot of time I just looked at the negative. I'd compare Gary to the other husbands. And when you look at someone else's husband, you just see the good side, not the bad one. Jan will point out to me, "You know Gary helps with the dishes"—or does this or that—"and Eddie never does." I'd start to think, "Gee, I really am lucky he does that. He's not all bad."

Occasionally, my friends will say something about Jeff that puts him in a different light and makes me appreciate him more. He impresses people in certain ways that I forget about because I live with it. Like someone will mention something he said that went right past me. And I'll think, "That's kind of nice."

Doreen tells me, "Jesse loves you." And he's this and he's that. She tells me his fine points and puts me in good spirits about him.

Humor is another frame-changing strategy that friends encouraged. A joke, usually self-deprecating, would make a noxious situation seem benign. Humor can instantaneously alter the frame and dissipate unwelcome emotions. "Sometimes when you've talked about something you've been upset about, you feel ridiculous being so upset. I'll just have to laugh. Just by laughing with me, friends have helped me not to worry."

Probing the emotions themselves can change them. This is a direct emotion-changing rather than frame-changing strategy. Anger, jealousy, shame, and other negative feelings are legitimate and acceptable to friends, women reported. These emotions can be expressed before close friends, their roots can be explored, and they can be worked over in cooperative reflection. Rita offered an example:

Sometimes, if I'm caught up in some emotions about an issue with Lloyd, I don't feel comfortable being there—in that state—right then. I feel a little shame, a little embarrassment. But by talking about it with June, I can bring it out and look at it. Then I don't feel so weird.

I'll even talk a bit about the shame or embarrassment. June's usually a little surprised, because she sees anger, and that sort of feeling, as very common. This just airs it out a little, and then I feel I can take care of it.

All the women without exception said they talked with friends about feelings of anger. Most of the time, the aim of these discussions was explicitly to defuse anger or other volatile emotions. But their method was not simply to suppress emotion. As Rita indicated above, working over emotion with friends enabled women first to express the emotion.

Using anger, we can study how women work over emotion with each another. A friend is not the object of the anger, so she can more easily sympathize, perhaps empathize, even collude: "If I say he's a son of a bitch, Loretta will say, 'You're darn right he is!'" Expressing the anger to an intimate who is not its object permits a woman to experience her feelings without escalating conflict or using strategies she might ultimately regret. Such an exchange empowers her by affirming her interpretation of reality. Its expression feels "safe" because it protects an emotion (and also affirms emotionality) and because it defuses further conflict with the spouse. "I told Gwen, 'I'm not going to take this stuff. I'm going to let him have it!' But when I talked it out with her, it took some of the stress out of it. Whew!"

I heard many examples of collective emotion management in accounts of discussion of marriage among friends. Friend helped friend to suppress unwelcome emotion and evoke desirable emotion for responding to problems in their marriages. Throughout this chapter, I explore these exchanges among friends to interpret the "conventions of feeling" and the conventions of framing marital encounters that emerged in my interviews.[5] The material just reviewed suggests that conducting emotion work with friends helps women to manage emotions within a context that allows them to acknowledge original feeling but to manage it so as to sustain their marriage commitment. There is a paradox here that this chapter also explores.

Situation Management

In the accounts I heard, "talking it out" with a friend almost always resulted in taking the edge off volatile emotion. Women wished to gain the emotional quiet to find constructive solutions to marital conflict. Friends joined them—oftentimes led them—in that search to explore strategies for changing their situation: "A few times I was ready to blow up, and after talking about it, I was able to quiet down and have the chance to look at things differently. And I said to myself, 'Maybe I don't have to act the way I've been acting.'"

I use the term *situation management* to refer to marriage work oriented to the world external to oneself. Talking with friends, women analyze marital situations and decide upon actions to change them. Often the adopted course is to talk over the problem with the mate. Thirteen of seventeen women reported such conferences, whose strategic advantages are suggested in these accounts:

Talking about the problem with June gives me a chance to sift through the issues and feelings and get to what I want to talk about with Lloyd.

Sometimes, I may be trying to get him to do something. I might talk first to Marla or my mom or Sue, because I may be mad about it and I don't want to come home and blurt it out. I figure there may be an easier way to do this than arguments. One of them might help me come up with a better alternative to yelling.

Friends sometimes related their own solutions to marital problems:

George and I were always fighting about household responsibilities and getting nowhere. I'd ask friends, "How does your husband feel? How do you divide up responsibilities?"

Catherine is in a very "like" marriage, so her solutions are especially helpful.

Or they joined in surveying alternative solutions.

Loretta will say, "Let's see, what are your options here? What if you tried this . . . or what if you said that. . . ? Rather than just being supportive, she'll be objective and say, "How do you think you can do that differently?"

I told her, "You should talk to him about it. Let him know what you think. Or you could go out at ten at night and see how he likes it."

Sometimes Sally just can't see the alternatives. I'll just state them as I see them, if I can be constructive.

Ultimately, friends might give explicit direction; the few women who reported receiving such firm advice seemed to appreciate it.

She says, "Just be straight with him—it's going to be all right."

Annette will say, "You've got to be more open and talk to Mike." Or, "Show more affection." She'll tell me to put more effort in specific areas.

Once after a big one, I left and went to stay with my sister. Lily called and said, "Janine, come on home. Your husband loves you. Don't do him that way."

Often, but not always, firm direction was an asymmetric exchange in a friendship with a mother-figure. Firm direction from actual mothers, however, was resented. The general symmetry and mutuality of friendships, even those with mother-daughter themes, admitted the strong advice that daughters had experienced as an intrusion when it occurred in real mother-daughter relationships.

Accommodative and Influence-oriented Marriage Work

These examples of marriage work illustrate a clear trend in the reports: with the help of friends, women solved marital conflicts by capitulation or adaptation. They used strategies of assertion, manipulation, and resistance far less frequently. Even Rita, who enthusiastically described how Loretta concurred that her husband was a "son of a bitch," continued with an account of her friend's more pacifying advice. Loretta supported Rita's ultimate aim of relieving herself of anger, rather than honing it as a weapon for marital combat.

Only a few times, in fact, did any answers recount discussions with friends aimed at sharpening or focusing anger to sustain or win a conflict. The first was Nancy, who spoke appreciatively of how talks with Helen strengthened her determination to impress Mike that "I'm a person too": "There's times I do rebel. I'll say, 'I'm not going to do such and such because I've talked to my girlfriends and we've agreed about it. They wouldn't do it either.' In talking to friends you can be reassured that you're right about things."

A second, more dramatic, account of close friends' reinforcing angry resistance was provided by Cass, who described how her family—who were her closest friends—helped her "throw out" her physically abusive husband:

I'd packed up and moved out and gone to their house a lot of times. . . . I wouldn't say they tried to talk me into feeling worse about him, because nobody could have felt worse about him than I did. But I knew they were in favor of getting rid of him.

One night he was ticked off about something and he went to bed. I went out for a bit, but when I got back he wasn't as asleep as I thought he was. He proceeded to go, Pow, pow, pow. I got my family; and my mother stuck a gun in him and told him to hit the road and he did. I was ready for him to go.

Although only a few women collaborated in angry resistance, others worked together in strategizing advantage and more subtle resistance to domination. Recall, for example, Karen's description of an unobtrusive power play that involved figuring out how to get David to cooperate with her plans: "I figure there may be an easier way to do this than arguments." She claimed her friends' cool-headed collective strategizing was often effective. Similarly, Janine described an occasion when Lily advised her to change her tactics to gain her husband's consent to a visit to faraway kin: "Lily said, 'Don't go getting into any more big hassles over it. Just wait a bit. He's not ready for it now. Go home and apologize. You'll be able to go.' So, I did that, and sure enough. . . ." Recall also how, in the last chapter, Jean characterized the discussion among a group of close friends scheduling their next get-together—each previewing her bargaining strategy for getting an evening off.

In Louise's case, consulting with Jan yielded useful strategies for asserting her needs to her oftentimes domineering husband. Louise herself believed, though, that what empowered her to change a lot that was wrong in her marriage was the fact of having a close friend. "Gary's had to learn to make some compromises. Before Jan and I were friends, I did all the compromising. It seems like it's kind of switching right now." In the early years of marriage,

Louise maintained, Gary's jealousy impelled her to detach from independent friendships. He sustained friendships, though; and the couple socialized with his friends and their wives. Louise continued: "I think it benefited him all around. He'd never admit that he loved it that way, but it's the truth. I sat home and took care of the house and had the dinner ready and the wash done. I was on top of things because I didn't have anything else to do."

Now, with both the shared activity of her new friendship with Jan and the independent projects Jan encouraged Louise to begin, Louise is less the perfect housewife she once was: "He used to feel sorry for his friend who complained he never had any clean underwear. Now, he'll come around saying, 'How do you work the washing machine? There's no underwear in my drawer again.'" Gary responded to Louise's ardent new friendship with considerable resentment. But Jan's importance to her fortified Louise to "work on" rather than appease her husband's jealousy. She believed that she and Gary were now steadily working out a resolution of marriage problems on much improved terms for her.

Although Cass had no regrets at having dealt so forcefully with her abusive husband, the subtler and more manipulative marital strategizing was the preferred method for the others. Nancy, who recounted how friends help her firmly stand her ground, analyzed its ambivalent legacy:

Men, in general, will walk over you unless you stand up to them. In talking to women, you can be reassured you're right to stand up. But it doesn't necessarily make things go smoothly. Friends can make you think a lot about the way things really are. But often you feel you're contradicting the way you've been brought up. You're not necessarily making your marriage work easier.

Nancy is forty, a housewife married to a hardworking small-businessman, and the mother of two teenagers. She described her husband as a "good friend" and her marriage as solid. Yet her marriage was more peaceable before she began to "think a lot about the way things really are." She and a few of her friends welcomed many of the egalitarian ideas that they had recently encountered and were at times exhilarated by their attempts to assert their own needs after many years of perceived self-sacrifice for family. But Nancy and some others I spoke to were not of one mind about these new ideas about women. Reflecting upon the mix of assertion with older, deep-rooted values can be painfully confusing.

Perhaps more troubling to Nancy than conflict of values or guilt was the discovery that an assertive or conflictive stance could be perilous. Taking combative stances after confirmatory discussions with friends, Nancy and others found they provoked husbands' rage and triggered a level of conflict they had not anticipated. Sometimes they found themselves experiencing an anger for which old tactics of emotion work no longer felt legitimate.

Most friends still helped Nancy to empathize with Mike or told her to "try harder." Yet even the maternal neighbor to whom Nancy turned anticipating the most accommodative advice, didn't "reach" her the way she used to. Increasingly, Nancy refrained from undertaking the emotion work Hochschild calls the "generous . . . self-persuasion [of] deep acting" in which an individual invests energy in trying to serve another's interests more and better than one's own.[6] Instead, she engaged in a more pragmatic overt adjustment. In this kind of collective marriage work, friends reminded each other how tough it is to survive outside the marriage, particularly for women of their age and their level of marketable skills. And then they used humor and "laugh[ed] at the ridiculousness of the whole thing."

This is marriage work, no doubt, and it is unquestionably accommodative. But it involves less profound emotion management than radical reframing does. Troubling vistas remain in the picture. By accommodating instrumentally, without renouncing either emotions or analysis of the situation, one challenges an authoritative ideology of wifely deference.

Seen in this light, emotion work (which reframes feeling and self-concept) shores up an ideology of female subordination, whereas lax emotion management (which rejects that strategy) challenges the ideology. The picture is the same, even when the outcome is accommodation.[7] I discuss below how collective marriage work can use pragmatic accommodation to resist subordination in marriage. Nonetheless, it is obvious why Nancy cautioned, in the epilogue to this energetic account of how friends participate in assertive marriage work: you don't necessarily make marriage go more smoothly that way.

Nancy thus provides clues to why accommodation might characterize the more pervasive forms of marriage work. In contrast to assertive situation management, the self-focused strategies require only one's own commitment to change rather than a husband's. These accommodative strategies do not risk incurring the recalcitrance, hostility, or resentment of another person, as do the strategies of talking it out, manipulating, or battling. In fact, emotion work may resolve a problem without even arousing a spouse's suspicion that a problem exists. Even though capitulation or adaptation may require the expenditure of voluminous resources of will, intelligence, imagination, and energy, these are resources that the relatively powerless retain at their disposal (depending more or less upon their level of subjection). This use of resources may be costly to women, given the alternate uses of these resources; but when marriage work is a primary goal, such choices seem logical enough.

Many scholars have observed the superior "emotional skills" women acquire to compensate for the material power and social privilege of men—or, alternatively, to equilibrate family life by functional specialization.[8] Their emotional skills include greater interpersonal observational acuity ("sensitivity"), faster interpersonal inductive calculation ("intuition"), more practiced indirect influence strategies ("feminine wiles," "maternal style"), and so on. Women may actively apply all of them to influencing others. Yet when the stakes are high—as they are in many marital conflicts— a woman may use more precise calculation of outcome and assume less risk by applying these skills to herself. Unlike outright and explicit capitulation, emotion work offers a reward beyond preserving marriage: a woman achieves an "improved" feeling about the situation, known in sociology of the family as "marital satisfaction."

In *The Future of Marriage*, Jessie Bernard summarizes several decades of family research to show, on the one hand, that women often perceive more marital problems than men do while both men and women report that wives make more marital adjustments and, on the other hand, that women nonetheless very often report themselves satisfied with their marriages.[9] The concept of accommodative emotion work may help explain such findings, once we clarify the impetus to accommodate.

Can I rely on women's self-reports of accommodation? It is possible, of course, that women emphasized accommodative marriage work in their reports and deemphasized manipulative or combative strategies. Perhaps more aggressive marriage work is more stigmatized and thus underreported. But, given that women did not hesitate to report that they gossiped and shared stigmatized feelings—like jealousy—with friends, it seems probable that the accommodative bias does predominate.

All this may begin to explain why the twenty women who recalled changed attitudes or feelings about their husbands virtually all gave accommodative accounts. Responding to another set of questions, sixteen of twenty-one women could think of times friends specifically had "talked them into feeling better" about their husbands; encouraging empathy with or ennobling the husband were the predominant methods they reported. Nine could think of times when friends had "talked them into feeling worse" about their mates. But those who recalled negative persuasion said it had occurred rarely—far less often than positive strategies. Significantly, except for one woman who said that the friend who talked her into feeling worse about her husband "didn't really bother me" and another who said she liked it because "they are being supportive of my interests," the rest of the women uniformly disliked such negative exchanges.

It's never happened. I probably wouldn't tolerate it.

Sometimes Wanda is very negative about Hal. Like, "He'll never change," and, "Oh, what you're going through!" And she'll comment on some of the stupid things he'll do. It's true, you know, but she doesn't have to tell me. I really don't like her coming back at it, though, because she really doesn't know.

If there was anything she disapproved of, she never said so. She was very wise. She never interfered.

When Carol criticizes Tom for his gambling, I get a little angry: "How dare you? I never say anything about your husband." She just doesn't hold anything back. I don't like it, but I just tell myself she doesn't understand.

No, nobody ever tried it. She probably wouldn't be that close a friend if she did.

Several of the women just quoted had marital problems—a few, quite serious—that they talked about with their friends (the seven who replied that they had marital difficulties all discussed these problems with close friends). These women were especially likely to report that they found themselves defending mates they had just been complaining about.

I'll be complaining to Lily about Dwight being gone most of the time, out with the guys, and she'll say, "He shouldn't be leaving you alone so much." I listen, but it just goes in one ear and out the other. I'd say I end up feeling more positive. Because she's telling me that and I'm defending him.

If anyone said anything against him, I'd say, "Well, it's not so bad." I might be really angry with him, but I'm real defensive as well.

Just before we got married, Marie would listen to my troubles and tell me I probably needed to find someone else. I didn't like that at all. When you complain to people, you really want them to find a solution for you. If they're negative, you start defending him.

Frances put it in classic terms: "I can call him a bastard, if I want to; but nobody else can."

The women who reported serious marriage problems and those who described their marriages as stable and untroubled all relied on friends to help build acceptance and optimism.

She makes me feel it's going to be all right. She reminds me that things take time.

If I'm down about him, they'd never down him too.

No more than "Stick it out. It'll blow over."

Sometimes I think she doesn't much care for him, but she's always encouraging.

They tell you you'll live through it, and you do.

A few times women reported feeling resentment that friends had not supported their assertiveness toward their husbands:

I think Margie has been uncomfortable with some of the changes in me. So, if I ever tell her about a conflict, she'll take his side. She's always afraid I'm going too far.

Paula took his side. Said I ought to stay home with the kids. She made me feel all the more guilty. I finally just quit the job. It was just too hard to defend it alone.

Rita and Kay are speaking above. Each believed she had changed in recent years, in ways some old friends could not understand or support. Both had enrolled in community college courses, seeking and finding new competencies in social and intellectual experiences. Both had explored ideas and opinions they had previously felt too timid to engage. They had also formed strong friendships with other "returning" women at school. Both of their closest friends were women they had met in school. For Rita and Kay and for other women I interviewed, the return to school meant disruptive shifts in marital power and sometimes long-lasting conflicts. (My sample reflects the educational opportunities that California's massive community college system has offered mature women; increasing numbers of working-class women have joined middle-class women in attending college classes.)

Like Nancy, whose "new ideas" questioning wifely submissiveness interfered with her typical practices of emotion work, Rita and Kay were less and less inclined to certain deferential forms of marriage work. They had acquired skills that translated into resources of marital power, and they had formed new friendship networks that circulated values favoring individual achievement and marital assertion as well as information about jobs and support for personal change. Rita and Kay could risk somewhat less deferential marriage work; they resented pressures from old friends to defer. Likewise, Thea's higher-income occupation and egalitarian ideals freed her to profess her dissatisfaction with friends' attempts to talk her into feeling less critical of her husband's faults; she could view friends' criticisms of him as supportive of her. Nevertheless, the accommodative balance of my responses reflects a sample that is not weighted toward the small privileged sector of American women.

Considering the moral rights and obligations of friendship, most women I spoke to felt a friend might appropriately criticize a friend's husband. Eighteen of twenty-one (and the same proportion of the married women) answered at least "Sometimes" to the question of whether friends had a right to do so. They believed in self-restraint, though. The hypothetical situations they suggested as warranting criticism were ones in which the wife suffered physical or psychological abuse. These extreme circumstances are of course, the most likely to come to mind. But the women's answers also reflected a respect for the moral autonomy of their friends.

I'd ask myself, "How does she see it?" You don't have a right to create a situation that doesn't exist.

Unless it's something like abuse, I'd let her open the conversation.

If the situation was so extreme and the person was so blind, [I would say something]. I would hope I wouldn't otherwise, though. Really.

They advocated a nonjudgmental and uncoercive delivery of criticism, so that the friend who received it would maintain her integrity. "You've got to do it carefully, not judging, not telling her what to do." Another explained, "I might say, 'If it were me, I think I would. . . .'"

In sum, women talked about marriage problems with friends to be able to think aloud; to let off steam; to reassess their perceptions and dissatisfactions; to plan communication with spouses; to reestablish empathy and appreciation for spouses; to effect changes in their own behavior, attitudes, and emotions; and to figure out how to change their husbands. From the accounts I heard, it appears that these women used marriage work to solidify and reinforce their own commitments to their marriages far more than to change their marriages to satisfy their own needs and wants. In a number of different ways, they expressed a desire that friends help them "work things out" in their minds. Presumably, marriage work could have the opposite effect. Women could ask for, and receive support for, more uncompromising stances in marital conflicts. Even in a society whose dominant expectation of wives is accommodation, friendships could form countercultural resistance. My general observation and a few segments of my interviews indicate that they sometimes do.

Thus, as I discuss the character and impact of marriage work, I must not repeat the error of network theorists who causally link the structure of friendship patterns to the content of normative exchange. This kind of mistake appears, for example, in the work of Elizabeth Bott. In her pioneering study of family and social network, Bott assumed the structure of a family's social network causes the marital role division, overlooking the variable practices a close-knit network might enforce in other circumstances (in an egalitarian kibbutz, for example).[10] In order to explain why their marriage work with friends is predominantly accommodative, we must understand the circumstances under which women seek or consent to this particular normative exchange. Once we have analyzed the aims of their marriage work, we will be better positioned to appreciate the impact of its collective form.

Why Marriage Work Reinforces Commitment to Marriage

I propose both structural and cultural explanations for the way women's marriage work reinforces their commitments to marriage. To begin with the structural factors, which appear to be at once simpler and more determinative, women reinforce each other's commitment because they are dependent upon marriage for survival or mobility.

Despite the fact that women increasingly work for pay, their salaries, relative to men's, have remained depressed over several decades. This fact means that marriage is still the best means of economic mobility for women. The median earnings of full-time working women are much closer to the poverty line than to the line of median family income.[11] For unemployed or low-income women, marriage might be the only decent avenue of survival; public assistance, varying by state, in no state awards even a poverty-level income. Nearly half of all female-headed families live below the federally established (and some argue, unreasonably low) poverty line. And poverty is much greater among minority women: in 1983, 63 percent of families headed by black women lived in poverty.[12] Moreover, in three out of ten impoverished female-headed households, the mother is employed. The employment ghetto of "women's jobs" and the fastest growing sectors of the employment market feature jobs with low wages, few or no crucial benefits, and short ladders of advancement (increasing numbers are part-time as well)—all conditions that are adding large numbers of women to the ranks of the working poor.[13]

Thus, for virtually all women, leaving a marriage—or being

left—means economic hardship. Half of divorced mothers do not receive the child support awarded to them, studies project; and the average yearly payment to those who do is around $2,000.[14] (These figures exclude, of course, the four of ten single mothers who are awarded no child support at all.) To the women I interviewed the gist of these facts is apparent. Many women are in age groups for which nearly half of all marriages end in divorce. Most have kin or friends who are divorced; and they see their situations clearly. A majority of women stated flatly that their biggest problem if their marriage ended would be economic survival. Several spontaneously mentioned the "lessons" they learned watching divorced friends manage. Only the divorced women, not the married ones, could see anything other than disadvantages in going it alone.

As heads of families and as friends, women experience the economic liabilities of gender. A woman might offer a divorcing friend emotional support, advice, a certain amount of daytime child care, and the like, but probably not money, room, or board. The most violent account of a husband's resentment of his wife's friendship involved an offer of temporary shelter to a divorcing friend. "She had left her husband and needed a place to stay for awhile. . . . Maybe she was intruding, but all I could think of was I was glad I was there. . . . He said she was breaking up our marriage, and he literally threw her out of the house. . . . It was my first bad experience with my husband. . . . She never came out here again."

A friend might offer information about how to apply for welfare aid, or she might have contacts at her own workplace who can get her friend a job; but whatever important role a woman plays for a friend whose marriage is dissolving, that role is not likely to include economic support. Women are likely to see marriage as the most certain source of economic security for themselves and for their friends.

The economic liabilities of gender might explain why women recommend marriage to their friends, but why do they reinforce commitments to existing marriages? Why don't women simply ratify the statistical trend toward serial monogamy and urge a friend with marital problems to try again and better luck next time? My respondents suggested that women surveyed the options available to themselves and their friends and concluded that the prospects were grim for better luck next time. Nancy summarized it quite plainly: "When I've just about had it, Annette will say, 'Stick it out, 'cause it could be a whole lot worse.' With all my friends, we look at how bad things could be. They just remind me, 'Hey, look around. . . .'"

Besides their economic options, Nancy and her friends look around at the marriage-market opportunities divorced women encounter. Divorcing young is not very damaging to women's chances of remarrying. Once they are in their thirties, however, women are less likely than men to remarry; and they take longer to do so. With increasing age at divorce, their remarriage opportunities drop drastically, compared to men's.[15] (Recall that the largest part of my sample was over thirty.) Since men tend to remarry much younger women, the years women have spent in a marriage subtract directly from their chances of remarriage. But women do not need statistics to assess the situation. Again, divorced friends and kin are poignant evidence that divorced women have no easy time of it. "I have girlfriends who are back out in the single world. I don't think I could take it." I suggest that these structured opportunities influence the algebra of marriage work among friends, weighting it toward making peace with existing circumstances.

The cultural factors shaping the content of marriage work are, on the one hand, too obvious and, on the other, too complex to review in detail. Suffice it to say that religion, secular philosophy, marriage counseling, and popular culture still elevate lifelong commitment and fidelity, in spite of the phenomenal growth in divorce. These cultural prescriptions apply to men as well as women, of course; but the gender structure of cultural production and consumption shapes the character and impact of these prescriptions. Quite simply, women are more extensively and more frequently exposed to these culture shapers. Because they are more religiously active than men and larger consumers of services, literature, and media dealing with marriage and family, women are often explicitly the audiences for whom the cultural messages are created.

The effects of this arrangement flow in both directions. Social-relations reformers must appeal to the desires or interests of women if they wish to build an audience and influence the behavior of women or men. Even themes of "male revolt" from marital commitment, like those Barbara Ehrenreich identified in the ideas of the human potential movement,[16] were transformed and harnessed to themes of marital struggle and redemption in the larger bulk of popular culture represented by marriage counseling and women's magazines.

Cultural messages about the best interests of children may also influence marriage work in favor of commitment. Yet my interviews showed women so acutely aware of the social privileges of children in two-parent versus single-parent families that their own independent assessments seemed to shape their behavior much more than cultural messages did. Children's evident material and emotional suffering in divorce and women's identification with the needs of children are enough to reinforce women's commitment to stability in marriage. I suspect that the popular transliterations of expert theory, which continue to link adequate nurture with female nature and adequate authority with male nature, operate more on alternate visions of the distant future than on considerations in the present. Women do not need to believe that women alone nurture children to know that if they do not nurture their children, no one else will.

I propose that these structural and cultural arrangements form an interest in stable marriage. The ethics of motherhood and marital fidelity, where marriage is a precondition of economic well-being for women and their children, create an interest in stable marriage that is greater for women than men. Further, this interest favors a moral order that appears to be eroding. To attempt to save other marriages by reinforcing one's highest commitment to stability is to attempt to shore up the cultural base of one's own marriage. If stable marriage is crucial to women's perceptions of survival or well-being, one of the few ways they can deny alternatives to men is to discourage them to other women.

Men's strongest interest in stable (as opposed to serial) marriage is their attachment to wives and children. In the wildfire spread of "fascinating womanhood" seminars, "fathering" workshops, and "marriage communication" theology, we can see how quickly women seize upon plausible means of increasing male attachments (and husbands' participation in the curriculum). Similarly, in the considerable female opposition to feminist and civil libertarian reforms like abortion rights and the ERA, we can see how dearly many women hold their interest in a moral order that disallows others' choices for an easy exit from marriage.[17]

What of the valuation of individual aspiration and autonomy that the last chapter showed to be characteristic of women's culture of friendship? Friends clearly draw upon these values in encouraging the expression of feelings and in collective strategizing for marital influence. Still, they more strongly emphasize individuality in treating other matters. In treating problems in marriage, they stress communal responsibility.

Do Husbands Do Marriage Work with Friends?

Moving from the social forms that shape marriage work among women friends to the impact of this collaboration on marriages, we must consider the marriage work of husbands as well. I cannot use the self-description I gathered in interviews with women to inspect men's close friendships. I can, however, interpret wives' statements about husbands' friendships, using the findings of other research on the topic. The similarities and parallels in these two sources of information constitute evidence that is reliable if I use it with care.

All but one of the married women I interviewed believed they talked personally with their friends more than their husbands did (Mary said, "I don't know what he does"). Although several women admired the strength and durability of the bonds between their husbands and their close friends, none of them believed that their husbands talked very intimately with their men friends about marital problems or anything else.

I don't think men pour out their emotional feelings to each other. When Jack does, it's to me.

Even though he's best friends with Frank, he's told me he can't talk to him about everything. They don't have an intimate relationship.

I feel better if I talk about stuff with my friend, but he's the other way: you keep your problems right here—you don't discuss them with anyone else.

Two-thirds of the married women also believed their husbands found it generally less easy to ask for friends' help.

The women I spoke to thought their husbands' friendships reflected those of most men. In answering questions about how men and women generally behave with friends, all but one or two women agreed that women turned more often to friends to talk about personal problems and that women talked more to friends about personal feelings and private details of their marriages (one or two said, "No difference"). According to their accounts, the vitality of men's close friendships lies elsewhere—in sociable camaraderie, loyalty, and generosity.

The wives' analyses corroborate other studies of men's friendships. An array of studies report that in comparison with women, men are less emotionally expressive, less empathetic, disclose less on intimate topics, and they have fewer friendships of intimacy and emotional exchange.[18] Fischer and Phillips found that, in general, men and women had equal numbers of friends in whom they confided but that men were more likely to have no one besides a spouse to confide in. My research suggests that surveys should specify the contents of personal confidences, since men and women might differ in what they consider "personal talk." Work by Reis, Senchak, and Solomon indicates such a gender difference.[19]

In many ways, the wives offered analyses of male friendships that seem more nuanced than those of social scientists, who collapse notions of intimacy, attachment, dependence, love, and loyalty into concepts like intimacy and self-disclosure. The women I talked to were quite certain that their husbands talked personally with their close friends less than they themselves did, but they varied in their assessments of their husbands' dependence, attachment, or loyalty to close friends: "I think he feels just as close to his friends as I do [to mine]. We just need them in a different way." Another, contrasting view: "They're close friends, but they're not intimately involved in each other's lives. Still, there's a permanence about his friendships that I don't feel even with my closest friends."

Since other research so strongly supports the women's descriptions of the intimacy of husbands' friendships, let us assume, for the moment, that the women noted facts—that their husbands are far less intimate with close friends. What, then, are the implications for our understanding of friendship and marriage work? It is tempting to speculate that marriage work is primarily women's work—that men and women contribute unequally to marital problem solving, compromise, and conflict resolution.

Tempting or not, the speculation on marriage work must wait: I have to answer other questions. How much marriage work do husbands and wives accomplish together, how much alone? Are there patterned gender differences in perception and emotion work that lead to accommodation, compromise, or capitulation? I cannot fully answer these questions. But there is research that bears on some of them. Bernard cites studies on women's greater adaptation in marriage; others report women more likely to perceive problems in marriage.[20] Certainly, if one does not perceive problems one cannot address them.

This much we can state with certainty: the marital problem solving and emotion management women and men do is asymmetric. My research offers preliminary evidence that the marriage work of women is considerably more socialized than that of men. Women are much more likely to undertake marriage work collectively, thinking, feeling, and deciding in dialogue with others. Assuming—only for purposes of argument—that men contribute quantitatively similar resources and energies to these matters, what kinds of qualitative differences in their contributions are likely to result from their private, as opposed to collective, methods?

The Concomitants of
Collective Marriage Work

Inevitably, when another person helps work out a personal problem, the work is not idiosyncratic or unmediated; the contribution shows. In short, problem solving and emotion work are subject to social control. Collective marriage work reinforces possibly latent but nonetheless influential values that are in theory variable. In my interviews, however, they varied little. Women reported that they sought accommodative marriage work with friends or met it regardless of their wishes. They did not describe this patterned influence as social control, however. Their language rarely evoked the quality of constraint. They called the influence "objective" or "unbiased," as did Rita and Karen, who stated without irony: "She'll be objective and say, 'How do you think you can do that differently?'" and, "Friends help you become more objective and accepting of how they [husbands] are."

When the women used terms like "objective" and "unbiased,"

they meant the advice was impartial, disinterested, not swayed by emotions. Yet most admitted that criticism of their mate, disinterested or otherwise, was unacceptable. The meaning of "objective" that is implicit in their examples is "determined by and oriented to a goal or object," the object being to keep commitment to marriage.

A friend's bias, then, turns not on favoring the interests of one partner or the other but on favoring individual needs and interests over fidelity to marriage. If we assume that in marriage work the goal of preserving a marriage and commitment to it overarches the goal of working out marital solutions that fit the needs of the individuals involved, then the discussions of marriage women reported were objective indeed. We need to evaluate the effect of this particular collaborative marriage work and then suggest different effects that marriage work might have in an alternate ideology or situation.

To appreciate the varied meanings of "objective" marriage work in the lives of different women, compare these three accounts. In chapter 2, Nancy described how Annette helped her work on her jealousy of her son's girlfriend. Annette found Nancy's jealousy understandable (she had sons of her own) but inappropriate, so she helped Nancy plan how to act in a way that reduced the jealousy. Confiding these uncomfortable feelings to Annette and allowing Annette to help her manage them, Nancy relieved undesirable emotion. And she found a strategy for handling residual feelings to avoid undesirable reactions, including her husband's disapproval.

In the second account, also introduced in chapter 2, Sally empathized with Arlene's periodic despair that everything her husband did was irritating; but Sally told her outright that this generalized fury was "ridiculous . . . you'll survive." Arlene told this story with amused appreciation and the conviction that her own current sense of contentment with her marriage proved her friend right.

In the third story, Mary told how, when she considered leaving Hal, Vera discouraged her by recounting the loneliness of a past separation of her own. "She tells me how she's been through the same thing and gotten herself out of it. She points out why Hal is doing these things, why I should understand him more and try to make a go of it."

In each example the friend's "unbiased" mediation moved the woman to a more "objective" state of mind or behavior. But the personal cost of her objectivity was different in each case. The first mediation tempered a mother's response that was irrational within a system where children marry outside their family. Following the dictates of jealousy promised Nancy nothing in either personal well-being or improved family relations. The second situation is more ambiguous, at least excerpted from context. Did Sally's exchange with Arlene simply intervene in an emotional eruption— the stuff of daily life in intimate relations—or did it subvert a charged but salutary attempt to insert long-denied personal needs into marriage bargaining? Arlene seemed firmly convinced that it was the former. She felt she had made her peace with the uncommunicativeness of her husband and wished to sustain this peace on the occasions when emotions eclipsed her reasons for the adjustment.

The last example is even more ambiguous. A few times in the past Mary had clutched at a last straw. She could no longer abide her husband's drinking and the chronic marital antagonism it created. Her job was secure; her son had grown and left home; she felt she no longer loved her husband; and she suffered daily anger, regret, and despondence. But Vera's objective mediation pressed Mary to endure, regardless of circumstances. Mary preferred to have a man in her life and knew the odds against a woman her age; how would she even try to find another? Vera's concern unquestionably spoke to one side of Mary's ambivalence. So Mary recounted this collaborative marriage work as appreciatively as she could. In her voice was not so much doubt as a weary wish not to think about it further.

Contrast the mediations already described with this one. Lee, a young, unencumbered single woman, described how her best friend, also young and single, helped her leave a relationship she was not at all sure she really wished to end.

I was choosing to leave a man who I absolutely adored. I said, "Look, I'm trying to leave him and I can't." She came and packed me up and moved me out of the apartment. She put me up, she made me tea, special meals. She'd take me out for walks and point things out. And when I wouldn't see them, she'd turn my head. It was the greatest help I've ever had from anybody.

Our earlier discussion of reasons for accommodative marriage work should indicate why the stories of young, single, childless women depart so sharply from the others. Indeed, women in one or more of these categories were more likely to have a friend discourage accommodation, criticize her partner, or strongly advocate individual self-interest over obligation to a relationship. This last mediation, Mary's story, and the following accounts of divorced women should establish that in collaborative marriage work friends do not simply discover and support a woman's basic intent, to stay married or move toward divorce. "Divorce work" emerged as a very different process in the friendships of the women I interviewed.

Divorced respondents told of support and sacrifice by friends after their marriages ended. Close friends were as dedicated to helping women "work out" their divorces as they had been to helping them "work out" their marriages. But *none* said she had been told "He's the wrong person, anyhow" before the decision, only afterward. "I know my friends would support me if I *did* go. But I've never heard any of them say, 'Go, he deserves it,' or, 'How can you put up with it?' and that sort of thing." Only two of the six ever-divorced women I interviewed identified themselves as the one who left the marriage; all of them claimed to have been very unhappy before divorce. Yet only Cass, who described how family members took a gun and chased out her abusive husband, received support for abandoning a marriage. Each of the others said friends responded with support for divorce only after her husband left or, in Lynn's case, after she firmly decided to leave.

Hilda divorced in an era when, she said, friends showed more reserve in talking about marital problems. She remembered her surprise when one friend came forward to confide the grave marital difficulties the friend had weathered and to persuade Hilda to try to do so as well. After she divorced, many friends helped her and her children. But not even witnesses to her husband's abuse had encouraged thoughts of divorce.

Help along the course of her decision to leave a relationship rarely appeared in the accounts of the women I interviewed—not just divorced women, but my entire sample. The exceptions involved Lee, the young, single woman; Cass, whose family gave material support throughout her marriage and finally rescued her from battery; and married women who recalled events from their youth. I would expect a larger study to reveal subtle variations in this pattern of response to evaluations of a friend's resources of survival. Here, support for divorce was primarily a post-divorce phenomenon. Marriage work was prescribed until divorce work became unavoidable.

For emotion management and marital recommitment, two heads are likely to be better than one; our examples illustrate the point. Collaborative marriage work is efficient as well as effective, although it is labor-intensive. Arlene explained why: "Had I spent some time thinking about it, I might have come to the same conclusion on my own. But she was there when I was still angry about it and not yet heading in the right direction. She helped me resolve that problem a lot quicker than I'd have done if I was doing it on my own."

Now that divorce is widespread, its threat hangs over marital conflicts as never before; the speed with which conflicts are resolved can be critical. Will this fight be the last straw; and if so, whose? Anger is especially resistant to deft emotion work, particularly when the only other person involved is one's combatant. Collectivizing marriage work is a particularly effective way of speeding up conflict resolution (if such is its aim). Further, its labor-intensiveness may not detract from its efficiency. By defusing conflict, collaborative marriage work may spare husband and wife the greater effort of repairing relations that deteriorate when there is no "objective" mediation.

It is evident that collaborative marriage work does something more than filter idiosyncratic or momentary emotional reaction. It allows (although it does not cause) a patterned injection of socially approved interpretations and responses. In the majority of instances reported, collective marriage work reinforced accommodation and recommitment to the marriage; "objectivity" replaced unreconstructive response to conflict. This objectivity generally casts a friend's (cold) eye on the sentiment and behavior that threaten to escalate marital conflict; it fatalistically views a woman's current situation as her best option. Even when stability in marriage is the utmost value, however, socialized marriage work assembles a curriculum of strategies that amplify the powers of the weak and that a different set of circumstances might transmute into a culture of resistance.

If, explaining why women want to remain in their marriages, I have argued well, I may have provoked a question about the causal efficacy of friends' marriage work in stabilizing marriage commitment. If women find ample reasons to stay in marriages, in what way is socialized marriage work crucial?

I think that collective marriage work operates most directly on the feelings and values of commitment rather than its logic. Women may adapt instrumentally (with calculation) because they perceive doing so is their safest or most reasonable alternative and yet not feel either satisfied or morally right. Collective marriage work often helps the cognitive process of commitment, but it probably operates with more independent effect on emotion and belief. Since larger structural and cultural forces may very well account for much of women's accommodation in marriage, collective marriage work contributes more to emotional and moral commitments, strengthening bonds that instrumental accommodation simply attaches. It is in this way that marriage work with friends may appropriately be said to shape and solidify commitments to marriage.

Implications for Male Power and Authority in Marriage

These observations suggest questions about the relation of collective marriage work to marital power and authority, questions compelling enough to prompt speculation. Since marriage work, as I observed it, presses the wife toward compromise, it solidifies the position of the person who does not need to budge. Since marriage work consumes the wife's time and energy and occupies her intelligence, the husband's unconsumed resources remain at his disposal (to invest perhaps in social mobility and prestige or in further marital power plays). Since marriage work uses dominant social norms, it reinforces traditional or rationalized forms of male authority and power in the family.

Yet when socially structured opportunities (created, for example, by a high-paying job, youth and beauty, no dependents) or individual motivation (of an ideological commitment, perhaps) move a woman to demand—or find friends who offer—influence-oriented marriage work, the effects of friends' collaboration may be very different: she may fight and win; his authority may be undermined; and her marriage work itself may be an organized power play. Although this pattern is not prevalent, for reasons discussed above, social changes some day may make it more widely applicable. In any case, it illustrates the double-edged quality and potential of women's patterns of intimate friendship.

Within the larger structure of gender power and authority, the prevalent pattern of marriage work has a parallel dynamic. Every exchange of marriage work among friends involves at least two women in a significant unfolding cultural exchange. One woman's act, a collectively generated accommodation or recommitment, entails the other's present moral consent and collaboration and obligates the woman to a future reciprocal exchange.

The resulting gender privileges go to the husband of the woman who acts and ultimately to the husbands of friends who participate in her decision. In this sense each husband benefits as an individual and as a member of a community of husbands—more abstractly, as a member of a gender-class. Private marital arguments resolved without the help of friends are influenced by a larger culture and structure of gender relations. Conflicts mediated by friends' marriage work, however, are more dynamically linked to a wide network that exchanges values legitimating male power and authority.

On this level, too, a contrasting process may unfold. Just as the individual example had a subversive version with transformative implications for the marriage, so this level has its countercultural version, heralding communal strategies of resistance to women's subordination in the family and in society. The extent to which women's friendship networks come to exchange the resources of resistance instead of adaptation depends on egalitarian change in women's economic and political position, and on arrangements to sustain families of women and children.

The women whom I interviewed talked about marriage problems with close friends. They did so, ultimately, to reinvigorate their own commitments to their marriages. Consulting with friends can give women help in changing their situations; they pool knowledge of influence and strategies; they implement their chosen courses with reason and confidence. In the accounts of the women I listened to, however, accommodative and self-changing strategies predominated. Women elicited—and their friends advocated—

marital strategies that posed less risk of escalating conflicts. In collective marriage work, women expressed anger and frustration; then they proceeded to rework their perceptions and feelings into more peaceable and adaptive modes.

Adaptive strategies are not the only modes of socialized marriage work: it has significant potential for communally supported resistance because it is a source of power that women have developed and men have not. Since men do not generally exchange intimate self-disclosure with friends, they lack this potentially vital communal exchange that women know.

And yet, without an intimate network that mediates conflicts in marriage, men are unlikely to engage in a communal discourse about responsibilities and commitments in marriage. They are socialized by more abstract and distant forces. To manage impulses, emotions, and perceptions in support of their marital commitment, husbands have only their mates to help them. Those who would establish in marriage a reign of aggressive impulse and will would encounter few communal sanctions. Regardless of its overt intent, the ethic of commitment in women friends' marriage work legitimates men's domestic authority; men's lack of a communal exchange bolsters their domestic power.

Chapter Six

Conclusion: Friendship and Community

Women's close friendships are an institution of personal life in which women find important emotional attachments, distinctive reflections of individual identity, and valued support for familial roles and commitments. In my interviews of twenty-one very different women, I heard accounts of friendships that, with few exceptions, would never fit the mold of emotionally shallow, morally insignificant relations cast by "decline of community" theory. Their friendships were unlike those of nineteenth-century middle-class women, enshrined in a culture of self-conscious romantic conventions. On the contrary, the women I spoke to had rarely even reflected on their friendships. Their statements about the quality and meaning of close friendship surprised them as much as they may have surprised some readers.

The women I interviewed sustained networks of close relationships with kin and friends. Within them, most had formed best friendships with women to whom they felt deeply and uniquely bonded. Women established bonds of best friendship by a mutual self-disclosure and empathy that most found unparalleled even in marriage. Some of the distinctiveness of this exchange lay in the willingness of friends to attend to the inner life and participate in another's emotions. Some of it lay in common experience, which they believed only other women could understand and dignify. Close friendships provided distinctive emotional gratifications, moral and intellectual engagement in critical life issues, and mutuality—values women said only their women friends could provide.

The intimacy and attachment of close friendship form part of the individual integration that is commonly assumed to take place only in family life. My research suggests that even though women do find unrivaled sources of personal integration in marriage and family, they conduct other relations of individuation and identity in intimate friendship. For many women, friends (and, to a lesser extent, women kin) are their primary support for individual aspiration and achievement.

The individuality that is positively recognized—constructed and enhanced—in friendship is a constrained individuality that is rooted in interdependence and communal responsibility. This responsibility applies to friends in the circumscribed obligations of close friendship; but primarily it applies to marriage and family. In several ways women's culture of friendship reinforces family commitments: the most subtle and important is its thorough subordination of the claims of friendship to those of marriage. By ethic and a complex array of practices, women friends make sure that the bonds of friendship never subvert the bonds of marriage. The harmony they sustain between the two spheres of deep attachments far exceeds that typically effected between strong attachments of kinship and nuclear family.

Women friends also devote a great deal of attention to problems of marriage and family—revealing, analyzing and strategizing private family matters. My research showed that best friends often direct their marriage work toward accommodation—women expect close friends to help them work out marriage problems, and the least risky solution is frequently accommodation and acceptance rather than conflictive struggle. As some evidence suggested, however, when a wife's social or marital position makes assertive marital problem solving less threatening, she can draw upon her close friendships as independent centers of emotional and moral support for her resistance or assertion.

I argued that historically, men and women have adapted affective individualism differently because of their differing social positions. I believe this is still true. Studies of men's friendships suggest that they reinforce a more individuated identity. Although they may reinforce marriage commitments, men's friendships employ very different values and exchanges in friendship. Eschewing self-disclosive intimacy as well as emotion management and marital problem solving, men's close attachments build through sociable camaraderie, task exchanges, and long familiarity. More often originating and taking place outside family contexts, in spheres of individual or nonfamilial collective achievement, they reinforce autonomous identities that are less rooted in the familial than women's are. Men's friendships may well reinforce familial commitment by an exchange of generalized social norms, but the exchange lacks both the explicitness and the power of personalized advice.

The Modernization of
Friendship and Marriage

My explorations of women's friendships and marriages provide a view of contemporary family and community that contradicts many scholarly accounts of the decline of community and the evolution of companionate marriage. My research suggests—but does not prove—a view of friendship and family that fits within the perspectives on the modernization of marriage and friendship I outlined in the opening chapter. Let me now situate my findings in that longer view of changes in family and friendship.

Modern friendship and marriage developed intertwined—infused by themes of affective individualism, mutuality, and romance. Nineteenth-century romantic friendships between women thrived because friendship ideals were practicable, whereas romantic companionate marriage was less practicable. As twentieth-century changes accelerated the companionship of men and women, romantic friendships withered. Even so, intimate friendships between women persisted. Indeed, they expanded as affective individualism spread to new sectors of society. In contrast to marriage, the reality of women's friendships outstrips the ideal.

Among contemporary women, friendships—most yet untouched by the sisterhood ideal of feminism—continue to grow in the shadow of the romantic companionate marital ideal. Women still need intimate women friends, and their friendships compensate the imbalance of conjugal ideals and realities. Further, intimate friendships among women provide the unfolding and oftentimes unique experience of mutual, empathic, intimate companionship that gives substance to the vision of communication, intimacy, and empathy that women hold for marriage.

The culture of women's friendship continues to nurture the companionate conjugal ideal for the same reasons it has for two centuries—dominant social values enshrine marriage; women need marriage for economic mobility; and the companionate ideal improves women's position in marriage. The romantic companionate marital ideal evolved in the nineteenth-century milieu of growing individualism and gender power difference. The individualism reflected a growing self-consciousness among middle-class women and a recognition that their survival depended on the volition and commitment of men—men who could survive quite well outside marriage. On the one hand, the ideal expressed newly tapped individualistic desires for self-development, emotional expression, and disclosive intimacy. On the other, it propounded a new set of interdependencies between husbands and wives, emphasizing mutual emotion over material dependence.

What may at first appear to be a contradictory stance—supporting an ideal as well as an accommodation to marriages that fall short of it—in fact reveals a consistency with women's interests in marriage. Women espouse an ideal that, if implemented, would improve their power and satisfaction in marriage. At the same time, women reinforce marriages that may represent the best chance of economic survival for them and for their children.

The modern culture of women's friendship took form within a nineteenth-century ideology of domesticity. Now, as then, women friends tend to focus their aspirations on adaptation and achievement in family life. From the eighteenth century until the middle of the twentieth, married women have carried out their friendships almost completely within the boundaries of private life. Since World War II, the increased participation of married women in the workforce has opened a workplace arena for friendships that could in theory emphasize the public (masculine) values of individualism, social achievement, and autonomy. But even workplace friendships still tend to channel women's aspirations back to private life.[1] In the low wages and scarce opportunities of the female employment ghetto, individual pursuits appear to offer perilous economic risks compared to a stable family life with a higher-earning partner.

Thus the friendships of married working women, like those of single working women of earlier eras, are likely to promote popular marriage ideals, commitments to stable marriages, and familial constraints on individual desires. Viewed in these terms, the accommodative emphasis in women's friendships contradicts neither the ideal of companionate marriage nor a widespread recognition of the gap between ideal and reality.

Beyond giving substance to a vision of marital intimacy, women's close friendships reduce the strain of the contradiction between that vision and the actuality of marriage. Responding to each other's needs for empathy, attended self-expression, and relational identity, women are able to limit their dissatisfaction and the potential risk of asserting these needs in marriage. This marriage work in friendship enabled the women I interviewed to report untroubled feelings about marriages of limited emotional intimacy.

Women's friendships defuse marital conflict in another way as well. Recognizing gender power differences, including women's material interests in marriage, women friends advocate strategies of marital accommodation and subtle influence; they discourage overt conflict and divorce. Even though the companionate ideal evolved as a modern vision of commitment, stability, and regeneration for an unstable marital system, individual attempts to implement the ideal often falter. In many marriages, stability still derives from traditional values of selflessness and duty, economic dependence, and passive emotional attachment. By reinforcing older values, particularly duty to children, women's friendships strengthen commitments in marriage that economic dependence alone might not ensure.

Another contribution friends make to marital adjustment and personal integration is their involvement with each other's children and with each other's identities as mothers. I propose that, like nineteenth-century women who forged an authoritative and dignified culture of motherhood in the social domain to which they were confined, contemporary friends conduct a female culture of motherhood in a domain still essentially their own. Providing this community of parenthood they also ease the strains on marriages that do not give such aid and recognition.

In most family sociology, the companionate ideal-type emphasizes the conjugal relationship as the unique site of "marital adjustment" and "adult personality stabilization."[2] As I noted previously, sociologists who analyze marital dynamics assume that as the marriage relationship became sentimentalized and emotionally primary, marriage and the family increasingly bounded the emotional lives of both women and men. These writers suggest the decline of kinship and community originally intensified the couple's emotional intimacy, but ultimately it is by its own internal dynamics that marriage comes to encompass the emotional lives of the partners and thus sustain commitment.[3]

I contend that marriage has never bounded the emotional lives of women. Women developed intimate friendships along with companionate marriages. In these friendships with other women they developed their emotional lives—in some eras, perhaps, more significantly than they did in relationships with men. As the companionate marriage ideal became more popular and more romantic, egalitarian, and empathic, women intensified their emotional investment in marriage. As they did, they relied increasingly on friendships for collaborative emotion management to sustain their emotional balance in marriage and their commitment to it. Thus, women conduct a considerable portion of what family theorists call "personality stabilization" and "marriage adjustment" within close friendships rather than marriage.

Women's friendships do accommodate women to strained marriages. But by serving as repository for marital ideals of reciprocity, emotional communion, and interdependent individuality, they do considerably more than accommodate some women to unequal, emotionally unsatisfying, and identity-submerging marriages. Friends' shared recognition of realities of gender power and their exchange of emotional self-awareness sustain a vision of gender power struggle and a strategic mode of thought about marriage. Writers like Christopher Lasch and Jean Elshtain have viewed such tendencies, as advocated by feminists, as a distorted or pseudo-politics. Yet I maintain that this befriended struggle constitutes a privately conducted politics of gender—not just "antagonism," as Lasch suggests, or manipulativeness and displaced public politics, as Elshtain suggests.[4]

The discourse that exposes gender inequality and erodes masculine authority has changed from nineteenth-century maternal piety to twentieth-century practical feminism ("I'm no women's libber, but . . ."). Yet it has kept consideration of the asymmetries of gender alive. At the same time that women friends' efforts to sustain marriage provide an example of time-consuming, energy-depleting women's work that men do not perform, they also create resources for women that men have not cultivated.

Close Friendship as Community

Do women's close friendships form community? If so, what kind of community? To answer these questions, I must begin with a conception of community rather than a knowledge of friendships. Above all, I do not wish to define community by simply summing up the positive dimensions of women's friendships. Doing so would cast this study in the tradition of evolutionary family theory that poses contemporary forms as the end of social evolution. Mine would be yet another cheerful network study that counters assertions of decline of community by asserting that modern sociability equals community. I would rather form a concept that preserves the deeper meanings present in traditional notions of community, a concept abstract enough to encompass as yet unforeseeable social changes that enlarge community. Defining community is difficult, however, even after centuries of exposition on the subject. I can do no more here than identify issues in conceptualizing community and suggest how my findings apply to them.

Most notions of community invoke premodern social organization—pastoral images of village, clan, parish, and neighborhood. Using these images, models of community inevitably emphasize corporateness, locality, permanence, and traditional authority. Claude Fischer condenses these notions into a sociological proposition about the affective and moral bases of community: "The more restricted their choice of associates, the more often and longer individuals must interact with, exchange with, and rely on a small number of people. Thus duration, interaction frequency, and material interdependence lead to communal ties."[5]

In this kind of communal perspective, dimensions like corporateness and locality have meaning because they limit the choices of community members and assure commitment through dependence. Fischer uses survey data from the 1950s and the 1970s to argue that these assumptions do not apply to modern community.

He concludes that in modern life, constraints that lead to localized, long-term, frequent, and multiplex relationships do not make these relationships intimate. On the contrary, with fewer structural restrictions on association people can choose relationships; their choices promote communal ties.[6]

Thomas Bender, among others, advances this argument along historical lines, citing an impressive array of historical scholarship that refutes the idealized image of community contained in much social theory. Traditional communities were not as stable, harmonious, intimate, or bountiful as the pastoral image suggests. Bender evokes Tönnies's emphasis on the persistence of community in modern society—of gemeinschaft in gesellschaft.[7] Theorists like Bender, Fischer, and Barry Wellman develop frameworks for modern forms of community and attempt to disengage a concept of community from traditional relations of corporate authority and constraint. Yet, in loosing the concept of community from these traditional restraints, the authors seem to drop the issue of communal constraint altogether. I think we should rework the component of moral constraint into our revised ideal-type of community.

Moral constraint is an important basis of commitment and the sustained experience of "we-feeling" that all writers identify in community. Shared moral values enable people to identify with and invest themselves in others and thus to build commitment; they deepen and extend relationships beyond self-interest. Moral bonds cognitively anchor emotional ones, steadying otherwise volatile attachments. They socialize relationships between self and social world and encourage people to act collectively. Moral constraint can lead to and strengthen communal resistance to larger authority, a communal attribute that contemporary writing on community must not ignore.

Robert Nisbet is a traditional theorist of community who insists on the importance of moral constraint. He both emphasizes moral authority and ties it to the social structures in which communities are embedded. Differentiating in theory two forms of constraint— social control and the constraint of shared values—he shows how they are tied in practice. Social control (in which a group functions to organize the individual's life and confer status) produces and maintains moral constraint. This is the communal dynamic of the preindustrial family, which determines the social roles its members will occupy and provides the skills to do so.[8] Nisbet's logic is undeniable. His premodern examples are too powerful, however, to allow him to imagine how less coercive communal functions might produce moral bonds. Nisbet calls for new forms of community rather than vain attempts to restore traditional forms, but he seems unable to imagine forms of dependence upon morally authoritative community that are not primordial, abject, or involuntary. My research suggests that women's close friendships show how moral constraint is generated in dependence expressed as voluntary mutual reliance on a relation that provides distinctive values. Women friends depend on the empathy and support they uniquely provide each other; they reciprocate and reinforce the moral constraint through their exchange on topics like motherhood and family obligations. The friendship creates a deep sense of meaning and belonging.

Nisbet similarly identifies the important communal attribute of mediating between the self and the society; but he focuses only on how communities mediate between individuals and public institutions. He insists—using the example of preindustrial family—that to be vital, communal structures must function directly in economic or political life.[9] But I propose that vital communities may also mediate between individuals and the institutions of private life, in the way that friendships mediate between women and their families. These communal functions are manifest to participants and generate moral authority, but their importance is in the realm of private life. Although such communal functions may not satisfy a full-blown ideal of community, they prefigure a more evolved community. Women's friendships hint at how more developed modern communities might evolve.

In spite of my disagreements with Nisbet's interpretation of the dynamics of community, I think his definition of communal relations remains useful:

[They] are characterized by a high degree of personal intimacy, emotional depth, moral commitment, social cohesion, and continuity in time. . . . Community . . . draws its psychological strength from levels of motivation deeper than those of mere volition or interest, and it achieves its fulfillment in a submergence of individual will that is not possible in unions of mere convenience or rational assent.[10]

How do women's close friendships satisfy this definition? The quality of intimacy and emotional exchange in close friendships easily meets this standard. The ties in each woman's small network of close relations outside the nuclear family are deeply affectionate, psychologically intimate, and emotionally secure. Women's best friendships develop mutual attentiveness and knowledge to an extent probably unparalleled in women's other close relations or in any of men's close ties. In this area of intimacy and attachment, women's best friendships may be exceptionally communal.

Commitment—an investment of self in a relationship—also characterizes close friendship. Women claim a subjective sense of commitment in close friendships, and they often report their beliefs have been confirmed by friends' sacrifices. Moreover, these commitments project continuity in time, and friendships endure separation. Friendships do, however, subordinate their obligations to those of family, which affects their commitments in significant ways. Commitments between women friends include mutable and even terminable bonds. Friends may not be able to sustain commitments if, for example, they have prior commitments to moving with husbands to new jobs. Committed friends understand that each other's ability to share resources of time, shelter, and money may be limited by superseding obligations to family. In traditional community, commitments to church, family, and village were permanent or long-term and fit together in a smoother, ideologically ordered pattern. Contemporary life refutes such permanence and order. And women may be restrained by their economic dependence on marriage from forming commitments that men can form with impunity.

Theories that define community in terms of permanence and locality imply that modern commitments must build over considerable time. But not all communal relations form the same way. My research suggests that the time required to form commitment in women's close friendship is different from that needed to form other commitments. The women I interviewed seemed to be quick to identify potential intimates, willing to disclose themselves to these attractive others, and thus able to attach and commit quickly. Of course it takes time to seal trust; but intimate self-disclosure, one of women's shared standards of commitment, binds friendships much faster than commitment that builds through long sociable association or the exchange of services (the pattern that studies of men's friendships suggest).

This capacity to form close friendship quickly has several implications. It probably assures women of close communities when they meet potential friends. In my interviews, women never expressed dismay at the prospect of having to find new friends, as they did when considering how they would meet men if they were no longer married. If women generally form close friendships more quickly than men, they can more quickly rebuild their close communities after moves, divorces, and deaths of friends or partners. Women's communal activity is resilient.

Because the intimate exchange of women's friendship satisfies deeply felt needs, including the desire for empathetic understanding—and because women *recognize* their dependence on friends and on the values of friendship—they experience in friendship a sense of belonging that may be distinctive to women's culture. Their profound reciprocal understanding and their recognition of a need for close relations create moral commitment. The sense of belonging must surely be much more tenuous if friends are loathe to admit such need and dependence. If men friends are both less intimate and less likely to acknowledge dependence, they are probably less likely to sustain the experience of belonging, particularly if time and trouble have not tried their commitment.

Women's close friendships are invested with moral obligations, both to respect individual liberty and to attend to each other's welfare and their children's. Friends' valuation of individual liberty (and also an aversion to conflict, which has other sources) appears to keep the scope of moral authority (if not discourse) narrow in most friendships. Some areas of conduct are subject to moral constraint and some are not. Nonetheless, that constraint applies to areas friends consider most important and that are grounds of common experience.

The area that women friends have significantly opened to moral exchange is childrearing. All of the mothers I interviewed discussed children and childrearing with friends in a way that communicated moral values and influence. This dialogue among women friends who are mothers seems to me to represent an unheralded example of vital community. It is unheralded because conventional studies focus on the nuclear family as the community of childrearing. Moreover, an intelligent but limited analysis of the penetration of expert authority into family life fails to perceive any process of communal authority able to mediate that influence.[11]

Writings on the family and social authority do not discuss the networks of exchange on childrearing that this study has discovered. The exchange among friends who are mothers not only solidifies trust and commitment in friendship, it also creates communities of resistance to social authority. Women friends discuss problems, values, and practices of childrearing, recognizing in each other the authoritative knowledge gained from experience that is undervalued and unattended in the larger social organization of honor and prestige. They recognize that childrearing is difficult and complex skill-developing work. They respect the knowledge and integrity of those who sacrifice to do it. And, in this process, they confer authority upon their network community of mother-friends, authority that they draw upon for sustenance and dignity. This exchange is far from impervious to outside influence; and it can, I am sure, serve as a conduit of expert influence.* Even so, outside authority is mediated by a discussion among mothers who recognize the authority of other mothers. They do not constitute a well-defended and unchanging community but one capable of change through dialogue and mutual adjustment.

We can also see evidence of communally generated resistance to authority in the relation between women's friendships and their marriages. Even in friendships in which the values of marriage translate into accommodative marriage work, the dialogue of friendship augments individual capacities for resistance to male authority. Because women friends analyze their relationships and strategize together, they collect knowledge on the dynamics of women's domestic subordination. When they subsequently accommodate, they are likely to do so instrumentally rather than passively—a tactical withdrawal rather than a rout. This process preserves a capacity for resistance that can be drawn on when resistance might succeed. The women's stories of marriage work

---

*The authors of *Crestwood Heights* show this process but do not distinguish between the deference women accord experts and their actual childrearing practices (John R. Seeley, R. Alexander Sim, and E. W. Loosley, *Crestwood Heights* [New York: Basic Books, 1956]).

illustrate many collectively plotted small resistances, often in the form of power plays for small advantages.

It is easy to imagine friends developing grander strategies to increase domestic power and authority when changing circumstances favor their success or decrease the costs of failure. When marriage represents most women's only opportunity to provide decently for their children, when women's opportunities to establish new heterosexual relationships decrease dramatically with age, when married women friends are powerless to share their material means of survival, the costs of resistance can be high. But when close friends provide support for struggle or provide emotional sustenance that enables emotional withdrawal from marriage, and when friends keep a vision of mutualistic companionate love alive (in ideals and by example), they undermine male domestic authority—even when they cannot radically erode men's power.

I do not wish to overstate the capacity for resistance to larger authority implicit in women's personal communities. Personal communities are not social movements. Women's friendships concentrate in private life and have their greatest communal impact there. Women have been excluded politically and economically from public life, and their ability to participate in public associations is limited by their domestic responsibilities. So, although friendships provide chains of recruitment into public life,* we would have to see a lifting of constraints on participation (in the form of child care, greater sharing of domestic responsibility) before a strong civil orientation occupies the dialogue of women friends. Men, who are freer to participate in public life, may be more oriented to public issues in their friendships.

What kind of community inheres in women's close friendships? Women's friendships create personal community—elective, essentially dyadic, intimate, oriented to mutual self-development and individual needs, and concentrating on the activities of personal life. Yet the benefits of women friends' community extend beyond

---

*Note how frequently working-class women, never before active in politics, have organized neighborhood networks to protest against toxic dumps that threatened their families' welfare. I have argued elsewhere that friendship networks rather than political outreach shaped many feminist organizations in the seventies (Oliker, "Sociology of Women," lectures presented at the Department of Sociology, University of California, Berkeley [Spring 1984]).

pairs of friends. Women's friendships influence their family lives, absorbing and transmuting tensions that originate in marriage and parenthood, recreating commitment, helping to effect change. They function very much like the "intermediate institutions" that theorists of community see mediating between the individual (or family) and larger social authority.

A woman's friendships mediate between the individual and her family, serving both her personal integration and the integration of her commitments to friends, kin, and family. Just as Nisbet's pre-industrial family manifestly served individuals in the larger society and in doing so created legitimacy for its authority, women's friendships manifestly serve women in the family. And in their evident importance, women's friendships also generate authority. The distinctive communal content of women's close friendships lies in their contribution to individual identity and needs and to women's family responsibilities. Through these valued exchanges, moral commitment and constraint evolve.

Most writers on modern community—both pro and con—agree that traditional community is gone and cannot be restored amid individualism, centralized authority, geographic mobility, and family privatization. Women's friendships contain elements of community not captured either by antimodernist sociological images of traditional community or by modernists' narrower images of community as intimacy or sociability. Beyond providing the bonds of psychological intimacy, women's close friendships forge, exchange, and preserve moral values that contradict rationalized, impersonal, instrumental, and individualistic values in the dominant culture. The structures of authority inherent in personal communities of women are difficult to delineate because they are informal and fluid. Personal communities of friends are generally loose networks of pairs and are therefore less cohesive and more subject to the idiosyncrasies of "dyadic withdrawal."[12] Nonetheless, women's personal communities generate authority that inheres in the unique and important contributions friends make—to satisfy needs generated by social structures that friendships both accommodate and resist.

The moral framework of modern women's friendships is radically different from that of traditional community. Friendships value voluntarism, mutability, and fluidity, which render their influence less absolute, more assailable, less punitively constraining, more (fallibly) porous and negotiable, and less directly and serviceably political than those of traditional community. In contrast, modern women's personal communities bind individuals without submerging individuality; sustain and reconstruct loyalty by a substantive rationality of befriended decision-making; and remain resilient and evolutionary by adapting to conditions of necessity while preserving transformative ideals and relations. They synthesize old values and new.

I do not intend to suggest that contemporary women's friendships offer a sufficient model of elective community. They are very loose networks of pairs and they contain many distorted reflections of women's powerlessness. Still, the quest for a vision of community whose benefits are ample and justly distributed requires a move beyond both premodern and extreme individualist conceptions. Contemporary women's friendships may suggest the makings of such a modern communal ideal.

Toward a More Inclusive Study of Women's Friendships

There is much more we need to know about friendships before we can evaluate them as community. My interviews with married women suggest that close friendships tend to buttress marriages and women's commitments to them. My few interviews with divorced women suggest that close friends labored to shore up their marriages until the divorce decision; then friends provided the emotional support and material aid (mostly child care) that helped them sustain lives outside marriage. Further study will have to examine whether and how married friends help women live through and work through divorce. What kinds of community do close friends provide divorced women, who now include the vastly increasing numbers of divorced women rearing children? How do friendships respond to the economic and emotional setbacks of divorce and to the asymmetries that such change introduces into friendship?

Future studies should also consider the friendships of single women, as the rate of single households among women increases and as more women defer marriage. Single women also balance commitments between close women friends and romantic attachments. Do their "rules of relevance" differ from married women's? Do they effect the same harmony between the two spheres of attachment? Do they exchange different kinds of support? My interviews with women not married and with wives talking about their single days suggest that single close friends have more rights to request a friend's time, shelter, and money and to criticize boyfriends and advise conflictive struggle. They also suggest more competition and bad feeling between the two spheres of commitment.

Interviews with single lesbians and women in lesbian couples would add a dimension absent from this research. Some intentional lesbian communities place strong moral emphasis on friendship.[13] Among these intentional, self-conscious communities of friends or among groups of feminists who have revived romantic friendship, we might learn how the cultural recognition of friendship's community affects that community. Studying lesbian friends would also let us separate issues of gender power and conflict from other issues of power and conflict in personal life. Thus, it would be an important viewpoint on gender stratification, as men's friendships would be.

Close friendships are only one kind of friendship. Sociable friendships, co-participation in organizations, and workplace collegiality all have benefits worth examining. I mention them here to evoke a wider picture of community and to remind the reader that the relations I have been describing are not women's friendships in general, but relations with best friends and others to whom women feel closest. Yet intimacy may be an overemphasized element of community. Intimacy creates burdens as well as blessings. The stresses that accompany emotional dependence and support may fray the looser bounds of modern community.[14] Other kinds of friendship may be more stabilizing or more satisfying in certain ways. The more distanced relations of sociability and civility may play more important roles in individual well-being and communal evolution than most modern conceptions of community suggest.[15]

Further studies of friendship and community should look more closely at the effects of the social roles women are increasingly undertaking, such as full-time jobs and careers, and political participation. Immersion in a career may inhibit the exchanges characteristic of the female friendships I identified. Such structures may affect patterns of friendship regardless of women's felt needs for intimacy and attachment. Lucrative and absorbing careers of the sort that still occupy few women today may shift resources in marriage and emphases in friendship. (Professional women who read this study commented that their close friendships are not as accommodation-oriented as those of the less occupationally privileged women I interviewed.) Political participation might introduce more civil issues into the conversation of friends. It might also expand, diversify, and loosen networks in ways that influence friendship practices. I interviewed a number of employed women (most of them in jobs rather than careers); but I mention them in this call for further research to remind the reader once again that hypotheses generated in exploratory research must be subjected to more conclusive methods. Such scholarship may contribute to an increasing recognition among women of the meaning of their close friendships. And this recognition may itself strengthen community among friends.

I have not answered two questions about friendship and marriage that people take great interest in: do differences in friendship and intimacy between men and women derive from gender differences in personality? can husbands and wives become each other's best friends? Although my study cannot answer whether or not gender differences in intimacy reflect deep differences in personality, I have found it worth exploring structural sources of differences that appear to be rooted in personality. Position in society and family may provide clues as to why certain intimacies like attentiveness and empathy, for example, may be preferred and practiced by some more than others—why they may be structured preferences rather than differential capacities. Nonetheless, my findings on women's friendships, and others on men's friendships, leave plenty of room for proposing deep gender personality differences that shape intimacy.

On the question of whether men and women can become each other's best friends, I am certain that some readers have already drawn pessimistic conclusions. And some may have taken this study as evidence that best friendships impede women's efforts to establish marital intimacy. Must we dim widespread hopes that men and women can struggle toward emotional intimacy and mutuality? My research offers no such implication. The women I interviewed often seemed to use intimate friendship to avoid the effort, disappointment, or risk involved in struggle in this area; nothing in my interviews indicates that a more direct strategy could not work. The women I interviewed generally did not see their limited marital intimacy as a major problem. Their reliance on best friends for certain kinds of intimacy tells us little about the chances of success for those women who do consider increased intimacy in marriage worth struggling for. Of those women who had tried to deepen marital intimacy or who had considered doing so, most believed their friends had helped them. Their belief does suggest that women's best friendships may further rather than impede such an effort; but nothing in my data indicates whether the effort can work. If there are reasons for pessimism over achieving contemporary companionate ideals of marriage, they will have to be drawn from a study of people who have actively pursued these ideals.[16] Good structural analyses should clarify patterns of accommodation without prescribing hopelessness.

I conclude that close friendship deserves recognition as a vital institution of private life. Women's close friendships are mutualistic, intimate, durable, and committed. They enmesh women in significant relations of individuation and community. They provide distinctive sources of interdependent individual identity and support for family commitment. If it is true that women have developed a form of community that men have not, then women may have accumulated resources to use with men in their struggles toward dignity, mutuality, and equality in marriage.

And yet sources of personal strength do not translate into significant social change without material or ideological means of organization. Mary Ryan, analyzing how nineteenth-century women translated sisterhood into public influence, commented on the paradoxical impact of effort that cemented women's domesticity as it manifested women's public power. Acting on their perceived interests as mothers, women organized to shape family values and public practices in ways that enforced the division between men's public roles and women's private ones. For Ryan, nineteenth-century sorority raises questions as to "whether women's cultural and female networks, which continue to be rooted largely in the relations of housewives and mothers, can generate much more than reflexive and defensive, rather than critical, responses to social and familial change."[17] My work appears to raise the same issue: autonomous networks of best friendships also seem to enforce marital accommodation. However, I believe our answer to this issue does not depend on whether the bonds among women exist in public or private networks. Feminists are realizing that they can and must organize women as wives and mothers, and they are reaching for a politics that bridges the gulf between private and public structures. How women use their networks depends not so much on their content per se as on the correspondence between women's public and private experience, and on the political, economic, and ideological resources available to women. It is from among them that women can gather resources and visions of change. Women's networks foster accommodation, survival, *and* resistance—the balance is struck in negotiations involving public experience as well as private life.

Appendix A:
Methods of Research

Extending the discussion I began in the introduction, this appendix describes elements of my method of research on contemporary women's friendships and marriage: respondents I interviewed, interview design, and problems of inquiry and inference that I encountered with this exploratory method (the interview schedule is reproduced in appendix B).

After open-ended "pre-test" interviews with men and women, I collected references from associates acquainted with women outside the sphere of university influence. My associates knew that friendship was the topic of my study. When I asked them for names, I told them I was looking for "ordinary" women; I stressed that I did not prefer especially sociable women, that I would like "just the first people who come to mind" who fit a set of characteristics—a few combinations of class, race, age, and life-cycle stage. Only two of twenty-three women I contacted declined to be interviewed. The women represented a range of statuses, personalities, and styles of friendship. Yet each seemed very much like others of her kind whom I have known in other places and times. This is no representative sample, of course, but it includes a variable range of women (which I described in the introduction).

In designing the interview, I standardized both questions and format across the interviews (in appendix B). I wanted to make it possible for others to replicate this study. I also wanted strong results, assuming that often-repeated themes would allow me to make more precise and confident theories. Finally, my standardized questions permitted maximum intrusion with maximum ethical control. I believed that a free-form discussion about the very intimate areas of friendship and marriage could easily range beyond areas where my subjects felt comfortable. Long experience in interviewing people about marriage has taught sociologists that many individuals are uneasy talking about sex and money. No comparable lore points to topics of intimate friendship that could cause discomfort or distress. By considering the ethics of each question as I developed it, I hoped to save myself the self-consciousness and distraction of constant ethical conundrums, and instead pay full attention to the woman I was interviewing.

As it turned out, the questions I developed worked very well from the beginning. Initial interviews prompted me to add and subtract a few questions, but I successfully used the remainder with all the respondents. Occasionally, I rephrased a question to be certain I understood the meaning it had for the woman I was interviewing. The answers convinced me that my questions were consistently interpreted by the variety of women I interviewed. To treat the related problem of internal reliability, I repeated some questions as the interview progressed.

Exploratory methods do not produce generalizable conclusions but, especially in an unexplored area, these methods can probe patterns and meanings that more conclusive methods are likely to miss. My favorite example derives from a criticism I received for "confounding" kinship and friendship by accepting some women's choice of sisters as best friends. My critic's suggestion to separate friendship from other kinds of primary relationships was perfectly appropriate. It alerted me to explain (in discussing close networks in chapter 3) how I discovered that women who call sisters best friends are describing relationships that, in important ways, are more like others' best friendships than they are like their own and others' sibling relationships. Had I begun by isolating friendship from kinship, I would have found that many women of few means and large families do not have best friends. But that is far from true. An exploratory method, which allowed careful probing for the unexpected, suggested that some women are more likely to select sisters as best friends, and that these relationships are properly considered best friendships as well.

My research design did leave problems of inquiry and inference, however. I describe these limitations here, to accomplish a second task as well: to remind the reader that the goal of this research is hypothesis-generation and invite a more conclusive investigative sequel.

I begin with a gaping problem of design: the missing men. It is surely obvious that a motivating interest in this research is gender difference and stratification; yet I interviewed only women. My goal of digging deep into the substance of women's friendships is well served by this focus.

But when the revelations about women prompt comparison with men's friendships, I am forced either to call forth evidence from other research—almost none of which is strictly comparable—or to rely on women's beliefs about men's friendships. I find it provocative to do both, but I remind the reader that nowhere in this work are the subjective voices of men.

Second, there is the risk of geographical fallacy: are Californians an American group? I did not aim at a random or representative sample; I selected respondents with a variety of characteristics that I believed would evoke a range of American women. I sampled heavily in two small cities, one suburb, an unincorporated area much like a small town, and finally, a large city. Although all Californians are reputed to have arrived here from somewhere else, about half of my respondents grew up in or near the city where our interview took place (one-fourth of them lived in the town where they grew up; another fourth, less than an hour's drive away; the number of those who had moved within the past five years was just below the national average of 20 percent).[1] Also defying the California stereotype, among the twenty ever-married women, the ratio of married to divorced women conformed to the national average. A slightly higher than average number of married women were in their first marriages (in 1977, 80 percent of all married couples were in their first marriages).[2]

I interviewed eighteen white and three black women, but not Hispanic or Asian women, who would have given this sample a richer California verity. I did, however, interview several women of southern white ancestry, a populous California ethnic minority; most of them were second-generation Californians. California has many of the clerical, service, electronics-assembly, and seasonal-agricultural industries that draw female labor forces. Exaggerating these peculiarities of the California labor market, employed women were vastly overrepresented in my sample. So were women with some community college education, which I believe is more pervasive among middle- and working-class Californians because of the state's large, accessible, and, until recently, free community college system. Rather than being representative, my sample reflected a variety of American women's experiences, emphasizing those— like work and higher education—that women, in general, are increasingly undertaking. Some characteristics of my twenty-one respondents may be summarized as follows:

Age		*Marital status*	
20–29	5	Single (never married)	1
30–39	10	Divorced (now single)	3
40–59	6	Married	17

Education
High school	6
Some college (including community college)	11
B.A.	2
M.A.	2

Family status
No children	2
At least one child under age 6	9
All children age 6 or older (at home)	5
All adult children	5

Employment
Not employed, not seeking job	4
Unemployed, seeking job	2
Employed part-time	7
Employed full-time	8

Most recent occupation
Pink-collar professional, administrative	3
Semi-skilled technical; skilled service, clerical	6
Low-skilled technical; semi-skilled service, clerical	9
Unskilled service	3

Husband's most recent occupation
Professional, executive managerial	2
Small business; middle-managerial; skilled industrial, technical sales	8
Semi-skilled industrial, sales	5
Unskilled service or production	2

My sampling method introduced systematic biases. By securing names from contacts who knew respondents, I began with a sample of women who were unlikely to be extremely isolated: somebody I knew, knew them. In general, I did not "snowball" sample (that is, interview people whom previous respondents identified) in order to avoid tapping networks of shared values or friendship cultures. I hoped instead to tap a variety of such values and avoid the demographic similarity that is a well-established characteristic of personal networks.[3]

Still, I chose to snowball sample three times. Twice, I interviewed best friends, to see if comparing friends' testimonies would prove fruitful. In one case, I interviewed two ardent, relatively new, best friends. In another case I interviewed the sister of one respondent, whom the respondent considered her best friend. The sister did not reciprocate the designation, however. So only one pair in my sample exaggerated the strength of some results by adding a second identical response to some questions. The variation among responses that should have been identical hints at the latitude a researcher must allow in factual self-reports. I compensated for these few parallel accounts when I described my findings in qualitative terms, but I did not adjust numbers when I counted responses. In the third case, I snowball sampled when a respondent who was particularly interested in the project thought of an acquaintance who fitted a number of characteristics I had been unsuccessfully seeking in a respondent. I saw no effect from this particular snowball.

Finally, I noted an interactive bias: it was much easier to establish a productive rapport with and ultimately "get to know" women who had very close friends. I do not wish to exaggerate this point for, with one possible exception, I was gratified to establish a comfortable trust and rapport with the women I interviewed. Still, women who engaged in very close friendships were practiced at endowing trust and sharing personal experience in a way that enabled me to glean a wealth of understanding in a relatively short period. I think this distinction did not significantly affect my conclusions, yet it is a methodological issue worth considering.

I would certainly expect interactive effects when interviewing on a topic like friendship. However loose its normative structure, friendship itself is widely considered a moral good. How could I interview people on this topic, asking them for all kinds of details about their friendships and their feelings about friends, without encouraging them to describe themselves favorably as people who have done and generally do what is good? I will describe the steps I took to limit this tendency, but I believe that only the addition of an unobtrusive method (some kind of hidden observation) would resolve doubts about this problem.

I did not introduce my project as a study of friendship. In my introductory letter, I stated I was conducting "a study of the everyday lives of Americans. The purpose . . . is to learn how friends, relatives, and family fit into the lives of people in various communities." In this way I was able to secure consent to the kind of interview I would conduct, without labeling my central interest. I began my interview with open-ended ambiguous questions about self, family, and friends and then moved to more pointed and specific questions. Occasionally, these unfocused questions elicited attitudes and feelings that women downplayed in more focused contexts. Such questions often made it easier to identify less "approved" themes in more defensively phrased answers. Finally, I asked a series of questions about how people "in general" conduct or feel about friendships. This left an opening for respondents to project inadmissible feelings they would not wish to claim for themselves.

My assessment of this last source of distortion is that it was not great, although I believe it was a faint and elusive note. For the most part, what could have been trite descriptions or sentiments led to detailed accounts of those experiences that proved them spontaneous and sincere and utterly defied a judgment of artificial or forced production. I frequently tested responses by asking for more details; my confidence in the sincerity of answers also grew every time one expressed an attitude that countered my own beliefs or expectations.

One aspect of my research strategy probably limited my findings. I was especially reluctant to probe areas that made women uneasy. At the outset I decided that before I intruded into areas that triggered unease I would have to know much more about the meaning of women's friendships. This is another way in which these interviews must be considered exploratory. I wanted to detect signs of perilous territory in friendships and carefully map the dynamics of friendships for further considerate investigation. A quick "No" that I interpreted to mean "Caution here!" may have indicated a simple moment of impatience rather than a wish to avoid the subject. Next time I might follow a "No" to a question like, Can you think of a time with your best friend when you felt you'd just "had enough"? with probes like, Never? I preferred to conduct a delicate first inquiry, accepting only that which women willingly offered.

Because it is a first inquiry on the relation between women's friendships and marriage, and because friendship has been studied so little, I would have considered a study of just about any size or method to be exploratory. Small-sample in-depth interviews allowed me to probe meanings in culture and dynamics of friendship; this would have been much more difficult with other methods. The same strategies that limited the generalizability of my conclusions opened avenues to new theory. If I have been successful, it is because my methods enabled me to explore some issues in depth and to organize observations on friendship and marriage into theory that will invite future research and that more conclusive methods will modify. The study of friendship is just beginning. In introducing it to sociological considerations of social structures in personal life, I aimed to make it theoretically fruitful.

Appendix B: Interview

Among these questions that make up my interview, some come from the Northern California Communities Study, conducted in 1977 by Claude S. Fischer, University of California, Berkeley.

1. How long have you lived in this neighborhood?
2. How long have you lived in this town?
3. Where did you live when you were growing up?
4. Tell me a little about yourself.
5. Would you tell me all the names of the people who live in this household—adults and children.
   Is this person male or female?
   How is [   ] connected to you? How old is [   ]?
   How long have you known [   ]?
   Is [   ] single, married, divorced, separated, or widowed?
   Is [   ] working? Part-time or full-time?
6. Who are the people you'd describe as most a part of your life?
7. (If single:) Do you have a fiancé or a special friend you're dating or seeing a lot of? (Name)
8. Tell me a little about your [husband, boyfriend, companion].
9. Tell me a little about your family [or kin].
10. Tell me a little about your friends.
11. Do you have any immediate family—parents, children, brothers, sisters, in-laws—living in this area, say within an hour's drive from here? How many?
12. Counting all your relatives (and your partner's relatives, if you

think of them as kin), about how many adult relatives live in this area?

13. How often do you visit or go out with someone who's a relative?
14. How many relatives do you think of as friends?
15. Do you ever visit with or go out with someone who's a neighbor? How often?
16. (If yes:) How many of your neighbors do you think of as friends?

(If respondent has job:)

17. What kind of work do you do? (Do you have more than one job?)
18. What are your working hours?
19. How many others work in the same office or work space?
20. Are any of them doing exactly the same job that you do?
21. How long have you been working there?
22. Some people don't talk about work—either on or off the job. Others discuss, with co-workers, friends, or family, things like work problems, or daily work events, or feelings about work. Is there anyone you talk with about your work? Who?

23. In the last three months, have you visited with anyone at your home or theirs, or gone out with anyone for a meal or a movie, or some other recreation? May I have the first names of these people?
24. (If in couple:) Do you and [partner] ever go out with or get together with other couples? What are the names of these couples? (For each couple:) How did you meet them? Who usually arranges these social times?
25. When you are concerned about a personal matter—for example, about someone you're close to or something you're worried about—how often do you talk about it with someone: usually, sometimes, or hardly ever?
26. When you do talk with someone about personal matters, with whom do you talk?
27. Sometimes people turn to others for advice in making important decisions about their lives—for example, decisions about relationships, family, or work. Is there anyone whose advice or opinion you consider seriously in making important decisions? Who?

(Record the following responses on a matrix:)

28. To whom would you say you feel closest? I'm going to write down their first names. (List names on matrix.)
    Anyone you feel closest to, whether they're nearby or far away?
    Are there any others you would say you feel closest to?

(For each name on list:)

29. Is this person male or female?
30. How is this person connected to you?

31. How long have you known her/him?
32. How did you first meet?
33. How old is she/he?
34. Is she/he single, married, divorced, separated, or widowed?
35. How often do you see her/him?
36. How long does it take to drive to her/his home?
37. How often do you talk on the phone?

(Show respondent the matrix.)

38. Some people are connected in a number of ways. They may be relatives and neighbors, or neighbors and co-workers. (Card lists categories of relation.) What are all the ways [name on list] is connected to you?
39. Do any of these people work? Is that part-time or full-time?
40. Do any of these people do the same kind of work as you? (or) Are any of these people full-time homemakers?
41. Do you have a religion? (If not:) Were you brought up in a religion?
42. (If yes:) Are any of these people also [religion]?
43. Some people describe themselves by their race, ethnicity, or national background. How would you describe yourself?
44. Are any of these people also [race/ethnicity]?
45. Is there any particular activity—like a club, association, sport, or spare-time interest—that you devote time to or find especially interesting?
46. Are any of these people also involved in [activity]?
47. Are any of these people in about the same income level as you?

48. Thinking of everyone you know, is there *one person* you feel closest to?
49. (If husband/boyfriend/parent/child:) Other than [   ], is there one person you feel closest to?
50. Can you tell me a little about [closest person]?
51. Would you say [closest person] is your best friend?
52. (If not:) Do you have a best friend? Can you tell me a little. . . .
53. Why did you become close friends with [closest friend]?
54. What do you like best or find most special about [closest friend]?
55. Can you think of areas you can talk about with [closest friend] that you can't discuss as well with your husband/boyfriend?
56. Are there some things you could tell [closest friend] that you wouldn't discuss *at all* with your husband/boyfriend?
57. Can you think of areas you can talk about with your husband/boyfriend that you can't discuss as well with [closest friend]?
58. Are there some things you could tell [husband/boyfriend] that you wouldn't discuss *at all* with [closest friend]?

59. (a) How does your husband/boyfriend feel about [closest friend]? Would you say he likes her, dislikes her, or doesn't feel either way?
    (b) Would you say he approves of your friendship, disapproves, or doesn't feel either way?
    (c) Is there anything about your friendship that he disapproves of?
60. (a) Do you trust [best friend]?
    (b) Why? How did you come to trust her?
    (c) Did anything ever happen to make you feel special trust? Did she ever do or say anything that made you especially trust her?
    (d) Has she ever done anything that made you trust her less?
61. (a) Can you think of a time that [best friend] disappointed you? What happened?
    (b) How did you feel?
    (c) At the time, how did you think you should feel?
    (d) Did that experience change your feelings about her in any way?
62. How does [closest friend] feel about [husband/boyfriend]? Would you say she likes him, dislikes him, or doesn't feel either way?
63. Is there anything about your marriage/relationship with your boyfriend that she disapproves of?
64. Have you ever been good friends with someone [husband/boyfriend] disliked or disapproved of? Can you tell me a little about that?
65. Has [husband/boyfriend] ever tried to discourage one of your friendships?
66. In general when you talk over a difficulty or disagreement with [husband/boyfriend], how often have you talked about it first with a friend or someone close: a lot of the time, some of the time, once in a while, or never?
67. Think back to the last time you and [husband/boyfriend] talked over a big difficulty or disagreement. Had you discussed it beforehand with anyone? Who?
68. What are some ways that your friends have helped you when you had difficulties with your husband/boyfriend?
69. Can you think of a time when talking with your friends changed your attitude toward your husband/boyfriend?
70. Can you think of a time when talking with your friends changed your feelings about a dispute or disagreement with your husband/boyfriend?

71. Can you think of some ways [closest friend] has helped you keep your marriage/relationship together?

72. If [closest friend] asked you to keep secret something you really wanted to share with your husband/boyfriend, how would you deal with that?

73. If [husband/boyfriend] asked you to keep secret something you really wanted to share with [closest friend], how would you deal with that?

74. (a) Have you and [husband/boyfriend] ever disagreed about where or when you ought to be able to go out with a friend or what you ought to be able to talk about?

    (b) Have you ever disagreed about [closest friend]?

75. (a) Have you ever felt you had to choose between [husband/boyfriend] and [closest friend]?

    (b) Have you ever felt you had to choose between your family and your friend?

    (c) (If yes to [b]:) How often do you feel you have to choose between your family and your friend: a lot of the time, some of the time, or once in a while?

76. How do you keep your obligations toward your friend from competing with your obligations to your family/relationship with [boyfriend]?

77. (a) Can you think of a time when friends ever tried to "talk you into" feeling better about [husband/boyfriend]—that is, when they've been more positive toward him than you were?

    (b) (If yes to [a]:) How often does this happen: a lot of the time, some of the time, or once in a while?

78. (a) Can you think of a time when friends ever tried to "talk you into" feeling worse about [husband/boyfriend]—that is, when they've been more negative toward him than you were?

    (b) (If yes to [a]:) How often does this happen: a lot of the time, some of the time, or once in a while?

79. When problems are on your mind, how often do you talk about it with friends: a lot of the time, some of the time, once in a while, or never?

    (a) problems raising children
    (b) problems in the marriage
    (c) how to talk to [husband/boyfriend] about something
    (d) marital sex life
    (e) problems with work
    (f) feelings of unhappiness
    (g) (*not used*)

(h) future dreams and ambitions
(i) feelings that family or household makes too many demands on you
(j) financial difficulties
(k) problems with other friends
(l) feelings of anger
(m) feelings about love
(n) your husband's job or work
(o) opinions about the news or politics
(p) feelings of self-doubt
(q) moral or religious beliefs

80. (a) Can you think of some kinds of things you care about or need from a relationship that only your women friends provide?
     (b) Do these things make your marriage/relationship with your boyfriend work more smoothly; do they interfere; both; or neither?

81. (a) What are the kinds of things you care about or need from a relationship that only a husband/boyfriend can provide?
     (b) If you weren't married/in a relationship with [boyfriend], to whom would you look for these things?

82. (a) Has there ever been a time during your marriage/relationship with your boyfriend when you had no close women friends?
     (b) How did you feel about that?
     (c) Did marriage satisfy your needs for friendship?
     (d) How did this affect your marriage/relationship with [boyfriend]?
     (e) Did you feel anything was missing from your life? How did you think you should feel?
     (f) (not used)
     (g) Do you think your marriage/relationship benefited in any way?
     (h) Do you think your marriage/relationship was harmed in any way?
     (i) Who became your first close friend after that period?
     (j) How did you meet?
     (k) How was your daily life affected by this friendship?
     (l) How much time did you spend together?
     (m) Did your daily routines change?
     (n) How did this new friendship affect your state of mind at the time?
     (o) Did you tell your husband/boyfriend about your new friendship?
     (p) How did this new friendship affect your marriage/relationship

with your boyfriend? How did it affect your feelings about [husband/boyfriend]?

(q) How did [husband/boyfriend] react to your new friendship?

(r) Can you think of ways your marriage/relationship benefited from your new friendship?

(s) Can you think of ways your marriage/relationship was harmed by your new friendship?

83. (If married:) If your marriage ended, what do you feel your biggest problems would be as an unmarried person?

(If has boyfriend:) If your relationship with [boyfriend] ended, what do you feel your biggest problems would be as a single person?

(If divorced:) When your marriage ended, what were your biggest problems as an unmarried person?

84. (If married/boyfriend:) How do you think your friends would react? (Would they feel or behave differently?)

(If divorced:) How did your friends react?

85. What would/did you miss most in your life?

86. (If single:) (If recently coupled, begin, "Thinking back" . . .) Can you think of ways that talking with friends makes it easier or harder to get along in a new relationship with a man?

87. Have friends ever helped out when a relationship with a man ended?

88. (a) Did a relationship with a man ever end when you had no friend to talk to?

(b) (If yes:) How did you feel then?

(c) (If no:) If a relationship ended when you had no friends to talk to about it, how would you feel?

89. I'd like to ask you for any of the people you think of when I ask you these questions. Just give me the first names that come to your mind. They can be adults or children, husband, family, friends, or anyone, whether nearby or far away.

Is there anyone . . .

1. who cheers you up when you're sad?
2. to whom you can talk about very personal problems?
3. who does regular child care or baby-sitting?
4. who would take care of you when you're ill?
5. who allows you to be completely yourself?
6. who makes you feel lovable?
7. who encourages you to try out new experiences or things?
8. to whom you've told things that you've never told anyone else?
9. whom you'd like to see every day?

10. who often makes you feel good about yourself?

11. whom you'd go out of your way to help out?

12. to whom you can show your worst side and know they'll still like you?

13. who usually makes you feel completely comfortable and at ease?

14. who recognizes your talents and abilities?

15. who can comfort you when you cry?

16. who would keep your most important secret?

17. whom you could call in the middle of the night, in case of emergency?

18. with whom you can tell private jokes?

19. to whom you expect you'll be close ten or twenty years from now?

20. with whom you can easily talk about your important beliefs?

21. to whom you can confide something you're ashamed of?

22. whom you'd try to help out of a serious problem, even if it meant a sacrifice on your part?

23. who knows and likes the real you?

24. who likes to hear something you're proud of?

25. about whom you would use the word "love" to describe your feelings?

26. whom you've seen the worst side of, and still care about a lot?

27. whom you can argue with and still remain close to?

28. who respects you as much as you respect them (a lot)?

29. whose personal problems you really take to heart?

30. from whom you don't mind hearing advice, even when you haven't asked for it?

31. who understands you better than anyone else?

32. who shares your most important values?

33. with whom you can talk about sex?

34. with whom you laugh a lot?

90. (a) Are there subjects or areas of life you would never talk about with [best friend]?

(b) What kinds of areas are these?

91. (a) Are there things you would never ask of [best friend]?

(b) What kinds of things are these?

92. (a) Has [best friend] ever tried to talk to you about issues or problems you didn't want to hear about or talk about?

(b) How did you react?

(c) (If no:) Has any close friend ever . . .

93. (a) Has [best friend] ever asked for more from you than a friend should ask?
    (b) How did you respond?
    (c) (If no:) Has any close friend ever . . .
94. (a) Has [best friend] ever made you feel like you've just had enough?
    (b) What was the situation? How did you react? How do you feel about it now?
    (c) (If no:) Has any close friend ever . . .
95. (a) How satisfied are you with your friendships?
    (b) Is there anything about your friendships or friends that you wish were different?
    (c) If you could have exactly the kind of social life or friendships or close friends you'd want, what would that be like?
96. Do you ever wish you had more friends you felt close to? Would you say this happens a lot of the time, some of the time, only once in a while, or never?
97. Do you ever wish you had more friends to have fun with? (Repeat choice.)
98. Do you ever wish you had more friends you could talk to about personal matters or feelings or problems? (Repeat choice.)
99. Do you ever wish you knew more people you could rely on for help—say, help with work, or around the house, or help in emergencies? (Repeat choice.)
100. Now I'd like to ask you some questions comparing men's and women's friendships. Just answer, "men" or "women" or "no difference." In general,
    (a) who have more friends, men or women, or no difference? (Repeat choice.)
    (b) whose friendships are closer . . .
    (c) who make new friendships more easily . . .
    (d) who are more loyal to their friends . . .
    (e) who depend more on their friends . . .
    (f) whose friendships are more emotional . . .
    (g) who are more likely to argue with friends . . .
    (h) who would try harder to cheer up a friend who's sad . . .
    (i) who need close friends more . . .
    (j) who turn to friends to solve personal problems more . . .
    (k) who are more likely to be jealous of a spouse or fiancé's friends . . .
    (l) whose friendships are more competitive . . .
    (m) who spend more time with friends . . .
    (n) who are more dependable as friends . . .

    (o)   who talk more about personal feelings with friends . . .
    (p)   who talk more about private details about marriage . . .
    (q)   who are more likely to be envious of a friend . . .
    (r)   who would be more likely to lend money to a friend . . .
    (s)   whose friendships last longer . . .
    (t)   whose friendships break up more easily . . .
    (u)   who are more likely to have one *best* friend . . .
    (v)   who are more likely to keep friends from childhood . . .
    (w)   who are more likely to trust friends . . .

(101–106: Ask if appropriate.)

101.   (a)   What were the names of your close women friends before you were married, when you were first seeing [husband]?
    (b)   Are you still friends with any of them?
    (c)   Are you still close with any of them?
    (d)   Can you tell me a little about what happened in those friendships once you were engaged/married?
    (e)   How did you feel about [friend]?
    (f)   How did you think you should feel?

102.   (a)   Can you think of a time that a close friendship changed when your friend got married?
    (b)   How did you feel at the time?
    (c)   How did you think you should feel?

103.   (a)   What were the names of your close women friends before you had your first child?
    (b)   Are you still friends with any of them?
    (c)   Are any of them close friends?
    (d)   Can you tell me a little about what happened in those friendships once your first child was born?
    (e)   How did you think you should feel?

104.   (a)   What were the names of your close women friends just before your divorce?
    (b–e: Same subquestions.)

105.   Would you say you had more close friends before you were married/engaged/with [boyfriend], fewer close friends, or about the same?

106.   Would you say you had more close friends before your first child was born, fewer close friends, or about the same?

Now I'd like to ask your opinion about friendships in general.
(Give respondent card listing choices: always, sometimes, or hardly ever. Probe, "When, for example, . . .")

107.   Should friends expect each other's first loyalty to be to a husband?

108. Does a friend have the right to ask an important favor that is likely to create conflicts or problems at home for the woman she's asking help from?

109. Do friends have the right to change a woman's attitude or belief, or way of doing things?

110. Do friends have the right to criticize the way a woman's husband or boyfriend treats her?

111. Do friends have the right to tell a woman her behavior is immoral and wrong?

112. Do friends have the right to criticize the way a woman raises her children?

113. If a friend seemed to be in trouble emotionally—having a breakdown—would her friends have a responsibility to try to get help for her?

114. If a woman were being beaten by her husband, would her friends have a responsibility to take her in if she asks?

115. If a friend were ill, or somehow unable to care for her children, would her friends have a responsibility to care for them?

116. If a friend were beating or abusing her children, would her friends have a responsibility to stop it?

117. In this same case, if all else failed, would they have a responsibility to call police or some outside agency?

118. (a) Did you have close friendships with other girls when you were in high school?

    (b) Were these friendships an important part of your life then? Would you say they were very important, somewhat important, or not very important?

    (c) How were close friendships in high school different from close friendships now?

119–120. (not used)

121. If you didn't have close friends right now, how would that affect you?

122. How would it affect your marriage?

123. To whom would you say your husband is closest? (List on matrix and, for each name, record the following information:)

    (a) Is this person male or female?

    (b) How is this person connected to him?

    (c) How long has he known him/her?

    (d) How did they first meet?

    (e) Is he/she single, married, divorced, separated, or widowed?

    (f) How often does he see him/her?

    (g) How often do they talk on the phone?

(Show list:)
- (h) How many are kin?
- (i) How many are co-workers?
- (j) How many are neighbors?
- (k) How many has he known since childhood?
- (l) How many has he known only a few years or less?

124. In what ways are [husband's/boyfriend's] close friendships different from yours?

125. Do you think he talks personally with close friends more than you do, less, or about the same?

126. Do you think he depends on his close friends more than you do, less, or about the same?

127. Do you think he feels closer to his close friends than you do, less close, or about the same?

128. Do you think he's more loyal to his close friends than you are, less loyal, or about the same?

129. Do you think his close friends are more loyal to him than yours are to you, less loyal, or about the same?

130. Do you think it's easier for him to ask help from his close friends, less easy, or about the same?

131. What kinds of things do you think he talks about or shares with his close friends that he doesn't talk about or share with you?

132. Can you think of a time when you felt jealous of [husband's/boyfriend's] close friendship with someone? (How did you think you should feel?)

133. Which of you could get along better without close friends if you were in a situation where you had to?

133-x. (For each question read alternatives: a lot of the time, some of the time, only once in a while, never.)
- (a) About how often do you feel that the people you live with make too many demands on you these days?
- (b) About how often do you feel that your friends and (other) relatives make too many demands on you?
- (c) How often do you feel unhappy or a bit depressed these days?
- (d) How often do you feel overwhelmed—that there is too much going on in your life for you to handle?
- (e) How often do you feel particularly excited about or interested in something these days?
- (f) How often do things get on your nerves so much that you feel like losing your temper?
- (g) How often do you find that you have time on your hands with little to do?

(h) How often do you feel that things are going the way you want them to?

(i) How often do you feel nervous, fidgety, or tense these days?

(j) How often do you feel pleased with what you're doing these days?

(k) How often do you feel you are boiling inside with anger because of others these days?

(l) How often do you feel worried or upset?

133-y. (a) Have you and [husband] been having any trouble getting along in the last year?

(b) (If yes:) How serious would you say these difficulties are: very serious, somewhat serious, or not too serious?

133-z. (a) Have you had any financial problems?

(b) (If yes:) How serious would you say they are: very serious, somewhat serious, or not too serious?

134. What was the highest grade or year you completed in school? (If college:) What was the highest degree you received?

135. (Show respondent card listing income categories.) Would you give me the letter of the income group that includes your personal income before taxes? Choose the figure that includes all your income: wages, salaries, interest, benefits, child support, and all other income.

136. Would you give me the letter of the income group that includes your household income before taxes? Choose the figure that includes all your household's income: wages, salaries, interest, benefits, child support, and all other income.

137. (If respondent has no job:)

(a) What kind of work did you do at your last job?

(b) When was that?

(c) How long did you do that work?

(d) What was the job before that?

138. What kind of work is [husband/boyfriend] doing now?

139. Was your father working while you were growing up? What kind of work did he do?

140. Was your mother working while you were growing up? What kind of work did she do?

(Open discussion, to ask respondent for impressions of interview and topics she would have included.)

Notes

Introduction

1. Some of the most interesting recent work includes Graham Allan, *A Sociology of Friendship and Kinship* (London: George Allen and Unwin, 1979); Jessie Bernard, *The Female World* (New York: Free Press, 1981); Nancy F. Cott, *The Bonds of Womanhood* (New Haven: Yale University Press, 1977); Lillian Faderman, *Surpassing the Love of Men* (New York: William Morrow and Co., 1981); Claude S. Fischer, *To Dwell Among Friends* (Chicago: University of Chicago Press, 1982); Mary P. Ryan, "The Power of Women's Networks: A Case Study of Female Moral Reform in Antebellum America," *Feminist Studies* 5 (Spring 1979): 66–87; Carroll Smith-Rosenberg, "The Female World of Love and Ritual," in *A Heritage of Her Own*, ed. Nancy F. Cott and Elizabeth H. Pleck (New York: Simon and Schuster, Touchstone, 1979); Lillian Rubin, *Just Friends* (New York: Harper and Row, 1985); Barry Wellman, "The Community Question," *American Journal of Sociology* 84 (1979): 1201–31; and the articles collected in Steve W. Duck and Daniel Perlman, eds., *Understanding Personal Relationships* (Beverly Hills, Ca.: Sage, 1985); Laura Lein and Marvin B. Sussman, eds., *The Ties That Bind* (New York: Haworth Press, 1983); Elliott Leyton, ed., *The Compact* (Newfoundland: Memorial University of Newfoundland, 1974); and Helena Z. Lopata and David Maines, eds., *Research in the Interweave of Social Roles*, vol. 2 (Greenwich, Conn.: JAI Press, 1981).

2. The contemporary exemplar of this tradition is Elizabeth Bott, *Family and Social Network*, 2d ed. (New York: Free Press, 1971).

3. See citations in Anne M. Seiden and Pauline B. Bart, "Woman to Woman: Is Sisterhood Possible?" in *Old Family/New Family*, ed. N. Glazer-Malbin (New York: D. Van Nostrand, 1975), 189–228; see also

Adrienne Rich, "Compulsory Heterosexuality and Lesbian Existence," *Signs* 5 (1980): 631–60.

4. Compare, for example, research on working-class women in the fifties by Komarovsky and by Young and Willmott, to findings on the seventies by Rubin and, once more, Young and Willmott (Mirra Komarovsky, *Blue-Collar Marriage* [New York: Random House, Vintage Books, 1967], chs. 5, 6; Michael Young and Peter Willmott, *Family and Kinship in East London* [Baltimore: Penguin Books, 1957], ch. 1; *The Symmetrical Family* [New York: Penguin Books, 1973], ch. 3; Lillian Breslow Rubin, *Worlds of Pain* [New York: Basic Books, 1976], ch. 7).

5. Carol B. Stack, *All Our Kin* (New York: Harper and Row, 1974), ch. 7.

6. Claude S. Fischer and Stacey J. Oliker, "A Research Note on Friendship, Gender, and the Life Cycle," *Social Forces* 62 (1983): 129–30; Fischer, *To Dwell*, 130–31.

7. Mary Jo Bane, *Here to Stay* (New York: Basic Books, 1976), 9.

Chapter 1: The Modernization of Friendship and Marriage

1. Eighteenth- and nineteenth-century writers often viewed changes in the institutional surroundings of family life as crucial determinants of family change. See Ferdinand Tönnies, *Community and Society*, trans. Charles P. Loomis (New York: Harper and Row, 1963): Frederic LePlay, *On Family, Work, and Social Change*, ed. Catherine Bodard Silver (Chicago: University of Chicago Press, 1982); Herbert Spencer, *The Principles of Sociology*, 3d ed., vol. 1 (New York: D. Appleton and Co., 1895); Emile Durkheim, *The Division of Labor in Society* (New York: Free Press, 1933); Friedrich Engels, *The Origin of the Family, Private Property, and the State* (New York: International Publishers, 1969).

2. Carle C. Zimmerman, *Family and Civilization* (New York: Harper and Brothers, 1947); Carle C. Zimmerman and Lucius F. Cervantes, *Marriage and the Family* (Chicago: Henry Regney Co., 1956) 38–39; Pitirim Sorokin, *Crisis of Our Age* (New York: E. P. Dutton, 1942), 187–92; Robert A. Nisbet, *The Quest for Community* (New York: Oxford University Press, 1953), 31, 70; Christopher Lasch, *Haven in a Heartless World* (New York: Basic Books, 1977), 143–47; Christopher Lasch, *The Culture of Narcissism* (New York: W. W. Norton, Warner Books, 1979), ch. 8; see Maurice Stein, *Eclipse of Community* (New York: Harper and Row, 1960).

3. Ernest R. Groves and Gladys Hoagland Groves, *The Contempo-

rary American Family (Chicago: J. B. Lippincott Co., 1947); William Ogburn, "Changing Functions of the Family," *The Family* 19 (1938): 139–43; Ernest W. Burgess, "The Family in a Changing Society," *American Journal of Sociology* 53 (1948): 417–23; William M. Kephart, *The Family, Society, and the Individual* (Boston: Houghton Mifflin Co., 1961); Talcott Parsons, "The American Family: Its Relation to Personality and Social Structure," in *Family, Socialization, and Interaction Process*, Talcott Parsons and Robert F. Bales (Glencoe, Ill.: Free Press, 1955); Philip Slater, "Parental Role Differentiation," *American Journal of Sociology* 67 (1961): 296–311; Mary Jo Bane, *Here to Stay* (New York: Basic Books, 1976).

4. Taking exception to this statement, Smelser, Greenfield, Goode, Harevan, and Hartmann all suggest that variables such as kinship organization, household authority, and gender ideology shaped or mutually interacted with industrial and urban forms. Neil Smelser, *Social Change in the Industrial Revolution* (Chicago: University of Chicago Press, 1959); Sidney Greenfield, "Industrialization and Family in Social Theory," *American Journal of Sociology* 67 (1961); William J. Goode, *World Revolution and Family Patterns* (New York: Free Press, 1963); Tamara K. Harevan, "Family Time and Industrial Time: Family and Work in a Planned Corporation Town, 1900–1924," in *Family and Kin in Urban Communities, 1700–1930*, ed. Tamara K. Harevan (New York: Franklin Watts, New Viewpoints, 1977); Heidi Hartmann, "Capitalism, Patriarchy, and Job Segregation by Sex," *Signs* 1 (Spring 1976): 137–69.

5. LePlay, *Family*, chs. 8, 20; George Elliott Howard, *A History of Matrimonial Institutions*, vol. 3 (Chicago: University of Chicago Press, Callaghan and Co., 1904), 225, 232, 258; Charles Horton Cooley, *Social Organization* (New York: Schocken Books, 1962), ch. 31; Ernest R. Mowrer, *The Family* (Chicago: University of Chicago Press, 1932), 14–19; Joseph Kirk Folsom, *The Family and Democratic Society* (New York: John Wiley and Sons, 1934), 222, 252, 679; Carl N. Degler, *At Odds* (Oxford: Oxford University Press, 1980), 191.

6. Mowrer, *Family*, 22; Ernest W. Burgess and Harvey J. Locke, *The Family: From Institution to Companionship* (New York: American Book Co., 1950), 289, 324; M. F. Nimkoff, *The Family* (Boston: Houghton Mifflin Co., 1934), 202; Goode, *Revolution*, 21; Robert O. Blood and Donald M. Wolfe, *Husbands and Wives* (New York: Free Press, 1960), 149; Edward Shorter, *The Making of the Modern Family* (New York: Basic Books, 1977), 15–16.

7. Mowrer, *Family*, 19–20; Reuben Hill, "Plans for Strengthening Family Life," in *Family, Marriage, and Parenthood*, ed. Howard Becker

and Reuben Hill (Boston: D. C. Heath, 1948), 782; Paul H. Landis, "The Changing Family," in *Readings in Marriage and the Family*, ed. Judson T. Landis and Mary G. Landis (New York: Prentice-Hall, 1952), 30; Philip Slater, *Footholds* (New York: E. P. Dutton, 1968), 40.

8. Nancy Chodorow, *The Reproduction of Mothering* (Berkeley: University of California Press, 1978); Parsons, "American Family"; Fred Weinstein and Gerald M. Platt, *The Wish to Be Free* (Berkeley: University of California Press, 1969); Jessica Benjamin, "The Oedipal Riddle: Authority, Autonomy, and the New Narcissism," in *The Problem of Authority in America*, ed. John P. Diggins and Mark E. Kann (Philadelphia: Temple University Press, 1981), 195–224.

9. See note 6 above.

10. Goode, *Revolution*, 19; see studies cited by Gary R. Lee, *Family Structure and Interaction* (Minneapolis: University of Minnesota Press, 1982), 229.

11. Shorter, *Modern Family*, 259.

12. Louise A. Tilly, Joan W. Scott, and Miriam Cohen have persuasively taken this line of argument in criticizing Shorter ("Women's Work and European Fertility Patterns," in *The American Family in Social-Historical Perspective*, ed. Michael Gordon, 2d ed. [New York: St. Martin's Press, 1978]).

13. Lawrence Stone, *The Family, Sex, and Marriage in England, 1500–1800* (New York: Harper and Row, 1977), 17, 93–102, 268.

14. Ibid., 8.

15. Ibid., 4, 268.

16. Quoted in ibid., 266–67; discussed on 258.

17. Ibid., 268.

18. Edmund S. Morgan, *The Puritan Family* (New York: Harper and Row, 1944); Mary Beth Norton, *Liberty's Daughters* (Boston: Little, Brown and Co., 1980), 17–25, 79–82.

19. Thomas Bender, *Community and Social Change in America* (Baltimore: Johns Hopkins University Press, 1978), ch. 3.

20. Nancy F. Cott, *The Bonds of Womanhood* (New Haven: Yale University Press, 1977), 66.

21. Stone, *Family*, 266.

22. Alexis de Tocqueville, *Democracy in America*, vol. 2 (New York: Schocken Books, 1961), 248.

23. Georg Simmel, *The Sociology of Georg Simmel*, ed. Kurt H. Wolff (New York: Free Press, 1950), 325.

24. Barbara Welter, "The Cult of True Womanhood: 1820–1860," in *The American Family in Social-Historical Perspective*, ed. Michael Gordon, 2d ed. (New York: St. Martin's Press, 1978), 325; see also Mary P.

Ryan, *Empire of the Mother* (New York: Institute for Research in History, 1982).

25. Cott, *Bonds*, 88; see also Mary P. Ryan, *Cradle of the Middle Class* (Cambridge: Cambridge University Press, 1981), chs. 2, 3.

26. Ann Douglas, *The Feminization of American Culture* (New York: Avon Books, 1977), 86.

27. Nancy F. Cott, "Passionlessness: An Interpretation of Victorian Sexual Ideology," in *A Heritage of Her Own*, ed. Nancy F. Cott and Elizabeth H. Pleck (New York: Simon and Schuster, Touchstone, 1979), 165; Philippe Ariès, *Centuries of Childhood* (New York: Random House, Vintage Books, 1962), 59–60; Richard Sennett, *The Fall of Public Man* (New York: Random House, Vintage Books, 1974), 162–68.

28. Cott, *Bonds*, 98; also see Barbara J. Berg, *The Remembered Gate: Origins of American Feminism* (Oxford: Oxford University Press, 1978), 220–22, 266–68.

29. Shorter, *Modern Family*, ch. 5; Ariès, *Centuries*, ch. 2; Jean-Louis Flandrin, *Families in Former Times* (Cambridge: Cambridge University Press, 1976), 203–7; Elizabeth Badinter, *Mother Love* (New York: Macmillan, 1981), 39–52, ch. 3.

30. Cott, *Bonds*, 189–90; on the antipatriarchal impact of Protestantism, see Stone, *Family*, 135–42, 241.

31. Welter, "True Womanhood."

32. Douglas, *Feminization*, 66; Mary P. Ryan, *Womanhood in America from Colonial Times to the Present*, 2d ed. (New York: Franklin Watts, New Viewpoints, 1979), 76–77.

33. Cott, "Passionlessness," 173; Linda Gordon, *Woman's Body, Woman's Right* (New York: Penguin Books, 1974), ch. 5; Daniel Scott Smith, "Family Limitation, Sexual Control, and Domestic Feminism in Victorian America," *Feminist Studies* 1 (Winter-Spring 1973): 40–57; see also Degler, *At Odds*, 271–78.

34. Mary P. Ryan, "The Power of Women's Networks: A Case Study of Female Moral Reform in Antebellum America," *Feminist Studies* 5 (Spring 1979): 66–87; Ryan, *Cradle*, ch. 3; Carroll Smith-Rosenberg, "Beauty, the Beast, and the Militant Woman," *American Quarterly* 23 (1971): 562–84; Berg, *Remembered Gate*, 134–37; Degler, *At Odds*, chs. 12, 13.

35. Ryan, *Womanhood*, 142; Degler, *At Odds*, 160–66.

36. Burgess and Locke, *Family*, 324; Herman Lantz et al., "Preindustrial Patterns in the Colonial Family in America: A Content Analysis of Colonial Magazines," *American Sociological Review* 33 (1968): 413–26; Blood and Wolfe, *Husbands and Wives*, 148–49.

37. Goode, *Revolution*, 19; Stone, *Family*, ch. 7; Shorter, *Modern*

Family, ch. 4; Daniel Scott Smith, "Parental Power and Marriage Patterns: An Analysis of Historical Trends in Hingham, Massachusetts," *Journal of Marriage and the Family* 35 (1973): 419–28.

38. Stone suggests that these changes showed up first among the English gentry, spread to American colonials, and later to the French and Italians. Free choice developed first among the "common people," say Shorter and Stone; they had no fortunes to control. Stone, however, astutely focuses on implications for "companionship" that the abrupt change in courtship offered the upper middle classes; companionship flourished there with other ideological and sentimental trends that were not typical of the working classes (Stone, *Family,* 320–24, 390–91). After Stone and Shorter, others have entered the debate with historical data that have made the question of priority even harder to resolve; their contributions include readings in R. B. Outhwaite, ed., *Marriage and Society* (London: Europa, 1983).

39. Stone, *Family,* 272–74; Shorter, *Modern Family,* 15–16, 259–60; Ian Watt, *The Rise of the Novel* (Berkeley: University of California Press, 1957), 138–39, 177.

40. Tocqueville, *Democracy,* 235.

41. Similar, but not identical. Even as formally free agents during a period of relative autonomy, women experienced an ambivalent, asymmetrical individualism. Economically, they had to marry. Tocqueville remarked that an American girl "had learned by the use of her independence, to surrender it without a struggle" for a married life of exceptional "abnegation" (Tocqueville, 240–41).

42. Degler, *At Odds,* 20; Cott, *Bonds,* 78–80; Willystine Goodsell, "The American Family in the Nineteenth Century," *Annals of the American Academy of Political and Social Sciences* 160 (1932): 13–22; Frank F. Furstenberg, Jr., "Industrialization and the American Family: A Look Backward," *American Sociological Review* 31 (1966): 326–37.

43. David Hunt, *Parents and Children in History* (New York: Harper and Row, 1970), 79.

44. John Demos, *A Little Commonwealth* (London: Oxford University Press, 1970), 83; Morgan, *Puritan Family,* 48–54; Laurel Thatcher Ulrich, *Good Wives* (New York: Alfred Knopf, 1982), 109.

45. Stone, *Family,* 272; Watt, *Novel,* 137–39.

46. Peter Gay, *The Tender Passion* (London: Oxford University Press, 1986); Degler, *At Odds,* 16.

47. Watt, *Novel,* ch. 5.

48. Gay, *Tender Passion.*

49. Degler, *At Odds,* ch. 2; Cott, *Bonds,* 22, 72; Carroll Smith-Rosenberg, "The Female World of Love and Ritual: Relations between

Women in Nineteenth-Century America," in *A Heritage of Her Own*, ed. Nancy F. Cott and Elizabeth H. Pleck (New York: Simon and Schuster, Touchstone, 1979), 331.

50. Smith-Rosenberg, "Female World," 322–23, 327–28; Degler, *At Odds*, 108.

51. Ellen Rothman, *Hands and Hearts: A History of Courtship in America* (New York: Basic Books, 1984), 63, 75; Steven M. Stowe, "The Thing Is Not Its Vision: A Woman's Courtship and Her Sphere in the Southern Planter Class," *Feminist Studies* 9 (Spring 1983): 128; Cott, *Bonds*, 80; also see Smith-Rosenberg, "Female World," 326.

52. Graves and Carlier, quoted in Goodsell, "American Family;" see also Furstenberg, "Industrialization," 332.

53. Tocqueville, *Democracy*, 247–48; Furstenberg, "Industrialization," 332.

54. John Mack Faragher, *Women and Men on the Overland Trail* (New Haven: Yale University Press, 1979), 147–51.

55. Elaine Tyler May, *Great Expectations* (Chicago: University of Chicago Press, 1980), 47.

56. Degler, *At Odds*, chs. 2, 7.

57. Lasch, *Haven*, 106.

58. Degler, *At Odds*, 26–29; Cott, *Bonds*, ch. 2; Eli Zaretsky, *Capitalism, the Family, and Personal Life* (New York: Harper and Row, Colophon Books, 1973), 66.

59. Shorter, *Modern Family*, 205–6, 227.

60. Ibid., 16, 166.

61. Burgess and Locke, *Family*, 203.

62. Ibid., 324. Works emphasizing romance: William L. Kolb, cited in William J. Goode, "The Theoretical Importance of Love," in *The Family*, ed. Rose Laub Coser, 2d ed. (New York: St. Martin's Press, 1974), 144; emphasizing partnership: Burgess and Locke, *Family*, ch. 11; Nimkoff, *Family*, 251; emphasizing complementarity: Kephart, *Family*, 465; Parsons, "American Family," 80–81; David R. Miller and Guy E. Swanson, *The Changing American Family* (New York: John Wiley and Sons, 1958), 200–201; emphasizing communication: see Goode, "Love"; and Sherod Miller, Ramon Corales, and Daniel B. Wackman, "Recent Progress in Understanding Marital Communication," *Family Coordinator* 24 (1975): 143.

63. Harvey J. Locke, *Predicting Adjustment in Marriage* (New York: Greenwood Press, 1968), 251; Ernest W. Burgess and Leonard S. Cottwell, Jr., *Predicting Sources of Failure in Marriage* (New York: Prentice-Hall, 1939); Gerald Gurin, Joseph Veroff, and Sheila Feld, *Americans View Their Mental Health* (New York: Basic Books, 1960), 101–10; Jessie

Bernard, *The Future of Marriage* (New York: Bantam Books, 1976), chs. 1–3; Joseph Veroff, Elizabeth Douvan, and Richard A. Kulka, *The Inner American* (New York: Basic Books, 1981), 24, 164, 178.

64. Robert S. Lynd and Helen Merrell Lynd, *Middletown* (New York: Harcourt, Brace and Co., 1929), 118, 311.

65. Kephart, *Family*, 465; see also John R. Seeley, R. Alexander Sim, and E. W. Loosley, *Crestwood Heights* (New York: Basic Books, 1956), 217–18, 382; Lillian Rubin, *Intimate Strangers* (New York: Harper and Row, 1983).

66. Hill, "Plans," 782; see also Slater, *Footholds*, 40; Folsom, *Family*, 190.

67. Louis Wirth, "Urbanism as a Way of Life," *American Journal of Sociology* 44 (1938): 13; Nisbet, *Quest*, 31.

68. Ariès, *Centuries*, part 3; Shorter, *Modern Family*, 5, 39–53; Flandrin, *Former Times*, ch. 2.

69. Demos, *Commonwealth*, 49–50; Lutz Berkener, "The Stem Family and the Developmental Cycle of the Peasant Household: An 18th-Century Austrian Example," in *The American Family in Social-Historical Perspective*, ed. Michael Gordon, 2d ed. (New York: St. Martin's Press, 1973), 37–38; Alexander Keyssar, "Widowhood in Eighteenth-Century Massachusetts: A Problem in the History of the Family," *Perspectives in American History* 8 (1974): 83–122; Flandrin, *Former Times*, 36; Stone, *Family*, 268; Shorter, *Modern Family*, 5–6, chs. 1, 2; Claude S. Fischer et al., *Networks and Places* (New York: Free Press, 1977), ch. 10.

70. Lionel Trilling, *Sincerity and Authenticity* (New York: Harcourt Brace Jovanovich, 1980).

71. Michael Anderson, *Family Structure in Nineteenth-Century Lancashire* (Cambridge: Cambridge University Press, 1971), ch. 9; Harevan, "Family Time."

72. Harevan, "Family Time," 156.

73. Sally Griffen and Clyde Griffen, "Family and Business in a Small City: Poughkeepsie, New York, 1850–1880," in *Family and Kin in Urban Communities, 1700–1930*, ed. Tamara K. Harevan (New York: Franklin Watts, New Viewpoints, 1977).

74. Stone, *Family*, 268; Cott, *Bonds*, ch. 5; Simmel, *Sociology*, 325; Philippe Ariès, "The Family and the City," in *The Family*, ed. Virginia Tufte and Barbara Myerhoff (New York: W. W. Norton and Co., 1978), 33–36.

75. Stone, *Family*; see also, Watt, *Novel*, ch. 5; and Sennett, *Public Man*, chs. 4, 5.

76. Michael Young and Peter Willmott, *Family and Kinship in East London* (Baltimore: Penguin Books, 1957), 188–90; Michael Young and

Peter Willmott, *The Symmetrical Family* (New York: Penguin Books, 1973), 91; Anderson, *Family Structure*, 178; Bender, *Community*, 71, 96.

77. Ryan, *Cradle*, chs. 3, 5, 236–37; Bender, *Community*, 79–100; Berg, *Remembered Gate;* Gerda Lerner, "Community Work of Black Club Women," *Journal of Negro History* 59 (April 1974): 158–67; Paula Giddings, *When and Where I Enter* (Toronto: Bantam Books, 1985), chs. 3–6; Sennett, *Public Man*, chs. 4, 5.

78. Ryan, *Cradle*.

79. Ibid., 236–38; Berg, *Remembered Gate;* for Europe, Ariès, "Family and City," 36–38.

80. Gunther Barth, *City People* (New York: Oxford University Press, 1980), 121, 129, 146.

81. Susan Strasser, *Never Done* (New York: Random House, Pantheon Books, 1982); Stuart Ewen, *Captains of Consciousness* (New York: McGraw-Hill, 1976); Lynd and Lynd, *Middletown*, 173, 253, ch. 18; Robert S. Lynd and Helen Merrell Lynd, *Middletown in Transition* (New York: Harcourt, Brace and Co., 1937), 245, 247–48, 267.

82. William H. Whyte, Jr., "The Wife Problem," in *Selected Studies in Marriage and the Family*, ed. Robert Winch, 2d ed. (New York: Holt, Rinehart and Winston, 1962), 111–25; Seeley, *Crestwood*, 135–36.

83. Herbert Gans, *The Levittowners* (New York: Random House, Pantheon Books, 1967), 154–62; William H. Whyte, Jr., *The Organization Man* (Garden City, N.Y.: Doubleday and Co., Anchor Books, 1956), 378, 389, 394; Helena Z. Lopata, *Occupation Housewife* (London: Oxford University Press, 1971), 241, 269–71; Nicholas Babchuk and Alan P. Bates, "The Primary Relations of Middle-Class Couples: A Study in Male Dominance," *American Sociological Review* 28 (1963): 377–85.

84. Nisbet, *Quest;* Folsom, *Family*, 190.

85. See Degler, *At Odds*, 145; Margaret Jones Bolsterli, "It Seems to Help Me Bear It Better When She Knows About It," *Southern Exposure* (March/April 1983): 58–61.

86. Smith-Rosenberg, "Female World"; Lillian Faderman, *Surpassing the Love of Men* (New York: William Morrow and Co., 1981); Cott, *Bonds*, ch. 5; Stone, *Family*, 336, 722, 386, 400–403.

87. Flandrin, *Former Times*, 36; Nathalie Zemon Davis, *Society and Culture in Early Modern France* (Stanford: Stanford University Press, 1965), 75; Mary P. Ryan, *Womanhood in America from Colonial Times to the Present*, 2d ed. (New York: Franklin Watts, New Viewpoints, 1979), 36; Martine Segalen, *Love and Power in the Peasant Family* (Chicago: University of Chicago Press, 1983), 138; Ulrich, *Good Wives*, 109.

88. Barbara Welter, "The Feminization of American Religion: 1800–1860," in *Clio's Consciousness Raised*, ed. Mary Hartman and Lois W.

Banner (New York: Harper and Row, Torch Books, 1974); Cott, *Bonds*, 126.

89. Cott, "Passionlessness," 173.

90. Cott, *Bonds*, 97; see also Degler, *At Odds*, chs. 4, 5; Welter, "True Womanhood," 326.

91. Cott, *Bonds*, ch. 5; Ryan, *Cradle*; Berg, *Remembered Gate*; Smith-Rosenberg, "Beauty." As Mary Ryan argues (in *Cradle*) voluntary organizations enabled women to define new bourgeois family ideals during this social transition.

92. On the literature of domesticity, see Douglas, *Feminization*; Degler, *At Odds*, 378–79. On female versus male sensibilities, see Cott, *Bonds*, 67–70, 98, 190; Douglas, *Feminization*, 54; Berg, *Remembered Gate*, 136.

93. Cott, *Bonds*, 105, 117; Degler, *At Odds*, 307.

94. Smith-Rosenberg, "Female World," 315, 328; Cott, *Bonds*, 173–78.

95. Cott, *Bonds*, 173; Faderman, *Surpassing*, 74–76.

96. Quoted in Faderman, *Surpassing*, 172.

97. Faderman, *Surpassing*, 145–204; Cott, *Bonds*, 185.

98. Smith-Rosenberg, "Female World," 320.

99. Ibid., 314.

100. Cott, *Bonds*, 176.

101. Degler, *At Odds*, 147.

102. Degler, *At Odds*, 149; Rothman, *Hands and Hearts*, 339.

103. Faderman, *Surpassing*, 82; Smith-Rosenberg, "Female World," 317; Degler, *At Odds*, 146; Cott, *Bonds*, 190.

104. Welter, "True Womanhood," 327.

105. Cott, *Bonds*, 80–81.

106. Lynd and Lynd, *Middletown*, 111; Faderman, *Surpassing*, 298; Paula S. Fass, *The Damned and the Beautiful* (Oxford: Oxford University Press, 1977), ch. 3; Niles Carpenter, "Courtship Practices and Contemporary Social Change in America," *Annals of the American Academy of Political and Social Sciences* 160 (1932), 38–44; John Modell, "Dating Becomes the Way of American Youth," in *Essays on the Family and Social Change*, ed. David Levine (Arlington: University of Texas Press, 1983), 91–127; Outhwaite, *Marriage and Society*.

107. Degler, *At Odds*, 150; Faderman, *Surpassing*, 308.

108. Faderman, *Surpassing*, 90, 229, 298; Nancy Sahli, "Smashing: Women's Relationships before the Fall," *Chrysalis* 8 (Summer 1979).

109. Folsom, *Family*, 39, 563; Christine Simmons, "Companionate Marriage and the Lesbian Threat," *Frontiers* 4 (1979): 54–59.

110. Nimkoff, *Family*, 251; see also Lasch, *Haven*, ch. 2.

111. Ewen, *Captains*; May, *Great Expectations*, ch. 8.

112. Locke, *Predicting*, 233; Burgess and Cottrell, *Sources of Failure*, 129; Kephart, *Family*, 465; Mirra Komarovsky, *Blue-Collar Marriage* (New York: Random House, Vintage Books, 1967), ch. 12; Gans, *Levittowners*, ch. 8; Marjorie Fiske Lowenthal, *Four Stages of Life* (San Francisco: Jossey-Bass, 1975), chs. 1, 2.

113. Theodore Caplow et al., *Middletown Families: Fifty Years of Change and Continuity* (Minneapolis: University of Minnesota Press, 1982), 125.

Chapter 2: Distinctive Values of Friendship

1. Robert O. Blood, "Kinship Interaction and Marital Solidarity," *Merill-Palmer Quarterly* 15 (1969): 171–82; Gary R. Lee, "Effects of Social Networks on the Family," in *Contemporary Theories about the Family*, vol. 1, ed. Wesley R. Burr et al. (New York: Free Press, 1979), 27–56; Michael Young and Peter Willmott, *Family and Kinship in East London* (Baltimore: Penguin Books, 1957), ch. 3; and Mirra Komarovsky, *Blue-Collar Marriage* (New York: Random House, Vintage Books, 1967), ch. 12.

2. Don H. Zimmerman and Candace West, "Sex Roles, Interruptions, and Silences in Conversation," in *Language and Sex*, ed. Barrie Thorne and Nancy Henley (Rowley, Mass.: Newbury House, 1975), 105–29.

3. Robert O. Blood and Donald M. Wolfe, *Husbands and Wives* (New York: Free Press, 1960), ch. 2.

4. Ibid., 42–43; Norval Glenn and Sara McLanahan, "Children and Marital Happiness: A Further Specification of the Relationship," *Journal of Marriage and the Family* 44 (1982): 63–72.

5. See also Claude S. Fischer and Stacey J. Oliker, "A Research Note on Friendship, Gender, and the Life Cycle," *Social Forces* 62 (1983): 126–30.

6. Philip Slater, "Social Limitations on Libidinal Withdrawal," *American Sociological Review* 28 (1963): 339–64.

7. Myra Marx Ferree, "Housework: Rethinking the Costs and Benefits," in *Families, Politics, and Public Policy*, ed. Irene Diamond (New York: Longman, 1983).

8. Blood and Wolfe, *Husbands and Wives*, 42–43.

9. Robert A. Nisbet, *The Quest for Community* (New York: Oxford University Press, 1953), 31.

10. Fischer and Oliker, "Friendship, Gender," 131; Edward A. Powers and Gordon Bultena, "Sex Differences in Intimate Friendships of Old Age," *Journal of Marriage and the Family* 38 (1976): 739–47.

11. Zick Rubin, *Liking and Loving* (New York: Holt, Rinehart and Winston, 1973).

12. Christopher Lasch, *Haven in a Heartless World* (New York: Basic Books, 1977), chs. 1, 8.

13. Willard Waller, *The Family* (New York: Dryden Press, 1938).

Chapter 3: Close Friendship as an Institution

1. Georg Simmel, *The Sociology of Georg Simmel*, ed. Kurt H. Wolff (New York: Free Press, 1950), 325.

2. Ralph Linton, cited by Cora DuBois, "The Gratuitous Act: An Introduction to the Comparative Study of Friendship Patterns," in *The Compact*, ed. Elliott Leyton (Newfoundland: Memorial University of Newfoundland, 1974), 30; Gerald D. Suttles, "Friendship as a Social Institution," in *Social Relationships*, ed. George McCall et al. (Chicago: Aldine Publishing, 1970), 96–98.

3. Robert Paine, "In Search of Friendship: An Exploratory Analysis in Middle-Class Culture," *Man* 4 (1969): 514.

4. Ibid.; DuBois, "Gratuitous Act," 17; S. N. Eisenstadt, "Friendship and the Structure of Trust and Solidarity in Society," in *The Compact*, ed. Elliott Leyton (Newfoundland: Memorial University of Newfoundland, 1974), 139.

5. Eisenstadt, "Friendship," 141; see also Max Scheler, *The Nature of Sympathy* (London: Routledge and Kegan Paul, 1954); and Lawrence A. Blum, *Friendship, Altruism, and Morality* (London: Routledge and Kegan Paul, 1980).

6. See discussions in Paine, "Search of Friendship"; DuBois, "Gratuitous Act," 17; and Eisenstadt, "Friendship," 140.

7. Simmel, *Sociology*, 78–79, 317–29. See chapter 4.

8. DuBois, "Gratuitous Act," 16, 28–29.

9. Paul Lazarsfeld and Robert K. Merton, "Friendship as a Social Process," in *Freedom and Control in Modern Society*, ed. M. Berger, T. Abel, and C. Page (New York: D. Van Nostrand, 1954), 18–66; Edward O. Laumann, *Bonds of Pluralism* (New York: John Wiley and Sons, 1973); Robert Max Jackson, "Social Structure and Process in Friendship Choice," in Claude S. Fischer et al., *Networks and Places* (New York: Free Press, 1977); Irwin Altman and Dalmas A. Taylor, *Social Penetration* (New York: Holt, Rinehart and Winston, 1973); and Steve W. Duck and R. Gilmour, eds., *Personal Relationship*, vols. 1–6 (London: Academic Press, 1981–1985).

10. Paine, "Search of Friendship," 510–11.

11. Graham Allan, *A Sociology of Friendship and Kinship* (London: George Allen and Unwin, 1979), 17.

12. Paine, "Search of Friendship," 512.

13. S. N. Eisenstadt, "Ritualized Personal Relations," *Man* 56 (1956):

90–95; Robert Paine, "Anthropological Approaches to Friendships," in *The Compact*, ed. Elliott Leyton (Newfoundland: Memorial University of Newfoundland, 1974), 4–6.

14. Eisenstadt, "Friendship," 140–41.

15. Paine, "Search of Friendship," 510–12; DuBois, "Gratuitous Act," 16.

16. See also Robert R. Bell, *Worlds of Friendship* (Beverly Hills, Ca.: Sage, 1981), 68.

17. Barry Wellman, "Paid Work, Domestic Work, and Network," in *Understanding Personal Relationships*, ed. Steve W. Duck and Daniel Perlman (Beverly Hills, Ca.: Sage, 1985), 169–70; Lillian Rubin, *Just Friends* (New York: Harper and Row, 1985), 68; see also Bell, *Worlds*, 60.

18. Carol B. Stack, *All Our Kin* (New York: Harper and Row, 1974), ch. 7.

19. Ibid., 39.

20. Nancy Chodorow, *The Reproduction of Mothering* (Berkeley: University of California Press, 1978), ch. 12.

21. Harry T. Reis, Marilyn Senchak, and Beth Solomon, "Sex Differences in the Intimacy of Social Interaction: Further Examination of Potential Explanations," *Journal of Personality and Social Interaction* 48 (1985): 1204–17.

22. See William J. Goode, "Why Men Resist," in *Rethinking the Family*, ed. Barrie Thorne (New York: Longman, 1982), 131–50.

23. Michael Argyl and Adrian Farnham, "Sources of Satisfaction and Conflict in Long-Term Relationships," *Journal of Marriage and the Family* 45 (1983): 490–91; Harriet Braiker and Harold H. Kelly, "Conflict in the Development of Close Relationships," in *Social Exchange in Developing Relationships*, ed. Robert L. Burgess and Ted L. Huston (New York: Academic Press, 1979), 152.

24. Deborah E. Belle, "The Impact of Poverty on Social Networks and Supports," in *The Ties That Bind*, ed. Laura Lein and Marvin B. Sussman (New York: Haworth Press, 1983), 89–104; Dair L. Gillespie, Richard S. Krannich, and Ann Leffler, "The Missing Cell: Amiability, Hostility, and Gender Differentiation in Rural Community Networks," *Social Science Journal* 22 (1985): 17–30; Claude S. Fischer, *To Dwell Among Friends* (Chicago: University of Chicago Press, 1982), 136; Ann Leffler, Richard S. Krannich, and Dair L. Gillespie, "Contact, Support, and Friction: Three Faces of Networks in Community Life," *Sociological Perspectives* 29 (July 1986): 337–56; Barry Wellman, "Applying Network Analysis to the Study of Support," in *Social Networks and Social Support*, ed. Benjamin H. Gottlieb (Beverly Hills, Ca.: Sage, 1981), 179–81.

25. Blum, *Friendship, Altruism*, 124.

26. Robert Jackson finds that people often perceive far-away friends

and kin as close; he maintains that otherwise they would probably not keep up the effort to stay in touch. Close far-away friends remain friends; others who are not close drop away (Jackson, "Friendship Choice," 48–49); Fischer, *To Dwell*, 172.

27. Fischer, *To Dwell*, 362.

28. Ibid., 90.

29. Ann Steuve and Laura Lein, "Problems in Network Analysis: The Case of the Missing Person," manuscript, Wellesley College Center for Research on Women, 1979.

30. Fischer, *To Dwell*, 106; Wellman, "Paid Work," 168–69; Claude S. Fischer and Stacey J. Oliker, "A Research Note on Friendship, Gender, and the Life Cycle," *Social Forces* 62 (1983): 126–27.

31. Fischer, *To Dwell*, 102; see Wellman, "Paid Work," 169, 186.

32. See also Fischer, *To Dwell*, 102.

33. Lazarsfeld and Merton, "Friendship"; Laumann, *Bonds;* Jackson, "Friendship Choice"; Fischer, *To Dwell*, 181.

34. Myra Marx Ferree, "Working-Class Jobs: Housework and Paid Work as Sources of Satisfaction," *Social Problems* 23 (1976): 431–41.

35. Jackson, "Friendship Choice," 73; Fischer, *To Dwell*, ch. 14.

36. Jackson, "Friendship Choice."

37. I am making a speculative comparison with Robert Jackson's large survey of men's friendships, which indicates greater economic similarity than I found here. And his category of "friends" includes kin friends, who tend to be less economically similar than nonkin. See also note 17 above.

38. See also Claude S. Fischer, "What Do We Mean By 'Friend'? An Inductive Study," *Social Networks* 3 (1982): 287–306.

39. See note 24 above.

40. Rubin, *Just Friends*, 139–40.

41. Nicholas Babchuk and Alan P. Bates, "The Primary Relations of Middle-Class Couples: A Study in Male Dominance," *American Sociological Review* 28 (1963): 380.

42. Other studies agree on the nature of men's networks: see Wellman, "Paid Work," 167–68; and Rubin, *Just Friends*, 60.

43. Fischer, *To Dwell;* Fischer and Oliker, "Friendship, Gender"; Claude S. Fischer and Susan L. Phillips, "Who Is Alone: Social Characteristics of Respondents with Small Networks," in *Loneliness: A Sourcebook of Theory, Research, and Therapy*, ed. L. A. Peplau and D. Perlman (New York: John Wiley and Sons, 1982).

Chapter 4: Friendship and Individuality

1. Robert Paine, "In Search of Friendship: An Exploratory Analysis in Middle-Class Culture," *Man* 4 (1969): 514; S. N. Eisenstadt, "Friendship

and the Structure of Trust and Solidarity in Society," in *The Compact*, ed. Elliott Leyton (Newfoundland: Memorial University of Newfoundland, 1974), 139–41.

2. Georg Simmel, *The Sociology of Georg Simmel*, ed. Kurt H. Wolff (New York: Free Press, 1950), 138, 130.

3. Talcott Parsons, "The American Family: Its Relation to Personality and Social Structure," in *Family, Socialization, and Interaction Process*, Talcott Parsons and Robert F. Bales (Glencoe, Ill.: Free Press, 1955), 3–21.

4. Peter L. Berger, *Facing Up to Modernity* (New York: Basic Books, 1977), 76.

5. Simmel, *Sociology*, 318–27.

6. Ibid.

7. Ibid., 138.

8. Ibid.

9. William F. Goode, "Why Men Resist," in *Rethinking the Family*, ed. Barrie Thorne (New York: Longman, 1982), 136–39.

10. For sources maintaining that married men perceive fewer problems in marriage and are more satisfied with communication, see Jessie Bernard, *The Future of Marriage* (New York: Bantam Books, 1976), 28.

11. Simmel, *Sociology*, 326.

12. Claude S. Fischer, *To Dwell Among Friends* (Chicago: University of Chicago Press, 1982), pts. 3, 4; Robert Max Jackson, "Social Structure and Process in Friendship Choice," in Claude S. Fischer et al., *Networks and Places* (New York: Free Press, 1977), 59–78.

13. Graham Allan, *A Sociology of Friendship and Kinship* (London: George Allen and Unwin, 1979), 51.

14. Barry Wellman, "Paid Work, Domestic Work, and Network," in *Understanding Personal Relationships*, ed. Steve W. Duck and Daniel Perlman (Beverly Hills, Ca.: Sage, 1985), 167–68; Nicholas Babchuk and Alan P. Bates, "The Primary Relations of Middle-Class Couples: A Study in Male Dominance," *American Sociological Review* 28 (1963): 380.

15. Ann Steuve and Laura Lein, "Problems in Network Analysis: The Case of the Missing Person," manuscript, Wellesley College Center for Research on Women, 1979.

16. Robert O. Blood and Donald M. Wolfe, *Husbands and Wives* (New York: Free Press, 1960), 39; Andrew J. Cherlin, *Marriage Divorce Remarriage* (Cambridge, Mass.: Harvard University Press, 1981), 50–54.

17. Jessica Benjamin, "The Oedipal Riddle: Authority, Autonomy, and the New Narcissism" in *The Problem of Authority in America*, ed. John

P. Diggins and Mark E. Kann (Philadelphia: Temple University Press, 1981), 208.

18. Ibid., 207.

19. Nancy Chodorow, *The Reproduction of Mothering* (Berkeley: University of California Press, 1978); for work on moral development in this tradition, see Carol Gilligan, *In A Different Voice* (Cambridge, Mass.: Harvard University Press, 1982).

20. See Benjamin, "Oedipal Riddle," 208–10.

21. Mirra Komarovsky, *Blue-Collar Marriage* (New York: Random House, Vintage Books, 1967), ch. 12; Michael Young and Peter Willmott, *Family and Kinship in East London* (Baltimore: Penguin Books, 1957), ch. 3; Carol B. Stack, *All Our Kin* (New York: Harper and Row, 1974), ch. 7; Robert Paine, "Search of Friendship," 508.

22. Simmel, *Sociology,* 325.

23. Ibid., 326.

Chapter 5: Women Friends and Marriage Work

1. Arlie Russell Hochschild, "Emotion Work, Feeling Rules, and Social Structure," *American Journal of Sociology* 85 (1979): 551–75; and Hochschild, *The Managed Heart* (Berkeley: University of California Press, 1983).

2. Hochschild, "Emotion Work," 552, 561.

3. Ibid., 562.

4. Ibid.

5. Ibid., 552, 566.

6. Ibid., 569.

7. On lax emotion work, see ibid., 567.

8. For a power analysis, see Hochschild, *Managed Heart,* ch. 8. For functionalist analyses, see Talcott Parsons, "The American Family: Its Relation to Personality and Social Structure," in *Family, Socialization, and Interaction Process,* ed. Talcott Parsons and Robert F. Bales (Glencoe, Ill.: Free Press, 1955); and David R. Miller and Guy E. Swanson, *The Changing American Family* (New York: John Wiley and Sons, 1958), 200–201.

9. Jessie Bernard, *The Future of Marriage* (New York: Bantam Books, 1976), 28.

10. Elizabeth Bott, *Family and Social Network,* 2d ed. (New York: Free Press, 1971).

11. At the time of the interviews median earnings for full-time female workers were $12,001 (Janet L. Norwood, "The Female-Male Earnings

Gap: A Review of Employment and Earnings Issues," U.S. Bureau of Labor Statistics, report 673 [Washington, D.C., 1982], 9).

12. Barbara R. Bergmann, *The Economic Emergence of Women* (New York: Basic Books, 1986), 230.

13. U.S. Bureau of the Census, *Poverty in the U.S.: 1985*, ser. P–60, no. 158 (Washington, D.C., 1987), 111; Diana M. Pearce, "Farewell to Alms: Women's Fare Under Welfare," in *Women: A Feminist Perspective*, 3d ed., ed. Jo Freeman (Palo Alto, Ca.: Mayfield, 1984), 508, 509; Bergmann, *Emergence*, chs. 6, 10.

14. Andrew J. Cherlin, *Marriage Divorce Remarriage* (Cambridge, Mass.: Harvard University Press, 1981), 82; U.S. Bureau of the Census, *Child Support and Alimony: 1983*, Current Population Reports, ser. 3, no. 141 (Washington, D.C., 1985).

15. Helen Koo and C. M. Suchindran, "Effects of Children on Women's Remarriage Prospects," *Journal of Family Issues* 1 (1980): 505; and Paul C. Glick, "Remarriage: Some Recent Changes and Variations," *Journal of Family Issues* 1 (1980): 475–76.

16. Barbara Ehrenreich, *The Hearts of Men* (Garden City, N.Y.: Doubleday, Anchor Press, 1983), ch. 7.

17. See Stacey J. Oliker, "Abortion and the Left: The Limits of 'Pro-Family' Politics," *Socialist Review* 56 (March 1981): 71–95; and Deirdre English, "The Fear that Feminism Will Free Men First," in *Powers of Desire*, ed. Ann Snitow, Christine Stansell, and Sharon Thompson (New York: Monthly Review Press, 1983), 477–83.

18. For findings that men are less expressive, see: John G. Allen and Dorothy M. Haccoun, "Sex Differences in Emotionality: A Multidimensional Approach," *Human Relations* 29 (1976): 711–22; Sandra Lipsitz Bem, Wendy Martyna, and Carol Watson, "Sex Typing and Androgyny: Further Explorations of the Expressive Domain," *Journal of Personality and Social Psychology* 34 (1976): 1016–23; Mirra Komarovsky, *Dilemmas of Masculinity: A Study of College Youth* (New York: W. W. Norton, 1976).——For findings that men are less empathetic, see: Martin L. Hoffman, "Sex Differences in Empathy and Related Behaviors," *Psychological Bulletin* 84 (1977): 712–22.——For findings that men disclose less on intimate topics, see: Paul C. Cozby, "Self-Disclosure: A Literature Review," *Psychological Bulletin* 79 (1973): 73–91; Brian S. Morgan, "Intimacy of Disclosure Topics and Sex Differences in Self-Disclosure," *Sex Roles* 2 (1976): 161–66; Sidney Jourard, *The Transparent Self*, (New York: D. Van Nostrand, 1971); Elizabeth J. Aries and Fern L. Johnson, "Close Friendship in Adulthood: Conversational Content Between Same-Sex Friends," *Sex Roles* 4 (1983): 1183–95; Komarovsky, *Dilemmas*.——For findings that men have fewer friendships of intimacy and emotional ex-

change, see: Barry Wellman, "Paid Work, Domestic Work, and Network," in *Understanding Personal Relationships,* ed. Steve W. Duck and Daniel Perlman (Beverly Hills, Ca.: Sage, 1985), 169–70; Lillian Rubin, *Just Friends* (New York: Harper and Row, 1985), 60; Mayta A. Caldwell and Letitia Anne Peplau, "Sex Differences in Same-Sex Friendships," *Sex Roles* 3 (1982): 721–32; Alan Booth, "Sex and Social Participation," *American Sociological Review* 37 (1972): 183–93; Marjorie Fiske Lowenthal and Clayton Haven, "Interaction and Adaptation: Intimacy as a Critical Variable," *American Sociological Review* 33 (1968): 20–30; Zick Rubin and Stephen Shenker, "Friendship, Proximity, and Self-Disclosure," *Journal of Personality* 46 (1978): 1–22; Michael P. Farell and Stanley Rosenberg, "Male Friendship and the Life Cycle," paper presented at the American Sociological Association, 1977; see also Joseph H. Pleck, *The Myth of Masculinity* (Cambridge, Mass.: MIT Press, 1981).

19. Claude S. Fischer and Susan L. Phillips, "Who Is Alone: Social Characteristics of Respondents with Small Networks," in *Loneliness: A Sourcebook of Theory, Research, and Therapy,* ed. L. A. Peplau and D. Perlman (New York: John Wiley and Sons, 1982), 21–39; Harry T. Reis, Marilyn Senchak, and Beth Solomon, "Sex Differences in the Intimacy of Social Interaction: Further Examination of Potential Explanations," *Journal of Personality and Social Psychology* 48 (1985): 1204–17.

20. Bernard, *Future,* 28; John Scanzoni, "Sex Roles, Economic Factors, and Marital Solidarity in Black and White Marriages," *Journal of Marriage and the Family* 37 (1976): 130–45; Gerald Gurin, Joseph Veroff, and Sheila Feld, *Americans View Their Mental Health* (New York: Basic Books, 1960), 101–10; Joseph Veroff, Elizabeth Douven, and Richard A. Kulka, *The Inner American* (New York: Basic Books, 1981), 24, 164, 175–78.

Chapter 6: Conclusion:
Friendship and Community

1. Leslie Woodcock Tentler, *Wage-Earning Women* (Oxford: Oxford University Press, 1979), 62–63; Rosabeth Moss Kanter, *Commitment and Community* (Cambridge, Mass.: Harvard University Press, 1972).

2. Talcott Parsons, "The American Family: Its Relation to Personality and Social Structure," in Talcott Parsons and Robert F. Bales, *Family, Socialization, and Interaction Process* (Glencoe, Ill.: Free Press, 1955), 17–20; Peter L. Berger and Hansfried Kellner, "Marriage and the Construction of Reality," in *The Family,* ed. Rose Laub Coser, 2d ed. (New York: St. Martin's Press, 1974), 161.

3. Parsons, "American Family."

4. Christopher Lasch, *The Culture of Narcissism* (New York: W. W. Norton, Warner Books, 1977), ch. 8; Jean Bethke Elshtain, "Feminists Against the Family," *The Nation*, 17 November 1979, 497–500.

5. Claude S. Fischer et al., *Networks and Places* (New York: Free Press, 1977), 12.

6. Ibid., 202.

7. Thomas Bender, *Community and Social Change in America* (Baltimore: Johns Hopkins University Press, 1978).

8. Robert A. Nisbet, *The Quest for Community* (New York: Oxford University Press, 1953), 50–52, 70.

9. Ibid., 48–52.

10. Robert A. Nisbet, *The Sociological Tradition* (New York: Basic Books, 1966), 47–48.

11. Christopher Lasch, *Haven in a Heartless World* (New York: Basic Books, 1977), chs. 1, 8.

12. Philip Slater, "Social Limitations on Libidinal Withdrawal," *American Sociological Review* 28 (1963): 339–64.

13. Susan Krieger, "Lesbian Identity and Community: Recent Social Science Literature," *Signs* 8 (1982): 91–108.

14. See chap. 3, note 24.

15. Claude S. Fischer, *To Dwell Among Friends* (Chicago: University of Chicago Press, 1982), 135; see also Richard Sennett, *The Fall of Public Man* (New York: Random House, Vintage Books, 1974).

16. See Lillian Rubin, *Intimate Strangers* (New York: Harper and Row, 1983).

17. Mary P. Ryan, "The Power of Women's Networks: A Case Study of Female Moral Reform in Antebellum America," *Feminist Studies* 5 (Spring 1979): 66–87.

Appendix A: Methods of Research

1. U.S. Bureau of the Census, *Geographical Mobility, March 1975–March 1980*, Current Population Reports, ser. P–20, no. 368 (Washington, D.C., 1981), 9.

2. U.S. Bureau of the Census, *Marriage, Divorce, Widowhood, and Remarriage*, Current Population Reports, ser. P–20, no. 312 (Washington, D.C., 1977), 1.

3. Lois M. Verbrugge, "The Structure of Adult Friendship Choices," *Social Forces* 56 (1977): 576–97; see chap. 3, note 9.

Bibliography

Allan, Graham. *A Sociology of Friendship and Kinship*. London: George Allen and Unwin, 1979.

Allen, John G., and Dorothy M. Haccoun. "Sex Differences in Emotionality: A Multidimensional Approach." *Human Relations* 29 (1976): 711–22.

Altman, Irwin, and Dalmas A. Taylor. *Social Penetration*. New York: Holt, Rinehart and Winston, 1973.

Anderson, Michael. *Family Structure in Nineteenth-Century Lancashire*. Cambridge: Cambridge University Press, 1971.

Argyl, Michael, and Adrian Farnham. "Sources of Satisfaction and Conflict in Long-Term Relationships." *Journal of Marriage and the Family* 45 (1983): 481–96.

Aries, Elizabeth J., and Fern L. Johnson. "Close Friendship in Adulthood: Conversational Content Between Same-Sex Friends." *Sex Roles* 4 (1983): 1183–95.

Ariès, Philippe. *Centuries of Childhood*. New York: Random House, Vintage Books, 1962.

———. "The Family and the City." In *The Family*, ed. Virginia Tufte and Barbara Myerhoff, 29–42. New York: W. W. Norton and Co., 1978.

Babchuk, Nicholas, and Alan P. Bates. "The Primary Relations of Middle-Class Couples: A Study in Male Dominance." *American Sociological Review* 28 (1963): 377–85.

Badinter, Elizabeth. *Mother Love*. New York: Macmillan, 1981.

Bane, Mary Jo. *Here to Stay*. New York: Basic Books, 1976.

Barker-Benfield, G. J. *The Horrors of the Half-Known Life*. New York: Harper and Row, 1976.

Barth, Gunther. *City People*. New York: Oxford University Press, 1980.

Bell, Robert R. *Worlds of Friendship*. Beverly Hills, Ca.: Sage, 1981.

Belle, Deborah. "The Impact of Poverty on Social Networks and Supports." In *The Ties That Bind,* ed. Laura Lein and Marvin B. Sussman, 89–104. New York: Haworth Press, 1983.

Bem, Sandra Lipsitz, Wendy Martyna, and Carol Watson. "Sex Typing and Androgyny: Further Explorations of the Expressive Domain." *Journal of Personality and Social Psychology* 34 (1976): 1016–23.

Bender, Thomas. *Community and Social Change in America.* Baltimore: Johns Hopkins University Press, 1978.

Benjamin, Jessica. "The Oedipal Riddle: Authority, Autonomy, and the New Narcissism." In *The Problem of Authority in America,* ed. John P. Diggins and Mark E. Kann, 195–224. Philadelphia: Temple University Press, 1981.

Berg, Barbara J. *The Remembered Gate: Origins of American Feminism.* Oxford: Oxford University Press, 1978.

Berger, Peter L. *Facing Up to Modernity.* New York: Basic Books, 1977.

Berger, Peter L., and Hansfried Kellner. "Marriage and the Construction of Reality." In *The Family,* ed. Rose Laub Coser, 2d ed., 157–76. New York: St. Martin's Press, 1974.

Bergmann, Barbara R. *The Economic Emergence of Women.* New York: Basic Books, 1986.

Berkener, Lutz. "The Stem Family and the Developmental Cycle of the Peasant Household: An 18th-Century Austrian Example." In *The American Family in Social-Historical Perspective,* ed. Michael Gordon, 2d ed., 34–58. New York: St. Martin's Press, 1973.

Bernard, Jessie. *The Female World.* New York: Free Press, 1981.

———. *The Future of Marriage.* New York: Bantam Books, 1976.

Blood, Robert O. "Kinship Interaction and Marital Solidarity." *Merill-Palmer Quarterly* 15 (1969): 171–82.

Blood, Robert O., and Donald M. Wolfe. *Husbands and Wives.* New York: Free Press, 1960.

Blum, Lawrence A. *Friendship, Altruism, and Morality.* London: Routledge and Kegan Paul, 1980.

Bolsterli, Margaret Jones. "It Seems to Help Me Bear It Better When She Knows About It." *Southern Exposure* (March/April 1983): 58–61.

Booth, Alan. "Sex and Social Participation." *American Sociological Review* 37 (1972): 183–93.

Bott, Elizabeth. *Family and Social Network.* 2d ed. New York: Free Press, 1971.

Braiker, Harriet, and Harold H. Kelly. "Conflict in the Development of Close Relationships." In *Social Exchange in Developing Relationships,* ed. Robert L. Burgess and Ted L. Huston, 135–68. New York: Academic Press, 1979.

Burgess, Ernest W. "The Family in a Changing Society." *American Journal of Sociology* 53 (1948): 417–23.

Burgess, Ernest W., and Leonard S. Cottrell, Jr. *Predicting Sources of Failure in Marriage.* New York: Prentice-Hall, 1939.

Burgess, Ernest W., and Harvey J. Locke, *The Family: From Institution to Companionship.* New York: American Book Co., 1950.

Caldwell, Mayta A., and Letitia Anne Peplau. "Sex Differences in Same-Sex Friendships." *Sex Roles* 8 (1982): 721–32.

Caplow, Theodore, Howard Bahr, Bruce Chadwick, Reuben Hill, and Margaret Williamson. *Middletown Families: Fifty Years of Change and Continuity.* Minneapolis: University of Minnesota Press, 1982.

Carpenter, Niles. "Courtship Practices and Contemporary Social Change in America." *Annals of the American Academy of Political and Social Sciences* 160 (1932): 38–44.

Cherlin, Andrew J. *Marriage Divorce Remarriage.* Cambridge, Mass.: Harvard University Press, 1981.

Chodorow, Nancy. *The Reproduction of Mothering.* Berkeley: University of California Press, 1978.

Cooley, Charles Horton. *Social Organization.* New York: Schocken Books, 1962.

Cott, Nancy F. *The Bonds of Womanhood.* New Haven: Yale University Press, 1977.

———. "Passionlessness: An Interpretation of Victorian Sexual Ideology." In *A Heritage of Her Own,* ed. Nancy F. Cott and Elizabeth H. Pleck, 162–81. New York: Simon and Schuster, Touchstone, 1979.

Cozby, Paul C. "Self-Disclosure: A Literature Review." *Psychological Bulletin* 79 (1973): 73–91.

Davis, Nathalie Zemon. *Society and Culture in Early Modern France.* Stanford: Stanford University Press, 1965.

Degler, Carl N. *At Odds.* Oxford: Oxford University Press, 1980.

Demos, John. *A Little Commonwealth.* London: Oxford University Press, 1970.

Douglas, Ann. *The Feminization of American Culture.* New York: Avon Books, 1977.

Douvan, Elizabeth, and J. Adelson. *The Adolescent Experience.* New York: John Wiley and Sons, 1966.

DuBois, Cora. "The Gratuitous Act: An Introduction to the Comparative Study of Friendship Patterns." In *The Compact,* ed. Elliott Leyton, 15–32. Newfoundland: Memorial University of Newfoundland, 1974.

Duck, Steve W., and R. Gilmour, eds. *Personal Relationship.* Vols. 1–6. London: Academic Press, 1981–1985.

Duck, Steve W., and Daniel Perlman, eds. *Understanding Personal Relationships.* Beverly Hills, Ca.: Sage, 1985.

Durkheim, Emile. *The Division of Labor in Society.* New York: Free Press, 1933.

Ehrenreich, Barbara. *The Hearts of Men.* Garden City, N.Y.: Doubleday, Anchor Press, 1983.

Eisenstadt, S. N. "Friendship and the Structure of Trust and Solidarity in Society." In *The Compact,* ed. Elliott Leyton, 138–45. Newfoundland: Memorial University of Newfoundland, 1974.

————. "Ritualized Personal Relations." *Man* 56 (1956): 90–95.

Elshtain, Jean Bethke. "Feminists Against the Family." *The Nation,* 17 November 1979, 497–500.

Engels, Friedrich. *The Origin of the Family, Private Property, and the State.* New York: International Publishers, 1969.

English, Deirdre. "The Fear that Feminism Will Free Men First." In *Powers of Desire,* ed. Ann Snitow, Christine Stansell, and Sharon Thompson, 477–83. New York: Monthly Review Press, 1983.

Ewen, Stuart. *Captains of Consciousness.* New York: McGraw-Hill, 1976.

Faderman, Lillian. *Surpassing the Love of Men.* New York: William Morrow and Co., 1981.

Faragher, John Mack. *Women and Men on the Overland Trail.* New Haven: Yale University Press, 1979.

Farell, Michael P., and Stanley Rosenberg. "Male Friendship and the Life Cycle." Paper presented at the American Sociological Association, 1977.

Fass, Paula S. *The Damned and the Beautiful.* Oxford: Oxford University Press, 1977.

Ferree, Myra Marx. "Housework: Rethinking the Costs and Benefits." In *Families, Politics, and Public Policy,* ed. Irene Diamond, 148–67. New York: Longman, 1983.

————. "Working-Class Jobs: Housework and Paid Work as Sources of Satisfaction." *Social Problems* 23 (1976): 431–41.

Fischer, Claude S. *To Dwell Among Friends.* Chicago: University of Chicago Press, 1982.

————. "What Do We Mean By 'Friend'? An Inductive Study." *Social Networks* 3 (1982): 287–306.

Fischer, Claude S., Robert M. Jackson, Ann Steuve, Katherine Gerson, and Lynn M. Jones. *Networks and Places.* New York: Free Press, 1977.

Fischer, Claude S., and Stacey J. Oliker. "A Research Note on Friendship, Gender, and the Life Cycle." *Social Forces* 62 (1983): 124–33.

Fischer, Claude S., and Susan L. Phillips. "Who Is Alone: Social Characteristics of Respondents with Small Networks." In *Loneliness: A*

Sourcebook of Theory, Research, and Therapy, ed. L. A. Peplau and D. Perlman, 21–39. New York: John Wiley and Sons, 1982.

Flandrin, Jean-Louis. *Families in Former Times.* Cambridge: Cambridge University Press, 1976.

Folsom, Joseph Kirk. *The Family and Democratic Society.* New York: John Wiley and Sons, 1934.

Furstenberg, Frank F., Jr. "Industrialization and the American Family: A Look Backward." *American Sociological Review* 31 (1966): 326–37.

Gans, Herbert. *The Levittowners.* New York: Random House, Pantheon Books, 1967.

Gay, Peter. *The Tender Passion.* London: Oxford University Press, 1986.

Giddings, Paula. *When and Where I Enter.* Toronto: Bantam Books, 1985.

Gillespie, Dair L. "Who Has the Power: The Marital Struggle." *Journal of Marriage and the Family* 33 (1971): 445–58.

Gillespie, Dair L., Richard S. Krannich, and Ann Leffler. "The Missing Cell: Amiability, Hostility, and Gender Differentiation in Rural Community Networks." *Social Science Journal* 22 (1985): 17–30.

Gilligan, Carol. *In A Different Voice.* Cambridge, Mass.: Harvard University Press, 1982.

Glenn, Norval, and Sara McLanahan. "Children and Marital Happiness: A Further Specification of the Relationship." *Journal of Marriage and the Family* 44 (1982): 63–72.

Glick, Paul C. "Remarriage: Some Recent Changes and Variations." *Journal of Family Issues* 1 (1980): 455–78.

Goode, William J. "The Theoretical Importance of Love." In *The Family,* ed. Rose Laub Coser, 2d ed., 143–56. New York: St. Martin's Press, 1974.

———. "Why Men Resist." In *Rethinking the Family,* ed. Barrie Thorne, 131–50. New York: Longman, 1982.

———. *World Revolution and Family Patterns.* New York: Free Press, 1963.

Goodsell, Willystine. "The American Family in the Nineteenth Century." *Annals of the American Academy of Political and Social Sciences* 160 (1932): 13–22.

Gordon, Linda. *Woman's Body, Woman's Right.* New York: Penguin Books, 1974.

Greenfield, Sidney. "Industrialization and Family in Social Theory." *American Journal of Sociology* 67 (1961): 312–22.

Griffen, Sally, and Clyde Griffen. "Family and Business in a Small City: Poughkeepsie, New York, 1850–1880." In *Family and Kin in Urban Communities, 1700–1930,* ed. Tamara K. Harevan, 144–63. New York: Franklin Watts, New Viewpoints, 1977.

Groves, Ernest R., and Gladys Hoagland Groves. *The Contemporary American Family*. Chicago: J. B. Lippincott Co., 1947.

Gurin, Gerald, Joseph Veroff, and Sheila Feld. *Americans View Their Mental Health*. New York: Basic Books, 1960.

Harevan, Tamara K. "Family Time and Industrial Time: Family and Work in a Planned Corporation Town, 1900–1924." In *Family and Kin in Urban Communities, 1700–1930*, ed. Tamara K. Harevan, 187–207. New York: Franklin Watts, New Viewpoints, 1977.

Hartmann, Heidi. "Capitalism, Patriarchy, and Job Segregation by Sex." *Signs* 1 (1976): 137–69.

Hill, Reuben. "Plans for Strengthening Family Life." In *Family, Marriage, and Parenthood*, ed. Howard Becker and Reuben Hill. Boston: D. C. Heath, 1948.

Hochschild, Arlie Russell. "Emotion Work, Feeling Rules, and Social Structure." *American Journal of Sociology* 85 (1979): 551–75.

———. *The Managed Heart*. Berkeley: University of California Press, 1983.

Hoffman, Martin L. "Sex Differences in Empathy and Related Behaviors." *Psychological Bulletin* 84 (1977): 712–22.

Howard, George Elliott. *A History of Matrimonial Institutions*. Vol. 3. Chicago: University of Chicago Press, Callaghan and Co., 1904.

Hunt, David. *Parents and Children in History*. New York: Harper and Row, 1970.

Jackson, Robert Max. "Social Structure and Process in Friendship Choice." In *Networks and Places*, ed. Claude S. Fischer, Robert M. Jackson, Ann Steuve, Katherine Gerson, and Lynn M. Jones, 59–78. New York: Free Press, 1977.

Jourard, Sidney. *The Transparent Self*. New York: D. Van Nostrand, 1971.

Kanter, Rosabeth Moss. *Commitment and Community*. Cambridge, Mass.: Harvard University Press, 1972.

Kephart, William M. *The Family, Society, and the Individual*. Boston: Houghton Mifflin Co., 1961.

Keyssar, Alexander. "Widowhood in Eighteenth-Century Massachusetts: A Problem in the History of the Family." *Perspectives in American History* 8 (1974): 83–122.

Komarovsky, Mirra. *Blue-Collar Marriage*. New York: Random House, Vintage Books, 1967.

———. *Dilemmas of Masculinity: A Study of College Youth*. New York: W. W. Norton, 1976.

Koo, Helen, and C. M. Suchindran. "Effects of Children on Women's Remarriage Prospects." *Journal of Family Issues* 1 (1980): 497–516.

Krieger, Susan. "Lesbian Identity and Community: Recent Social Science Literature." *Signs* 8 (1982): 91–108.

Landis, Paul H. "The Changing Family." In *Readings in Marriage and the Family*, ed. Judson T. Landis and Mary G. Landis, 27–31. New York: Prentice-Hall, 1952.

Lantz, Herman, Margaret Britton, Raymond Schmitt, and Eloise C. Snyder. "Pre-industrial Patterns in the Colonial Family in America: A Content Analysis of Colonial Magazines." *American Sociological Review* 33 (1968): 413–26.

Lasch, Christopher. *The Culture of Narcissism*. New York: W. W. Norton, Warner Books, 1979.

————. *Haven in a Heartless World*. New York: Basic Books, 1977.

Laumann, Edward O. *Bonds of Pluralism*. New York: John Wiley and Sons, 1973.

Lazarsfeld, Paul, and Robert K. Merton. "Friendship as a Social Process." In *Freedom and Control in Modern Society*, ed. M. Berger, T. Abel, and C. Page, 18–66. New York: D. Van Nostrand, 1954.

Lee, Gary R. "Effects of Social Networks on the Family." In *Contemporary Theories about the Family*, vol. 1, ed. Wesley R. Burr, Reuben Hill, Ivan Nye, and Ira L. Reiss, 27–56. New York: Free Press, 1979.

————. *Family Structure and Interaction*. Minneapolis: University of Minnesota Press, 1982.

Leffler, Ann, Richard S. Krannich, and Dair L. Gillespie. "Contact, Support, and Friction: Three Faces of Networks in Community Life." *Sociological Perspectives* 29 (July 1986): 337–56.

Lein, Laura, and Marvin B. Sussman, eds. *The Ties That Bind*. New York: Haworth Press, 1983.

LePlay, Frederic. *On Family, Work, and Social Change*, ed. Catherine Bodard Silver. Chicago: University of Chicago Press, 1982.

Lerner, Gerda. "Community Work of Black Club Women." *Journal of Negro History* 59 (April 1974): 158–67.

Leyton, Elliott, ed. *The Compact*. Newfoundland: Memorial University of Newfoundland, 1974.

Locke, Harvey J. *Predicting Adjustment in Marriage*. New York: Greenwood Press, 1968.

Lopata, Helena Z. *Occupation Housewife*. London: Oxford University Press, 1971.

Lopata, Helena Z., and David Maines, eds. *Research in the Interweave of Social Roles*. Vol. 2. Greenwich, Conn.: JAI Press, 1981.

Lowenthal, Marjorie Fiske. *Four Stages of Life*. San Francisco: Jossey-Bass, 1975.

Lowenthal, Marjorie Fiske, and Clayton Haven. "Interaction and Adaptation: Intimacy as a Critical Variable." *American Sociological Review* 33 (1968): 20–30.

Lynd, Robert S., and Helen Merrell Lynd. *Middletown*. New York: Harcourt, Brace and Co., 1929.

————. *Middletown in Transition*. New York: Harcourt Brace and Co., 1937.

May, Elaine Tyler. *Great Expectations*. Chicago: University of Chicago Press, 1980.

Miller, David R., and Guy E. Swanson. *The Changing American Family*. New York: John Wiley and Sons, 1958.

Miller, Sherod, Ramon Corales, and Daniel B. Wackman. "Recent Progress in Understanding and Facilitating Marital Communication." *Family Coordinator* 24 (1975): 143–52.

Modell, John. "Dating Becomes the Way of American Youth." In *Essays on the Family and Historical Change*, ed. David Levine, 91–126. Arlington: University of Texas Press, 1983.

Morgan, Brian S. "Intimacy of Disclosure Topics and Sex Differences in Self-Disclosure." *Sex Roles* 2 (1976): 161–66.

Morgan, Edmund S. *The Puritan Family*. New York: Harper and Row, 1944.

Mowrer, Ernest R. *The Family*. Chicago: University of Chicago Press, 1932.

Nimkoff, M. F. *The Family*. Boston: Houghton Mifflin, 1934.

Nisbet, Robert A. *The Quest for Community*. New York: Oxford University Press, 1953.

————. *The Sociological Tradition*. New York: Basic Books, 1966.

Norton, Mary Beth. *Liberty's Daughters*. Boston: Little, Brown and Co., 1980.

Norwood, Janet L. "The Female-Male Earnings Gap: A Review of Employment and Earnings Issues." U.S. Bureau of Labor Statistics, report 673. Washington, D.C., 1982.

Ogburn, William. "Changing Functions of the Family." *The Family* 19 (1938): 139–43.

Oliker, Stacey J. "Abortion and the Left: The Limits of 'Pro-Family' Politics." *Socialist Review* 56 (1981): 71–95.

————. "Sociology of Women." Lectures presented at Department of Sociology, University of California, Berkeley, Spring 1984.

Outhwaite, R. B., ed. *Marriage and Society*. London: Europa, 1983.

Paine, Robert. "Anthropological Approaches to Friendships." In *The Compact*, ed. Elliott Leyton, 1–14. Newfoundland: Memorial University of Newfoundland, 1974.

————. "In Search of Friendship: An Exploratory Analysis in Middle-Class Culture." *Man* 4 (1969): 505–24.

Parsons, Talcott. "The American Family: Its Relation to Personality and Social Structure." In Talcott Parsons and Robert F. Bales, *Family, Socialization, and Interaction Process*, 3–21. Glencoe, Ill.: Free Press, 1955.

Pearce, Diana M. "Farewell to Alms: Women's Fare Under Welfare." In *Women: A Feminist Perspective*, 3d ed., ed. Jo Freeman, 502–15. Palo Alto, Ca.: Mayfield, 1984.

Pleck, Joseph H. *The Myth of Masculinity*. Cambridge, Mass.: MIT Press, 1981.

Powers, Edward A., and Gordon Bultena. "Sex Differences in Intimate Friendships of Old Age." *Journal of Marriage and the Family* 38 (1976): 739–47.

Reis, Harry T., Marilyn Senchak, and Beth Solomon. "Sex Differences in the Intimacy of Social Interaction: Further Examination of Potential Explanations." *Journal of Personality and Social Psychology* 48 (1985): 1204–17.

Rich, Adrienne. "Compulsory Heterosexuality and Lesbian Existence." *Signs* 5 (1980): 631–60.

Rothman, Ellen. *Hands and Hearts: A History of Courtship in America*. New York: Basic Books, 1984.

Rotundo, E. Anthony. "Body and Soul: Changing Ideals of American Middle-Class Manhood, 1770–1920." *Journal of Social History* 16 (Summer 1983): 23–38.

Rubin, Lillian Breslow. *Intimate Strangers*. New York: Harper and Row, 1983.

————. *Just Friends*. New York: Harper and Row, 1985.

————. *Worlds of Pain*. New York: Basic Books, 1976.

Rubin, Zick. *Liking and Loving*. New York: Holt, Rinehart and Winston, 1973.

Rubin, Zick, and Stephen Shenker. "Friendship, Proximity, and Self-Disclosure." *Journal of Personality* 46 (1978): 1–22.

Ryan, Mary P. *Cradle of the Middle Class*. Cambridge: Cambridge University Press, 1981.

————. *Empire of the Mother*. New York: Institute for Research in History, 1982.

————. "The Power of Women's Networks: A Case Study of Female Moral Reform in Antebellum America." *Feminist Studies* 5 (Spring 1979): 66–87.

————. *Womanhood in America from Colonial Times to the Present*. 2d ed. New York: Franklin Watts, New Viewpoints, 1979.

Sahli, Nancy. "Smashing: Women's Relationships before the Fall." *Chrysalis* 8 (Summer 1979).

Scanzoni, John. "Sex Roles, Economic Factors, and Marital Solidarity in Black and White Marriages." *Journal of Marriage and the Family* 37 (1975): 130–45.

Scheler, Max. *The Nature of Sympathy.* London: Routledge and Kegan Paul, 1954.

Seeley, John R., R. Alexander Sim, and E. W. Loosley. *Crestwood Heights.* New York: Basic Books, 1956.

Segalen, Martine. *Love and Power in the Peasant Family.* Chicago: University of Chicago Press, 1983.

Seiden, Anne M., and Pauline B. Bart. "Woman to Woman: Is Sisterhood Possible?" In *Old Family/New Family,* ed. N. Glazer-Malbin, 189–228. New York: D. Van Nostrand, 1975.

Sennett, Richard. *The Fall of Public Man.* New York: Random House, Vintage Books, 1974.

Shorter, Edward. *The Making of the Modern Family.* New York: Basic Books, 1977.

Simmel, Georg. *The Sociology of Georg Simmel.* Ed. Kurt H. Wolff. New York: Free Press, 1950.

Simmons, Christina. "Companionate Marriage and the Lesbian Threat." *Frontiers* 4 (1979): 54–59.

Slater, Philip. *Footholds.* New York: E. P. Dutton, 1968.

———. "Parental Role Differentiation." *American Journal of Sociology* 67 (1961): 296–311.

———. Social Limitations on Libidinal Withdrawal." *American Sociological Review* 28 (1963): 339–64.

Smelser, Neil. *Social Change in the Industrial Revolution.* Chicago: University of Chicago Press, 1959.

Smith, Daniel Scott. "Family Limitation, Sexual Control, and Domestic Feminism in Victorian America." *Feminist Studies* 1 (Winter–Spring 1973): 40–57.

———. "Parental Power and Marriage Patterns: An Analysis of Historical Trends in Hingham, Massachusetts." *Journal of Marriage and the Family* 35 (1973): 419–28.

Smith-Rosenberg, Carroll. "Beauty, the Beast, and the Militant Woman." *American Quarterly* 23 (1971): 562–84.

———. "The Female World of Love and Ritual: Relations between Women in Nineteenth-Century America." In *A Heritage of Her Own,* ed. Nancy F. Cott and Elizabeth H. Pleck, 311–42. New York: Simon and Schuster, Touchstone, 1979.

Sorokin, Pitirim. *Crisis of Our Age.* New York: E. P. Dutton, 1942.

Spencer, Herbert. *The Principles of Sociology.* 3d ed. Vol. 1. New York: D. Appleton and Co., 1895.

Stack, Carol B. *All Our Kin.* New York: Harper and Row, 1974.

Stein, Maurice. *Eclipse of Community.* New York: Harper and Row, 1960.

Steuve, Ann, and Laura Lein. "Problems in Network Analysis: The Case of the Missing Person." Manuscript. Wellesley College Center for Research on Women, 1979.

Stone, Lawrence. *The Family, Sex, and Marriage in England, 1500–1800.* New York: Harper and Row, 1977.

Stowe, Steven M. "The Thing Is Not Its Vision: A Woman's Courtship and Her Sphere in the Southern Planter Class," *Feminist Studies* 9 (Spring 1983): 113–30.

Strasser, Susan. *Never Done.* New York: Random House, Pantheon Books, 1982.

Suttles, Gerald D. "Friendship as a Social Institution." In *Social Relationships*, ed. George McCall, Michal M. McCall, Norman K. Denzin, Gerald D. Suttles, and Suzanne B. Kurth, 95–135. Chicago: Aldine Publishing, 1970.

Tentler, Leslie Woodcock. *Wage-Earning Women.* Oxford: Oxford University Press, 1979.

Tilly, Louise A., Joan W. Scott, and Miriam Cohen. "Women's Work and European Fertility Patterns." In *The American Family in Social-Historical Perspective*, ed. Michael Gordon, 2d ed. New York: St. Martin's Press, 1978.

Tocqueville, Alexis de. *Democracy in America.* Vol. 2. New York: Schocken Books, 1961.

Tönnies, Ferdinand. *Community and Society.* Trans. Charles P. Loomis. New York: Harper and Row, 1963.

Trilling, Lionel. *Sincerity and Authenticity.* New York: Harcourt Brace Jovanovich, 1980.

Ulrich, Laurel Thatcher. *Good Wives.* New York: Alfred Knopf, 1982.

U.S. Bureau of the Census. *Child Support and Alimony: 1983.* Ser. P–23, no. 141. Bureau of the Census. Washington, D.C., 1985.

———. *Geographic Mobility, March 1975–March 1980.* Current Population Reports, ser. P–20, no. 368. Bureau of the Census. Washington, D.C., 1981.

———. *Marriage, Divorce, Widowhood, and Remarriage.* Ser. P–20, no. 312. Bureau of the Census. Washington, D.C., 1977.

———. *Poverty in the U.S.: 1985.* Ser. P–60, no. 158. Bureau of the Census. Washington, D.C., 1987.

Verbrugge, Lois M. "The Structure of Adult Friendship Choices." *Social Forces* 56 (1977): 576–97.

Veroff, Joseph, Elizabeth Douven, and Richard A. Kulka. *The Inner American*. New York: Basic Books, 1981.

Waller, Willard. *The Family*. New York: Dryden Press, 1938.

Watt, Ian. *The Rise of the Novel*. Berkeley: University of California Press, 1957.

Weinstein, Fred, and Gerald M. Platt. *The Wish to Be Free*. Berkeley: University of California Press, 1969.

Wellman, Barry. "Applying Network Analysis to the Study of Support." In *Social Networks and Social Support*, ed. Benjamin H. Gottlieb, 171–200. Beverly Hills, Ca.: Sage, 1981.

———. "The Community Question." *American Journal of Sociology* 84 (1979): 1201–31.

———. "Paid Work, Domestic Work, and Network." In *Understanding Personal Relationships*, ed. Steve W. Duck and Daniel Perlman, 159–92. Beverly Hills, Ca.: Sage, 1985.

Welter, Barbara. "The Cult of True Womanhood: 1820–1860." In *The American Family in Social-Historical Perspective*, ed. Michael Gordon, 2d ed., 313–33. New York: St. Martin's Press, 1978.

———. "The Feminization of American Religion: 1800–1860." In *Clio's Consciousness Raised*, ed. Mary Hartman and Lois W. Banner, 137–57. New York: Harper and Row, Torch Books, 1974.

Whyte, William H., Jr. *The Organization Man*. Garden City, N.Y.: Doubleday and Co., Anchor Books, 1956.

———. "The Wife Problem." In *Selected Studies in Marriage and the Family*, ed. Robert Winch, 2d ed., 111–25. New York: Holt, Rinehart and Winston, 1962.

Wirth, Louis. "Urbanism as a Way of Life." *American Journal of Sociology* 44 (1938): 1–24.

Young, Michael, and Peter Willmott. *Family and Kinship in East London*. Baltimore: Penguin Books, 1957.

———. *The Symmetrical Family*. New York: Penguin Books, 1973.

Zaretsky, Eli. *Capitalism, the Family, and Personal Life*. New York: Harper and Row, Colophon Books, 1973.

Zimmerman, Carle C. *Family and Civilization*. New York: Harper and Brothers, 1947.

Zimmerman, Carle C., and Lucius F. Cervantes. *Marriage and the Family*. Chicago: Henry Regney Co., 1956.

Zimmerman, Don H., and Candace West. "Sex Roles, Interruptions, and Silences in Conversation." In *Language and Sex*, ed. Barrie Thorne and Nancy Henley, 105–29. Rowley, Mass.: Newbury House, 1975.

Index

Capitulation, marital conflicts solved by, 118, 129
Careers, 167–68. *See also* Work
Caretaking: in marriage, 49, 50. *See also* Child care; Economic support
Childbirth, 41, 42, 44
Child care: exchanges in, xix, 40–41, 65, 67, 75–76, 166. *See also* Parenting
Children: in colonial America, 7; friends meeting through, 93–94; husbands' value with, 50–51; and marriage commitment, 141; in postrevolutionary America, 10, 12; rearing of, 38–42, 74–76, 81–96 passim, 101, 156, 162–63; in women's close networks, 76–77, 78. *See also* Family status, of interviewees
Chodorow, Nancy, 68, 110
Christianity, 6
Class. *See* Middle class; Upper class; Working class
Close networks, of interviewees, 76–78, 82, 83, 88, 90–91. *See also* Best friends; Intimacy
Clubs, 89
Cognitive techniques, of emotion work, 124
Cohen, Miriam, 194n.12
Collective identifications: gender, 11–13, 28, 36. *See also* Woman's culture
Collective marriage work. *See* Marriage work
College friendships, 79–80. *See also* Community college
Commerce: and marital feeling, 18; and market individualism, 7–9 (*see also* Capitalism). *See also* Consumerism
Commitment: community, 158, 159; in friendship, 62, 63–68, 72, 84, 88, 89, 96, 161–62, 166–67; in marriage, 48–49, 52, 62, 137–57 passim, 166; standards of, 62, 63–68, 84, 88, 89, 96, 111
Communal responsibility: for family, 111–21, 153; friends exchanging, 40–41, 65, 67, 73, 75–76. *See also* Moral role
Community, xi–xii, 1, 2; concepts of, xiv, xvi, 158–62; decline of, xii, xiv, 1, 3–4, 22, 32, 58, 152, 154; and family change, 1, 3, 22–24, 192n.1; friendships and, xii, xvi, 2, 22, 25, 58, 121, 152–70; marriage and, 1; modernization of, 22–25, 158–59, 165–66; moral, 58, 159–60, 162–63, 165; personal, 164–65; sociology of, xii, xiii, xiv, 1, 2, 3–4, 32, 158–59; traditional, 7, 22–23, 165–66. *See also* Communal responsibility

Community college: women attending, 80, 81, 136, 173
Companionate marriage, xvii, xx, 59, 66–67, 79, 169; evolution of, xv, 1, 3, 4, 14–22, 29–32 passim, 96, 154, 155, 156; friendships compared with, 47, 53, 55, 57, 106–8, 154–57; and romantic friendship, xv, xvii, 29–33 passim, 154; unique values in, 48–49, 51, 52, 156–57
Companionship, 14, 196n.38
Confidences, in friendship, 104–5, 143. *See also* Intimacy
Configurations, of association, 91–96
Conflicts, 167; friends avoiding, 70–72, 76; between friendship and marriage, 112–13; in marriage, 71–72, 122–51, 156
"Consciousness-raising" groups, xiv
Constraints: community moral, 58, 159–60, 162–63, 165; in friendship, 98, 99, 111, 112–21, 134, 153, 162
Consumerism, xx–xxi, 13, 24–25, 30, 31. *See also* Shopping
"Conventions of feeling," 127
Corporateness, community, 158–59
Cott, Nancy, 11–12, 18, 26, 27, 29
Counseling, marriage, 140–41
Couple-socializing, xix, 25, 30, 92–93, 102, 131
Courtly love, romantic love vs., 16
Courtship: dating in, 29; in England, 16–17, 196n.38; free, 15–17, 196n.38; romance in, 15–16, 19
Co-workers, in close network, 78, 81–83, 155
Crestwood Heights, 163n
Cultural messages, and marriage commitment, 140–42
Culture, women's. *See* Women's culture
"Cultures of resistance," xv. *See also* Resistance

Dating, 29
Decision making, on household purchases, 38
Degler, Carl, 18, 28
Democracy, 4, 5, 13
Dependence: economic, 51, 59, 111, 161; emotional, 46, 74; on friends, 46, 74, 79–80, 111–12, 162; individuality and, 109–11; moral constraint and, 160
Disclosure. *See* Self-disclosure
Discretion: in friendship, 112–13, 117, 119–21. *See also* Constraints
Division of labor, sexual, 68, 99, 100, 110